D1479024

Colonists from Scotland:

EMIGRATION TO NORTH AMERICA,

1707–1783

Published under the direction of the American Historical Association from the income of the Albert J. Beveridge Memorial Fund.

For their zeal and beneficence in creating this fund the Association is indebted to many citizens of Indiana who desired to honor in this way the memory of a statesman and a historian.

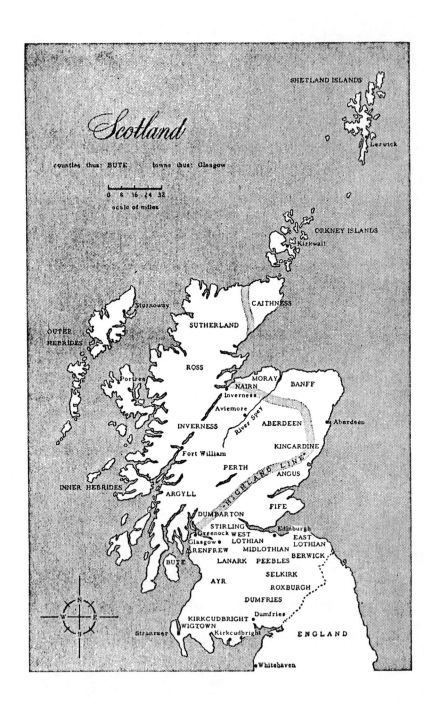

Scotland

counties thus: BUTE   towns thus: Glasgow

0   8   16   24   32
scale of miles

SHETLAND ISLANDS

Lerwick

ORKNEY ISLANDS

Kirkwall

Stornoway

CAITHNESS

OUTER
HEBRIDES

SUTHERLAND

ROSS

MORAY

NAIRN

BANFF

Portree

Inverness

Aviemore

River Spey

ABERDEEN

Aberdeen

INVERNESS

KINCARDINE

Fort William

PERTH

ANGUS

INNER HEBRIDES

ARGYLL

FIFE

DUMBARTON

STIRLING

WEST

Edinburgh

Greenock

LOTHIAN

EAST
LOTHIAN

Glasgow

MIDLOTHIAN

RENFREW

BERWICK

BUTE

LANARK

PEEBLES

SELKIRK

AYR

ROXBURGH

DUMFRIES

KIRKCUDBRIGHT

Dumfries

WIGTOWN

Stranraer

Kirkcudbright

ENGLAND

Whitehaven

HIGHLAND LINE

N
W   E
S

Colonists from Scotland:

EMIGRATION TO NORTH AMERICA, 1707-1783

By Ian Charles Cargill Graham

CLEARFIELD COMPANY

Reprinted for
Clearfield Company, Inc. by
Genealogical Publishing Co., Inc.
Baltimore, Maryland
1994

International Standard Book Number 0-8063-4517-9

Preface

STUDENTS of immigration to the United States have long regretted the lack of a reliable survey of British settlement in North
America, or, indeed, of the detailed studies upon which such a
survey might be based. Interest in the social and economic history
of British migration has usually been subordinated to genealogical
considerations. The older accounts tend to be narrative and local
in emphasis rather than interpretive and general.

This book attempts to give a wider perspective and to reach
some general conclusions about a small part of that large field of
study. At first I had hoped to look into the influence of Scottish
thought upon pre-Revolutionary America. But I was soon forced
to recognize that such a task would be severely inhibited by the
absence of a systematic treatment of Scots settlement in the
colonies. The problem of Scottish emigration and settlement was
finally isolated and attacked for its own sake as a result of the
helpful suggestions of Professor Richard Hofstadter.

Thanks are due to many for assistance in research and in the
preparation of the manuscript. Professor Frederick C. Dietz of the
University of Illinois enabled me to concentrate my whole attention
upon the work by granting me the Kendric C. Babcock Fellowship
in history for the session 1953–1954. I am grateful for guidance in
research to Professor Raymond P. Stearns. I owe much to the

thoughtful teaching and thorough methods of Professors Arthur E. Bestor and Richard N. Current.

I wish to express my thanks to the staffs of the following institutions: the University of Illinois Library, the National Archives, the New York Public Library, the Virginia State Library, the Library of William and Mary College, and the Institute of Early American History and Culture in Williamsburg, Virginia.

Finally, I must thank an old friend, Herbert Sterrett of the art department of the University of Illinois Press, for drawing the map that appears as the frontispiece of this book.

The manuscript has been read by Professor Stearns at various stages of its preparation and by the Committee on the Albert J. Beveridge Award of the American Historical Association. These friendly critics have saved me from many pitfalls.

A work such as this, which touches on a wide variety of social and economic problems, is sure to contain statements that will be questioned. I hope that the discussion of these questions will prove sufficiently interesting to compensate in some measure for whatever errors remain.

IAN C. C. GRAHAM

New York City
January 16, 1956

Contents

Abbreviations Used in Footnotes

Canad. Claims: "United Empire Loyalists: Enquiry into the Losses and Services in Consequence of Their Loyalty: Evidence in the Canadian Claims." In Ontario Bureau of Archives, *Second Report,* 1904. Toronto: L. K. Cameron, 1905.

Colden Papers: Cadwallader Colden. *The Letters and Papers of Cadwallader Colden.* 9 vols. (New-York Historical Society, *Collections,* vols. L–LVI, LXVII–LXVIII.) New York: Printed for the Society, 1918–37.

D.A.B.: *Dictionary of American Biography.* 21 vols. Published under the auspices of the American Council of Learned Societies. New York: Charles Scribner's Sons, 1928–44.

D.N.B.: *Dictionary of National Biography.* 66 vols. London: Smith, Elder, & Co., 1885–1901.

Ga. Recs.: *The Colonial Records of the State of Georgia.* Ed. by Allen D. Candler. 26 vols. Atlanta: Franklin Printing and Publishing Company, 1904–16.

Johnson Cal.: New York State Library, Albany. *Calendar of the Sir William Johnson Manuscripts in the New York State Library.* Comp. by Richard E. Day. Albany: University of the State of New York, 1909.

Johnson Papers: Sir William Johnson. *The Papers of Sir William Johnson.* 10 vols. Albany: University of the State of New York, 1933.

Md. Archives: *Archives of Maryland.* 65 vols. Baltimore: Maryland
                  Historical Society, 1883–1952.

N.C. Recs.:   *The Colonial Records of North Carolina.* Ed. by Wil-
                  liam L. Saunders. 10 vols. Goldsboro and Raleigh,
                  1886–90.

N.J. Archives: *Documents Relating to the Colonial History of the State
                  of New Jersey.* 1st ser., 33 vols. Newark, 1880–1928.

N.Y. Cal.:   New York State. *Calendar of Historical Manuscripts Re-
                  lating to the War of the Revolution.* 2 vols. Albany,
                  1868.

I

Introduction

DOWN to the end of the eighteenth century the poverty of Scotland
was proverbial. Before 1750 manufactures were negligible, and subsistence agriculture was the rule. In the hundred years before the
battle of Culloden, wages, the rent of land, and the price of necessi-
ties remained virtually unchanged. Enterprise and industry hardly
existed, while trade stagnated. Over most of the Highlands and much
of the Lowlands the peasants accepted grinding poverty and squalor
with a resigned hopelessness and even a careless contentment.[1]

The barbarous mode of agriculture practiced in most of the country, especially in the Highlands, coupled with a severe climate and
a poor soil in the mountainous north, brought periodical calamities
accompanied by famine. With the land uncleared, undrained, un-
limed, and unmanured, crops were often insufficient to feed the inhabitants dependent on it. Men renting forty or even a hundred
acres had to buy meal for their families. Whole districts depended
on a single crop—usually gray oats—so that a bad season inevitably
brought destitution. Years of dearth came frequently, and general
disasters took place in the late 1690's, 1709, 1740, and 1760.[2]

In the eighteenth century the condition of the Lowlands was de-

[1] Henry Grey Graham, *The Social Life of Scotland in the Eighteenth Century*,
4th ed. (London, 1937), pp. 183–185.
[2] *Ibid.*, pp. 159, 153.

plorable; that of the Highlands was even worse. In almost every respect, whether economic, social, political, or cultural, the High-lands differed from, and compared unfavorably with, the Lowlands. An eighteenth-century traveler passing from one area to the other would have been impressed immediately with the change. He would have noticed first the topographical transformation. Wherever he entered the Highlands the land took on a new appearance. As he approached the hills across the flat or gently rolling fields of the Low-lands, a wall of barren mountains faced him, the rounded peaks gray under streaks of patchy rain, while here and there a shaft of sunlight gave depth to the view, bringing forth patches of green and purple on the mountainside. As he entered this region with few laws and no roads, the traveler crossed an unofficial frontier, christened some-what later the "Highland Line." The geographical boundary between Highlands and Lowlands has generally been held to lie along this mountain line, which is in most places well defined by the contours of the land itself. It runs across the north side of the Clyde Valley, then north and east through Perthshire and Angus, and so around the east side of Scotland close to the coast. Reaching the boundary of the counties of Sutherland and Caithness, it turns northwest to end on the northern shore near the Pentland Firth, leaving Caithness as a remote outpost of the Lowlands. In the eighteenth century the cultural and linguistic boundary approximated very closely to this geographical line. The Western Isles, or Hebrides, have always be-longed to the Highlands in every respect, while the Northern Isles, consisting of the Orkneys and Shetlands, possessed in the eighteenth century, as they do today, some of the characteristics of both High-lands and Lowlands.

Since 1750 the language, culture, and customs of the Lowlands have gradually permeated the Highlands and islands, so that only in the Outer Hebrides is there any considerable area where Gaelic is the everyday language of the people. The process of Anglicization is still going on. There are now a mere two thousand persons in Scotland whose only language is Gaelic. But in the middle of the eighteenth century the linguistic frontier coincided almost every-where with the geographical one. The military and feudal life of the clans prevailed in the entire Highland area, and the clansmen con-tinued to make forays into the neighboring Lowlands to carry off

Introduction

cattle. A man's first loyalty was to his chief, who could still indulge in private war and administer private justice on the lands of his clan. The law of Scotland possessed little force beyond the Highland Line. The Reformation had never penetrated many of the Highland glens and Western Isles.

The people of each area were ignorant of the other, holding them in contempt in proportion to their ignorance. The English, thought Dr. Johnson, should pay little heed to "*Scotch* authority; for of the past and present state of the whole *Earse* nation, the Lowlanders are at least as ignorant as ourselves." And again: "To the southern inhabitants of Scotland, the state of the mountains and the islands is equally unknown with that of *Borneo* or *Sumatra:* Of both they have only heard a little, and guess the rest. They are strangers to the language and the manners, to the advantages and wants of the people, whose life they would model, and whose evils they would remedy." The Highlanders, on their side, were unwilling to be taught by Lowlanders, "for," wrote Johnson, "they have long considered them as a mean and degenerate race." [3]

The disruption and dissolution of the old Highland way of life took place in the generation after the defeat of the Stuart cause at Culloden in 1746. In this period the British government made a determined effort to assimilate the Highlands to the rising commercial and industrial civilization of the Lowlands.[4] They spent the revenue from the estates forfeited after the 1745 rebellion to send schoolteachers, Presbyterian missionaries, and Lowland craftsmen to the remotest glens of the north.[5] The legislation of 1747–1748 proscribed the Highland dress and arms and curtailed the heritable jurisdictions through which the Highland lairds administered justice. Clan ties weakened and fell away. Within a generation, the new measures brought about a social and economic transformation of the Highland area. The so-called "civilizing of the Highlands" gave a clear field to the avaricious landlord and encouraged him to

[3] Samuel Johnson, *Journey to the Western Islands of Scotland,* ed. by R. W. Chapman (Oxford, Eng., 1924), pp. 108, 79, 31.

[4] George Pratt Insh, *The Scottish Jacobite Movement* (Edinburgh, 1952), pp. 147–164.

[5] The Church of Scotland supervised the program of re-education. See the reports to the General Assembly in the *Scots Magazine,* XXVIII (1766), 457–463, 513–520, 573–578, 680–688.

exploit his lands as a new field for capital investment. The chiefs of an older day lost their traditional responsibilities and acquired an absolute title to their lands. The clan's territory became private property. Lowlanders brought capital to the Highlands. When the forfeited estates were returned to private ownership in 1784, the recipients no longer belonged to a class of paternal chieftains in a primitive society, but rather to a dwindling group of large landowners who invested capital in whatever use of the land was most profitable to themselves, even when it meant eviction for their undertenants.

In the long run, of course, the improvements introduced by the new capitalist farmers were to bring benefits to the whole country. But the advancement of agricultural knowledge and practice was not accomplished without some temporary dislocation and suffering.[6] The consolidation of small farms into large, the enclosure of the open fields (or "runrig," as land divided into strips was known in Scotland) and the conversion of arable land into pasture called for the resettlement of some at least of the peasantry—the crofters and cotters. So attached was the peasant to his locality, especially in the Highlands, that to move only a few miles often seemed as much of a hardship for him as to cross the Atlantic. When, for various reasons, it became fashionable and even commonplace to emigrate, the peasant farmer was inclined to gamble on the longer journey rather than the shorter.

Never at any time during the eighteenth century, however, was eviction a major cause of emigration from Scotland. The greatest single element among those causes was perennial, grinding poverty. Behind the proximate inducements to migrate—the immediate forces of "push" and "pull," which will be discussed shortly—was still the age-old problem of the pressure of population upon a meager stock of the means of subsistence. Even where the emigrants were people of some small substance, as in the 1770's, the psychological pressure upon them was the fear of slipping back to the poverty and insecurity of the masses.

Scotland had fallen behind the other small countries of northern Europe. At the opening of the eighteenth century, according to a

[6] Margaret I. Adam, "The Causes of the Highland Emigrations of 1783–1803," *Scottish Historical Review*, XVII (1919–20), 73–89.

contemporary Scottish economist, Scotland had "by nature many advantages for trade. . . . But numbers of people, the greatest riches of other nations, are a burden to us; the land is not improv'd, the product is not manufactur'd; the fishing and other advantages for foreign trade are neglected. . . . If the same measures," he suggested, "had been taken in Scotland for encouraging trade, as were taken in Holland, we had been a more powerful and richer nation than Holland." [7]

In fact, beginning in 1681, the Scots Privy Council and Parliament had passed a series of vigorous measures to promote trade and industry. There was a considerable upsurge of mercantile enterprise culminating in the disastrous attempt to colonize Darien.[8] From this period, just before the Union of the Parliaments in 1707, dates the beginning of the industrialization of the Scottish Lowlands. But little advance was made in the general prosperity of the country until that union brought to Scotland free trade with the English colonies.

On the eve of the Union, England, with a population perhaps six times that of Scotland, enjoyed a public revenue thirty-five times as great and a customs yield forty times as great as Scotland's.[9] Even with due allowance for the comparative inefficiency of the Scottish customs authorities, these figures show the Scottish economy in a very unfavorable light.

The Union inaugurated an era of unprecedented prosperity in Scotland. It did not come all at once, and at first the development was uneven, affecting only a few industries. A general improvement did not occur in the Lowlands until after the middle of the century, when even the fringes of the Highlands began to share in the economic advance. Linen was then the chief manufacture of Scotland. In 1775 the quantity of linen manufactured for the market was six times that of 1728. At the time of the Union the annual value of exports by sea from Scotland was about £500,000; by the time of the American Revolution it had reached £1,800,000. The correspond-

[7] John Law, *Money and Trade Considered,* 2nd ed. [?] (Glasgow, 1760), pp. 209–210.

[8] Insh, *Jacobite Movement,* pp. 32–77.

[9] George Chalmers, *An Estimate of the Comparative Strength of Great-Britain, during the Present and Four Preceding Reigns,* "A New Edition" (London, 1794), pp. 199–200.

ing figures for shipping entering Scots ports were 10,000 and 93,000 tons respectively.[10]

The commercial and industrial structure built up in Scotland between 1681 and 1776 lay almost wholly in the Lowlands. The Lowland merchants interested in it protected their investments by unstinting loyalty to the ruling Hanoverian dynasty. The Highlands and the Episcopalian northeast did not have such an investment to consider. In these areas the hereditary landowners enjoyed great respect and power. Extremely conservative in an age of important social changes, they gave their loyalty, for the most part, to the house of Stuart. In the economic sphere the commercial development of the Lowlands during the eighteenth century served to intensify the contrast between that region and the rest of the country, while in the political and military sphere the Jacobite rebellions of 1715 and 1745 served to point up the differences still further.[11] The suppression of the latter rising gave the British government an almost unique opportunity to make over the Highlands in the image of the Lowlands. From 1755 on, the commissioners for the estates forfeited by the rebels established manufacturing centers in various parts of the lands they administered. At the same time, the Board of Manufactures fostered the northward spread of flax cultivation and linen manufacture. New communities sprang up, to which Lowland craftsmen and cultivators migrated, bringing their much-needed skills to the Highlands. Under state encouragement, smiths, wrights, spinners, weavers, and schoolmasters came to these villages and helped make them self-sufficient. During the whole period of their management the commissioners spent over six thousand pounds on the development of manufactures generally, and three thousand more on the training of agricultural and industrial apprentices.[12]

To those who lost their heritable jurisdictions by the law of 1748 the government paid £152,000 in compensation, which the recipients were free to invest, if they wished, in the improvement of their estates. About 1760 banks appeared in the country towns of the Lowlands. The "nabobs" brought back fortunes from the East, while the Virginia merchants accumulated them in Glasgow. At last ade-

---

[10] *Ibid.*, p. 201 and n.   [11] Insh, *Jacobite Movement*, pp. 89–90.
[12] John Mason, "Conditions in the Highlands after the 'Forty-five,'" *Scottish Historical Review*, XXVI (1947), 142–143.

quate capital was available for agricultural and industrial progress. The Lothians led the way in increasing the productivity of land. Knowledge and interest regarding such matters spread rapidly among the landed gentry of the Lowlands, and more slowly among those of the Highlands. The Montgomery Act of 1770 encouraged the carrying out of improvements on entailed property by authorizing the owners to settle part of the cost on their successors.[13]

The first improvements were confined to the planting of timber, a commodity of which Scotland had long since been almost denuded. In the thirty years after 1716, Grant of Monymusk planted fifty million trees, chiefly spruce and fir. In 1767 Lord Finlater began planting eleven million in Nairnshire. The Duke of Atholl covered sixteen thousand acres with twenty-seven million larches. But as late as 1773 it was still possible for Dr. Johnson to remark upon the enormous districts still bare of trees, especially along the route northward and westward which he traveled.[14]

The main problem for the landlord who wished to raise the output of his lands was the fragmentation of farms and the division of the open fields into "runrig," or strips. In the middle of the eighteenth century even principal tenants often had rather small farms. Of those at Monymusk in Aberdeenshire, just inside the Highlands, 95 had less than 50 acres, and of these 73 had less than 20. Moreover, the small farms of the Highlands were commonly worked by several tenants. Of 109 farms surveyed on Lochtayside in 1769, only 10 were held separately by single tenants. Two farms had as many as 10 tenants, one had 9, and several had 8.[15]

One important purpose behind the early enclosures, which began before midcentury, was consolidation of the smallest holdings into more efficient and sizable farms. As they carried out such consolidation, landlords with a strong taste for agrarian improvement converted the usual short leases into longer ones to foster more intelligent methods of cultivation. The standard improving lease on the vast Argyll estates was for nineteen years. These measures were usually followed by the fencing, draining, liming, and manuring

---

[13] Graham, *Social Life*, pp. 205–207.   [14] *Ibid.*, pp. 218–220.
[15] Henry Hamilton, ed., *Selections from the Monymusk Papers* (*1713–1755*) (Edinburgh, 1945), p. lxxviii; Margaret M. McArthur, ed., *Survey of Lochtayside 1769* (Edinburgh, 1936), p. xxxvi.

of the fields, the leveling of the rigs (ridges) between the strips, the reclaiming of waste land from moor and marsh, and the diversification of crops. The consolidation of the "mailings," or small farms and crofts, into larger units forced many people into the towns and contributed to emigration.[16]

By the time of the Peace of Paris (1763), the effects of the Union and the measures taken after the '45 were too obvious to be denied. Scotland's economic condition compared very favorably with what had gone before. But she was prosperous only by comparison with the wretchedness of her own past. She had by no means caught up with her sister kingdom to the south. English visitors still regarded her poverty with a blend of contempt and amusement. By comparison with her later achievements Scotland was miserably poor in agriculture and almost barren of manufactures. The beginnings of an industrial revolution, which she was experiencing, were confined as yet almost entirely to the Lowlands. Agricultural improvements, other than afforestation, had scarcely penetrated beyond the fringes of the Highlands. Outside the Lowlands, dykes, or stone walls, the commonest type of fence used in Scotland, were uncommon even between properties. "Speaking generally," said a traveler in 1790, "the Highlands may be said to lie in an open state." [17]

Scotland's economic achievement in the eighteenth century, remarkable as it was by the standards of her own past, was only a foundation for things to come. Such new wealth as she enjoyed was far from evenly distributed, and most of her people shared in it hardly at all. The very improvements in agriculture, which were indispensable to any permanent improvement in the condition of the whole people, were achieved at the cost of eviction or resettlement for some of them. By raising the value of land they sometimes tempted the landlord to raise his rents to a prohibitive level.

Emigration from Scotland in the eighteenth century grew from a trickle to a stream in the very years when the country experienced an unprecedented accession of wealth. The statement is not as paradoxical as it sounds. As has been emphasized, the economic progress was only relative. High rents and other forms of localized suffering

[16] Graham, *Social Life*, pp. 201–202, 208.

[17] John M. Dickie, "The Economic Position of Scotland in 1760," *Scottish Historical Review*, XVIII (1920–21), 16–17; Graham, *Social Life*, p. 221.

were necessary by-products of agricultural advance, which contributed to emigration while it enriched posterity. More important,
emigration to what had been down to 1707 English colonies provided a natural "safety valve" for Scotland's surplus population and
an obvious remedy for the worst evils of poverty. In spite of the
lamentations of Scottish patriots for nearly two centuries, emigration and economic progress were, in an important sense, comple-
mentary phenomena.

II

During the seventeenth century, and especially after the Restoration, many Scots emigrated or were exiled to America. The emigrants
fall naturally into a number of fairly distinct categories.

Between the Restoration and the Union of 1707 the English government barred Scots, as well as Dutch and other foreigners, from
trade with the English colonies. In doing so they curtailed the opportunities for Scots to emigrate to the plantations as indentured
servants. Few who wished to go could afford to do so on any other
terms. Ships taking over Scots servants required a special warrant
from the English Privy Council. Enough warrants were issued to
allow a good many Scots into the English colonies.

The West Indian planters, who held the Scottish servants in high
esteem, complained bitterly at the restrictive action of the English
administration. So profitable was a shipload of Scotsmen to the merchant that, during the period 1665–1685, the Privy Council issued at
least twenty-six warrants for conveying them to the English settlements in America.[18]

Before the Union, it was not uncommon for Scots judges to sentence criminals or vagrants to transportation to the English colonies. The penalty of banishment, unknown to English law, was a
punishment familiar to Scottish courts. Sometimes the felon was
ordered to the plantations, but more often he was simply banished
from the country.[19] Soon after the Restoration, it became customary
for the Scots Privy Council to issue warrants for the transportation

[18] Abbot Emerson Smith, *Colonists in Bondage* (Chapel Hill, N.C., 1947),
pp. 38, 146, 289.
[19] *Ibid.*, p. 133.

of petty malefactors and homeless paupers, in order to clear the overcrowded prisons. In 1695, for example, the city treasurer of Edinburgh made a contract with a merchant in Glasgow for transporting to America certain women out of the House of Correction. The merchant was to get thirty shillings sterling for every person so conveyed and was to pay a fine if he failed to fulfill his contract. In addition, he was to pay five hundred merks if he suffered one particularly troublesome female prisoner to escape after he took charge of her in Glasgow.[20]

Four years later, a pauper of Stirling and his family became a burden on the Over Hospital of that burgh. One of the masters of the hospital gave him three pounds Scots. Soon afterward the town magistrates ordered the masters of the hospital to advance him money for clothes and necessaries whenever he should give assurance of his readiness to embark for America in the next outgoing vessel, "quherby the said hospitall may be disburdened of them." Not all those ordered to emigrate departed quietly. In the same year, the Stirling burgh accounts mention the purchase of two fathoms of rope, "to tye Laurance M'Lairen quhen sent to America." [21]

At various times in the seventeenth century, military and political prisoners were sent from Scotland to the English colonies. During the later campaigns of the English Civil War, Cromwell's troops took many prisoners, most of whom were Scots. Of 4,000 able-bodied captives taken at Dunbar, at least 1,250 were ordered to America, but there is record of the arrival of only 150. A week after the battle of Worcester, in 1651, 1,610 prisoners were granted as servants to persons desiring them for Virginia, upon the assurance that they would be well treated. Of these at least 150 were sent to Virginia, and 272 to Massachusetts. In 1665 a correspondent in Virginia reported that many of the Scots there were better off than their forefathers, having progressed from the degradation of servitude to be themselves the masters of many servants.[22]

After each of the crises in the long struggle between the Crown

[20] *Ibid.*, pp. 144–145; David Robertson, *The Princes Street Proprietors and Other Chapters in the History of the Royal Burgh of Edinburgh* (Edinburgh, 1935), p. 125.

[21] *Extracts from the Records of the Royal Burgh of Stirling*, A.D. 1667–1752, ed. by R[obert] Renwick (Glasgow, 1889), pp. 90–91, 345.

[22] Smith, *Colonists in Bondage*, pp. 152–154, 157.

and the Scottish Covenanters, numbers of prisoners went to America. After Bothwell Brig (1679), the Scots Privy Council obtained authority from the king to transport their captives to the English colonies. Upon the defeat of Argyll's rebellion in 1685, the Council ordered the branding of prisoners about to be sent to America, so that they could not return to Scotland without being recognized. Hundreds of Covenanters were forced to go to the colonies, great numbers of whom were the victims of shipwreck on the journey.[23]

George Scot of Pitlochy received over a hundred of the prisoners of 1685 for transportation to East New Jersey, an English colony in which several prominent Scots had just acquired an interest as merchants and coproprietors. The Scottish members among the twenty-four proprietors of East Jersey induced many hundreds of Scots to settle in and around their new capital at Perth Amboy, named after the Earl of Perth. In 1684 another group of men founded Stuart's Town in southern Carolina as a refuge for Scottish Covenanters, but the Spaniards destroyed it two years later. These were the only attempts of an organized kind made by private persons before the Union to plant Scots in the English colonies.[24] Both undertakings, it will be noted, were launched soon after the Act for Encouraging Trade of 1681. They represent the colonial aspect of the movement then beginning to expand the commerce and industry of Scotland. They bear witness unfortunately to the failure of Scotland to establish colonies of her own. The name of Nova Scotia survives as a monument to the first of these failures.

In 1621 the Scots Privy Council, at the desire of James VI, made a grant of Nova Scotia (including what is now New Brunswick) to Sir William Alexander of Menstrie, later Earl of Stirling, who sent out a few settlers, only to have his plans frustrated and ruined by the diplomacy of Charles I, whose concessions to French demands included the abandonment of the new colony. The grant was to be held of the Crown of Scotland. The king, therefore, extinguished a purely Scottish enterprise in order to reconcile England and France.[25]

Throughout the seventeenth century—the period of united crowns

[23] *Ibid.*, pp. 180, 183–185.
[24] George Pratt Insh, *Scottish Colonial Schemes 1620–1686* (Glasgow, 1922), chs. v, vi; William A. Whitehead, *East Jersey under the Proprietary Governments* (New York, 1846), *passim.*
[25] Insh, *Colonial Schemes*, ch. ii.

and separate parliaments and administrations—the kings at Westminster, close physically and intellectually to the English government, sacrificed the interests of their northern kingdom to those of
England. In the long run both countries were forced to recognize
the need for either complete separation or complete union with one
another. The crisis which led to the Union of 1707 grew out of the
second and final attempt of Scotland as a nation to establish her
own colonies.

III

Much has been written about the 'Company of Scotland Trading
to Africa and the Indies and of its disastrous effort to set up an exclusively Scottish colony in Central America. Chartered in 1695, the
company presented a serious challenge to the monopoly of the English East India Company. It was largely this conflict of interests that
induced the English Parliament to urge a union of the legislatures.
When this union came about, its terms included the final dissolution of the Company of Scotland, but Scotland insisted on and won
the right to trade freely with the English colonies. Since trade and
emigration went hand in hand, it is worth while to consider briefly
the history of Scottish trade with the English colonies in America
before 1707.

Excluded from trade with the English colonies by the Navigation
Acts of the Restoration, Scotland turned, in 1681 under the leadership of the Duke of York (later James VII), to a policy of protective
mercantilism, whose beginning was marked by the passage in the
Scots Parliament of the Act for Encouraging Trade and Manufactures. The new policy brought almost immediate disaster to the
Scots linen industry, for the retaliatory measures taken by England
cut off the market for linens in that quarter. The Lords of the Scots
Privy Council had no idea how to cope with a setback which they
had not foreseen. But following the lead of the merchants, they realized that the loss of old markets required a search for new ones—
hence, a generally renewed interest in colonial schemes.[26]

Colonization was not the primary aim of the founders of the
Company of Scotland, or the Darien Company, as it is familiarly

[26] Insh, *Jacobite Movement*, pp. 32, 57–58.

known. Three distinct forces went into its making. A group of merchants, chiefly in Glasgow, wished to establish a colony in America; another group in Edinburgh wanted to build up an African trade; a third body, consisting of merchants in London, hoped to use the new company to break through the monopoly of the East India Company. By 1698 the first group had pushed their desires to the point of action. In that and the following year the company sent out two expeditions to settle New Edinburgh, on Caledonia Bay in the Gulf of Darien. The first carried twelve hundred planters, of whom, after some months of privation, a few hundred half-starved survivors found their way to Jamaica, New York, or back to Scotland. The Spaniards, defeated by Captain Campbell of Fonab at Toubacanti, invested and blockaded Fort St. Andrew, which surrendered on March 31, 1700, along with the second body of settlers at New Edinburgh. Thus ended the most elaborate attempt made by Scotland to establish a colony of her own.[27] The company continued to exist for a few years, while Anglo-Scottish relations continued to deteriorate.[28] Meanwhile Scotland's growing interest in the American trade and her developing relations with America were producing other effects tending toward a crisis in these relations.

From about 1670 onward Scottish illegal trade with America gradually increased, reaching a considerable volume by the end of the century. Even before the formulation of Scotland's new commercial policy in 1681, the English Surveyor-General of Customs in America was complaining to the London commissioners that much merchandise was finding its way illegally from Scotland to the mainland colonies in America. The Scottish trade, he wrote, was being conducted by "Legerdemain jugles." A ship would call in at some English port, take on a little coal or other cargo of small bulk, proceed to Scotland where it would load great quantities of linen and other Scottish goods and continue on her voyage to America with the clearings obtained at the English port.[29]

Though the illegal trade suffered from growing measures of op-

[27] George Pratt Insh, *The Darien Scheme* (London, 1947), pp. 9, 18–20.
[28] *Ibid.*, pp. 20–21; Albert V. Dicey and Robert S. Rait, *Thoughts on the Union between England and Scotland* (London, 1920), p. 125.
[29] Theodora Keith, *Commercial Relations of England and Scotland, 1603–1707* (Cambridge, Eng., 1910), p. 118; Robert Holden, Boston, Mass., to the Commissioners of Customs, London, June 10, 1679, in *N.C. Recs.*, I, 244–245.

position, it continued to develop down to the Union of 1707. The War of the League of Augsburg (1689–1697) fostered it, as did the immigration of Scots to the English colonies. These immigrants began to fill more and more offices in the colonial administrations, when, abetted by sympathetic Americans, especially in the proprietary provinces, they could turn a blind eye to the illicit traffic. In 1695, for example, the brigantine *William and Mary* took a cargo from Scotland to Pennsylvania. The collector of the colony admitted her to an entry, but a customs official afterward seized her in West Jersey. The case came up in a court presided over by Andrew Hamilton, the Scots governor of the Jerseys, notoriously "a great favourer of the Scotch Traders his Countrymen." Patrick Robinson, the Scottish secretary of Pennsylvania, attended the court in West Jersey to defend the vessel against the Crown prosecutors. Needless to say the master was acquitted.[30]

Such partisanship led the English to demand the exclusion of Scots from offices in the plantations, a matter which will be discussed later in connection with Scottish political activities in America.

According to Edward Randolph, who held the office of Surveyor-General of Customs in America, the recently passed act of the Scots Parliament constituting the Darien Company meant that "under pretence of erecting an East India Company in that Kingdome They do engage themselves with great sums of money in an American Trade." To evade the terms of the English Navigation Acts, Randolph informed the Commissioners of Customs, the masters of Scottish ships sailing from Scotland to the plantations traveled as "supercargoes" or as itinerant merchants, taking along counterfeit masters to satisfy the English law. Late in 1695 Randolph suspected the Scots of planning to purchase a settlement in one of the three lower counties of the Delaware, adjacent to Pennsylvania. He feared they might set up on some West Indian island a staple for the exchange of European manufactures and colonial commodities, as the Dutch had done, "with great abuse," at Curaçao. Randolph's solution was to reduce the number of proprietary colonies, where the Navigation

---

[30] Keith, *Commercial Relations*, pp. 124, 128; Edward Randolph, Surveyor-General of Customs in America, to the Commissioners of Customs, London, Nov. 10, 1696, in *N.C. Recs.*, I, 467–469; *N.J. Archives*, 1st ser., II, 120–122, where the same letter is printed, with the original spelling preserved.

Laws were poorly enforced, and to extend the direct rule of the Crown representatives. He pointed up the role of the new Scots settlements in the Jerseys, "in the very center of Trade and business," in fostering the illicit commerce. The Commissioners of Customs grew thoroughly alarmed at the prospect of a more open trade between Scotland and the plantations, "under Colour of a law lately past in Scotland for a joint Stock to Affrica & the Indies," and recommended that the Privy Council take measures to suppress it. In the following February, the Council informed the colonial governors in a circular letter that the king was aware how prejudicial the Darien Act might be to the trade of England, as well as to the plantations. He expected the governors to use their utmost endeavors to enforce the Navigation Laws.[31]

Between 1691 and 1702 at least thirty-one vessels were definitely recorded as engaged in illegal trade with the colonies, of which eleven can be positively identified as Scottish or trading to Scotland. Almost all of these ships were seized.[32] There must have been many others which escaped seizure among the innumerable bays and rivers of the Atlantic coast, and which were therefore not recorded.

These international rivalries in trade were making the Union of 1603 impossible to continue. Since the Revolutions of 1688–1689, which affected both countries, the independence of the Scots Parliament had been translated from theory into fact. No longer subservient to the royal will after 1689, this body, now more representative of Scottish opinion than ever before, embarked on a seventeen years' career of vigorous legislation, which benefited Scottish interests only to embarrass the Crown. Scotland's growing political independence of Westminster, which had been gradually eaten away between the Union of the Crowns and the Revolutions, contributed

[31] Edward Randolph to Commissioners, Dec. 7, 1695, in *N.C. Recs.*, I, 440–442; Commissioners of Customs to Commissioners of Treasury, 1695, in *ibid.*, pp. 439–440; English Privy Council to colonial governors, Feb. 13, 1695/6, in *ibid.*, p. 458.

[32] Margaret Shove Morriss, *Colonial Trade of Maryland 1689–1715* (Baltimore, 1914), pp. 117–118. At p. 118, n. 159, the author gives a detailed list for each year, showing the number of ships caught illegally trading, with citations from the sources for each entry. At p. 119, n. 160, she gives a further list of "more or less specific reports" of the illegal trade with Scotland, between 1690 and 1699. "Some of these cases," she adds, "are mentioned in the study by T[heodora] Keith, . . . p. 125."

much to the desire of far-seeing statesmen on both sides of the Border that a more complete union be negotiated.

Conferences between commissioners from both countries met in 1702–1703 and in 1706. The former failed to agree on a plan of union chiefly because of "the resolution of England to retain an exclusive commerce." [33] The Treaty of Union, drawn up in 1706, passed as an act by both parliaments and put into force on May 1, 1707, stipulated in its fourth article:

THAT all the Subjects of the United Kingdom of Great Britain shall from and after the Union have full Freedom and Intercourse of Trade and Navigation to and from any port or place within the said United Kingdom and the Dominions and Plantations thereunto belonging.[34]

The Treaty of Union was one of the most statesmanlike and successful arrangements of its kind ever devised. Concerning it and the men who designed it a leading English jurist and a leading Scots historian have combined in this judgment:

The whole aim of the men who drafted the contract was to give the English and the Scottish people the benefits which each of such people mainly desired to receive under the Treaty and the Act of Union. Hence inevitably resulted the further effect that the men who drafted the Treaty of Union carefully left every institution in England and every institution in Scotland untouched by the Act, provided that the existence of such institution was consistent with the main objects of the Act. It destroyed everything which kept the Scottish and the English people apart; it destroyed nothing which did not threaten the essential unity of the whole people; and hence, lastly, . . . while creating the political unity it kept alive the nationalism both of England and Scotland.[35]

In the long run the bitterness of opposing nationalities was to give place to friendly rivalry and mutual respect, but not in the eighteenth century. Not until the age of Burns and Scott were the foundations laid for a union of mind and feeling.

After 1707 Scots found their way in growing numbers to London and to the former English colonies, where they seized every oppor-

[33] Dicey and Rait, *Thoughts on the Union*, p. 126.
[34] Text of the Treaty of Union, in George S. Pryde, *The Treaty of Union of Scotland and England: 1707* (London, 1950), p. 84.
[35] Dicey and Rait, *Thoughts on the Union*, pp. 361–362.

tunity to advance themselves, acquiring like most enterprising and homogeneous minorities a reputation for boldness, acquisitiveness, and clannishness. In the eighteenth century, these qualities, when displayed by Scots in England and America, were not especially admired by the English or the Americans. Only in the nineteenth century did their boldness come to be regarded as a virtue and their clannishness as a charming idiosyncracy.

Before the Union of the Parliaments, Scotsmen had been accustomed to seek their fortunes in European countries. Apart from the commercial community at Veere in the Netherlands, there were Scots all over northern Europe, some of them in high military and governmental positions. The eighteenth century, it is true, found John Law of Lauriston as finance minister of the infant Louis XV, the Earl Marischal Keith as the trusted adviser of Frederick the Great, and Admirals Gordon and Greig highly esteemed by the Russian monarchs they served, but after the Union the Scots enjoyed and exploited to the full the new privilege of migrating freely to the English colonies in America and the opportunity to seek employment there or at Westminster, through the patronage afforded by a unified British administration.

IV

What has been said of the relationships between Scotland and England does not apply to those between the Ulster Scots and the English. Although Ulster received constant reinforcements of population from Scotland down to the beginning of the eighteenth century, her people had by then developed their own traditions and outlook, so that they formed virtually another nationality. Only by understanding the many factors which then distinguished Scot from Ulsterman can the student of emigration from Scotland itself arrive at sound conclusions. The Scots have too often been subsumed under the heading "Scotch-Irish," and much confusion and loose thinking have resulted.

Writing of the contribution of Ulster in men and ideas to the making of the United States, the author of a well-known survey of immigration to North America has made the statement: "A list of distinguished Scotch-Irish leaders would begin with James Wilson and John Witherspoon." [36] Both these gentlemen were born, brought up, and educated in Scotland; both emigrated directly from Scotland to the American colonies in middle age. To write of them as "Scotch-Irish" is to misuse a somewhat controversial term.

Lord Adam Gordon, a Scottish nobleman who traveled through the colonies in the 1760's, described Winchester, Virginia, as "inhabited by a spurious race of mortals known by the appelation of Scotch-Irish." Since then, few Scots have questioned the integrity of the race, but many have denied the legitimacy of the term applied to it by Americans. George S. Pryde, a Scots historian in America, after stating the usual objections to the word "Scotch" as a general adjective, condemns the term "Scotch-Irish" for its implication (as it seems to him) of a mixture of races, arguing with doubtful accuracy that "nothing could be further from the actual state of affairs in Ulster in the Seventeenth and Eighteenth centuries." Pryde insisted that the Ulster immigrants from Scotland were almost exclusively of Lowland Scots blood and always kept themselves a race apart.[37] Even allowing this to be true, it does not follow, as some have supposed, that the Ulstermen continued to regard themselves as Scots. They maintained their Protestantism, their hatred of Catholicism, and their contempt for the "mere Irish." But their environment and the divergence of their history from that of the parent country seem to have given them a sense of distinctness from all other peoples, even including the Scots themselves. Their separate role in history is nowhere more evident than in the story of their emigration to America in the eighteenth century. The size and fame of this movement have obscured and confused a good many accounts of the migration directly from Scotland. For this reason it is worth while to be clear as to the salient points in the Scotch-Irish story.

When the Ulster Scots began to arrive in the North American colonies, they were not a little chagrined to find themselves dubbed "Scotch-Irish." The term was used by an American resident as far back as 1695. In 1720 the Ulstermen of Londonderry, New Hampshire, expressed surprise at hearing themselves termed *"Irish people,*

---

[36] Carl Wittke, *We Who Built America: The Saga of the Immigrant* (New York, 1948), p. 65.

[37] *Ibid.*, p. 52; George S. Pryde, "The Scots in East New Jersey," *Proceedings of the New Jersey Historical Society*, n.s., XV (1930), 3, n. 2.

when we so frequently ventured our all for the British Crown and Liberties against the Irish Papists." Colonial Americans indeed made little effort to differentiate the Catholic Irish and the Ulster Scots, as in later times American orators of Scottish descent overlooked the historical distinctness of Scot and Ulsterman.[38]

By 1672 Sir William Petty estimated that there might be 100,000 Scots in Ulster. Around the end of the century the discriminatory legislation of the English Parliament brought ruin to the Ulster wool-growing and cloth-manufacturing industries and excluded the Presbyterians from all offices. Rising rents and the harshness of landlords added to the suffering. The great movement to America began, ministers in some instances leading whole congregations across the sea. Most of the emigrants traveled as indentured servants. By the time of the American Revolution perhaps 150,000 had settled in the colonies of North America. During the three years 1771–1773 the figure was 28,600 by exact statistics. It should be noted in passing that only about one-third as many Scots emigrated directly from Scotland to America in the same period, although this was the peak period of Scots migration before the American Revolution. This is one of several respects in which Scottish and Scotch-Irish immigration to America differed during the eighteenth century: the numbers of the Ulstermen were far greater than those of the Scots proper. For several years after the famine of 1740–1741, twelve thousand emigrants are said to have left Ulster annually for the plantations.[39]

The Scotch-Irish settlements in America were distinguished from those of the Scots of Scotland by geographical location and by other special characteristics which followed from this primary fact. The Ulster immigrants began to settle along the Eno and the Haw in western North Carolina about the year 1738. Coming south from Pennsylvania with Germans, Englishmen, and Welshmen, they filled up a great tract of back country around the headwaters of the rivers rising in the central Appalachians. In North Carolina they were cut off from the sea coast by the intervening back country, by the pine

[38] Carl Bridenbaugh, in *William and Mary Quarterly,* 3rd ser., III (1946), 139–140; Wittke, *We Who Built America,* pp. 49, 46.
[39] D[onald] MacDougall, ed., *Scots and Scots' Descendants in America* (New York, 1917), pp. 17–18; Thomas Jefferson Wertenbaker, *Early Scotch Contributions to the United States* (Glasgow, 1945), pp. 20–21; Wittke, *We Who Built America,* p. 50; Smith, *Colonists in Bondage,* p. 313.

barrens, and by the Highland settlements of the Cape Fear Valley. They did their trading with the coast through the Highland Scottish settlers at Cross Creek, so that they had no direct contact with the planter class near the sea. Their few religious and cultural contacts were with the northern colonies. Their Presbyterian ministers came from the synods of New York or Philadelphia. Their own candidates for the ministry went to Princeton to be educated—hence in part their resentment at the political and legal dominance of the Carolina coast, and hence their willingness to follow the leaders of the rebellion called the Regulation. The Scots proper played little part in this pattern of development. A few Scots lived among the Scotch-Irish. The best known of these, perhaps, was Henry Patillo, a minister who would have nothing to do with the Regulation, although he later urged independence of Britain on several occasions. In this he identified himself with the interests and opinions of the seaboard area, rather than with those of the Scotch-Irish frontiersmen.[40]

The Scotch-Irish have long been famous for their exploits as pioneers of the Appalachian frontier. The Scots, on the other hand, played only a minor role as frontiersmen. They were often pioneer farmers in virgin soil, but seldom Indian fighters and explorers. They mingled with the Scotch-Irish only in a few areas, notably in western Pennsylvania and some parts of New England.

As is well known, the Ulster immigrants and their descendants played a vigorous part in the American Revolution, especially in Pennsylvania, where their prompt alignment with the American cause was perhaps of decisive importance. The Scots, as will shortly appear, were overwhelmingly loyal to the Crown, maintaining a deep attachment to their country of origin. There is a certain irony in the fact that, before the Revolution, the Virginia planter was hostile to the commercial power and conservative loyalism of the Lowland Scots in the Upper South; after the peace of 1783 he turned his ire upon the "banditti of low Scotch-Irish," despising them as leveling democrats.[41] In the Revolutionary period, in spite of many in-

[40] *N.C. Recs.*, V, 1214; John Spencer Bassett, "The Regulators of North Carolina (1765–1771)," *Annual Report of the American Historical Association for the Year 1894* (Washington, 1895), pp. 143, 145–147; Charles L. Wells, in *D.A.B.*, XIV, 295.

[41] Wittke, *We Who Built America*, pp. 55, 58–59.

dividual exceptions, the Scots and Scotch-Irish were at opposite political poles.

It is the Ulstermen who have provided material for the "Scottish
contribution" school of American Presbyterian historiography, with
its insistence on the Scot's part in founding the United States and on
the major role of the covenanting tradition in bolstering republican
sentiment in the rebellious colonies.[42] There is more sentiment and
romance in such views than soundness of judgment. The Presbyterian
tradition of thought, while not incompatible with a conservative re-
publicanism, can hardly be regarded as the core of the revolutionary
impulse when the bulk of the Scots in America, who were of course,
with few exceptions, staunch Presbyterians, held aloof from it.

The history of the direct migration from Scotland to North America
cannot be properly understood if it is to be subordinated to the long
familiar, but largely unrelated, saga of the Scotch-Irish. The Scots
deserve a separate treatment not only because the Ulstermen even
as early as the eighteenth century constituted a new national group
with its own, independent sense of community, but also—and far
more important from a historical point of view—because the stories
of the two migrations touch at very few points. The Scotch-Irish
story does not elucidate the Scottish one; it merely serves to point up
here and there certain contrasts between the two movements.

The two migrations differed not only in over-all scale but in the
incidence of their peak periods. The Scotch-Irish emigration went
through two intensive and protracted phases, one roughly between
the years 1710 and 1730, and the other from 1765 to 1775. The Scottish emigration, on the other hand, was fairly gradual until about
1768, when it gathered unprecedented momentum and continued to
grow in scale down to the Revolution. This "rage for emigration,"
as James Boswell called it, was common to both Lowlands and Highlands, but it affected the latter more than the former.

In spite of the intense migration just before the Revolution, which

---

[42] Among many examples see particularly Rev. Thomas Smyth, *Complete
Works*, ed. by J. William Flinn (Columbia, S.C., 1908–12), III, *passim*, especially pp. 421, 446, 459, where Smyth quotes a Mr. Reed for the ridiculous statement: "A Presbyterian loyalist was a thing unheard of." For a cruder expression
of this attitude to Presbyterianism and the "Scots contribution" to American independence, see MacDougall, ed., *Scots in America*, p. 28.

seems to set that short period apart, the whole movement from the
Union of 1707 to 1783 possesses certain pronounced characteristics
not present either before or after. The emphasis already placed on
the importance of the Union in Scottish history will perhaps sufficiently explain the choice of that date as a beginning for the present
study. The end of the American Revolutionary War forms a convenient and suitable stopping place. Various factors, including the
war itself, brought about an almost complete cessation of the migration, which resumed quite suddenly in the years 1782–1784. In
the meantime the character of the movement had changed. The in-
terlude of the war separated two fairly distinct phases in the whole
story of Scottish emigration. The period of the present study was
distinguished particularly as that in which the Scots made many
attempts to transfer their traditional ways of life, both Highland and
Lowland (but especially the former), to the New World. All such
clan-building and feudalizing schemes were vitiated by the American environment with its abundant land and finally brought to nothing by the American Revolution. It is more than convenient, it is
necessary for a true comprehension of the problems of social history
involved, to treat this phase of the movement from 1707 to 1783 as
a separate unit of study. Moreover, consideration of a shorter period
would oversimplify and distort the forces at work behind the emigration. These forces have never been adequately explained.[43]

[43] [Janet Schaw], *Journal of a Lady of Quality,* ed. by Evangeline Walker
Andrews and Charles McLean Andrews (New Haven, 1921), p. 257. The editors,
one of whom was the doyen of American colonial historians, published this opinion a generation ago, but after the appearance of Margaret I. Adam's articles
in the *Scottish Historical Review* (see Bibliography), than which nothing better
has been written since. The judgment, therefore, still holds true.

II

Forces behind Emigration: Lowlands and Highlands

IN THE spring of 1774 the ship *Bachelor* sailed from the Shetland Isles with a cargo of emigrants from the north of Scotland. One Sutherland farmer gave the customs authorities at Lerwick four distinct reasons for leaving the country. Two of his sons were already in Carolina and had written begging the rest of the family to come over. He wanted to improve the lot of his remaining children. He had lost his cattle in the severe winter of 1771. The land he occupied had often changed masters, and every change had brought a rise in rent. Intervening between himself and the superior landlord was the tacksman (middleman leaseholder), William Baillie of Rosehall, who must have his share of the profit of the land. The result was that he was paying sixty merks Scots for a holding which had cost his grandfather only eight. Another Sutherland farmer on the same ship mentioned crop failures, dear bread, low cattle prices, and favorable accounts of Carolina from his friends in America. But he insisted that his rents had not been raised by the wadsetter (minor tacksman) of the Sutherland family, who was his immediate landlord. A third farmer, this one from Caithness, stressed the arbitrary and unlimited services exacted by the factor of the absentee landlord. Most members of this party had suffered from rising rents and hard times, but each family had its own set of reasons, some special combination of circumstances, which had induced it to break the ties with home.[1]

If people from the same county, leaving for America at the same time, had a variety of reasons for emigrating, one would expect these differences a fortiori among people leaving at various times from a number of scattered areas. The evidence confirms this deduction. While some of the motives for emigration were common to both Highlands and Lowlands, others were peculiar to one of these regions. Still others operated in very small areas and for very short periods of time.

In discussing the causes of emigration, it is not uncommon to begin by dividing them into two groups. The first group consists of forces tending to *push* the people from their old homes, while the second comprises those which *pull*, or attract, the emigrant toward a particular area of resettlement. The hardships of the old country are often contrasted with the attractions of the new. It is probably unwise to make such a rigid division in the causes of Scottish migration. It is likely to obscure the simultaneous and interdependent working of the two categories, especially noticeable in the period of intensive migration just before the American Revolution.[2] The simplest treatment of a complex subject may be to take the Highlands and Lowlands separately and then to see how far the smaller subdivisions depart from the norms established for the two major regions.

In considering the causes of the eighteenth-century emigration from Scotland one must always bear in mind that the scale of the movement increased quite suddenly about 1770, after a more gradual increase in the preceding five years. This was true of both Highlands and Lowlands, but for different reasons. There were certain broad trends in the social history of both major regions which go far to explain emigration throughout the period. In each region there were specific and local causes for the increasing tempo of emigration between 1765 and 1775.

[1] A. R. Newsome, "Records of Emigrants from England and Scotland to North Carolina, 1774–1775," *North Carolina Historical Review*, XI (1934), 130–138.

[2] Adam, "Highland Emigration of 1783–1803," p. 77. Some of the discussion in this article applies to the period before 1783. The author concentrates her attention on the "pushing" forces.

II

Throughout the eighteenth century, following the pattern laid down before the Union, there was a steady, but moderate, flow of indentured servants from the Scottish Lowlands to the mainland colonies in America, especially to Pennsylvania and the Southern colonies. The liberal policy of Pennsylvania toward settlers is well known, while the Southern colonies held out various inducements to immigrants. A few went to the West Indies, but their numbers appear to have diminished during the course of the century, as the growth of the slave labor force lowered the demand for white servants. Prospective settlers tended to avoid Jamaica, where the cost of living was high.

No extraordinary causes need be sought for the drift of Lowlanders to America before 1772. Indentured service and cheap land offered obvious opportunities for personal improvement. The growing commercial connections between Glasgow and the colonies after 1707 provided a convenient outlet for the surplus population of the Lowlands.

There was little promotion of emigration in bulk. An exception was the venture of Samuel Waldo in Maine. In 1753 Waldo issued a circular in Glasgow in which he offered lands free of rent for nineteen years to emigrants from the Lowlands. After that time the settlers were to pay a small quitrent of from ten to forty shillings per hundred acres. Waldo offered to transport certain types of craftsmen free and to provide them with employment in America. He named agents in Glasgow to negotiate particular agreements with those persons interested in the scheme. About seventy people from Glasgow, Stirling, and other Lowland towns, including ten children, arrived at George's Bay, Maine, in September, and settled the newly laid-out town of Stirling.[3] But Waldo's colony was not typical. Most Lowland Scots who emigrated in the middle decades of the century went to the Southern colonies, mainly to the tobacco country, as indentured servants. Considerable numbers seem to have gone to Pennsylvania.

[3] Cyrus Eaton, *Annals of the Town of Warren; with the Early History of St. George's, Broad Bay, and the Neighboring Settlements on the Waldo Patent* (Hallowell, Me., 1851), pp. 83–85.

Shortly before the Revolution, Scottish economic conditions gave a sudden boost to emigration from the Lowlands. In 1772 a startling change took place in the fortunes of Lowland Scotland. Having enjoyed the fruits of growing trade and industry for several decades, the Lowlands now experienced one of those sudden shocks which periodically afflict most industrial societies. The panic of 1772, and the ensuing depression in commerce and manufacturing, affected considerably the relations between Scotland and America and gave an impetus to the emigration of skilled craftsmen to the colonies.

The crisis followed a period of extravagant speculation. In the 1760's a number of wealthy Scots began to invest heavily in the improvement of recently annexed West Indian islands. Others put money into agricultural developments at home. After 1767 there was a heavy demand for capital to build the large and elegant houses that were designed for Edinburgh's New Town. Some of the private bankers in Edinburgh took part in the fashionable speculation. Requiring a larger capital than they had on hand, they had recourse "to the ruinous mode of raising money by a chain of bills on London." When the more cautious of the Scottish banks refused to expand the fictitious paper further, a large number of prominent Scots, none of whom had any banking experience, took steps to set up the so-called "Ayr Bank" of Douglas, Heron, and Company.

The contract of copartnery of the Ayr Bank, providing for a capital of £150,000 sterling, was concluded on August 24, 1769. Among the original 136 stockholders there was not a single banker. Within three years the company had put into circulation bills totaling £400,000 in face value, while others among the less cautious Scots banks had issued together a similar amount. These Scottish bills of credit rapidly fell into discredit in London, until their further expansion was checked suddenly by the failure of the London banking house of Neale, James, Fordyce, and Downe.

On the afternoon of Friday, June 12, 1772, a horseman rode into Edinburgh, after a breakneck journey of forty-three hours from London. He brought the news of the collapse of the Neale and Fordyce concern. Other London houses had gone down immediately afterward, and a widespread panic ensued. All those houses in London which had accepted substantial numbers of bills drawn on them from Scotland had to follow Neale and Fordyce in stopping payments. The Edinburgh drawers of bills had to do likewise. The "circle" was broken.

Douglas, Heron, and Company's bank suspended payments in specie, and offered interest on their outstanding notes. The Dukes of Queensberry and Buccleugh, with other leading shareholders, approached the Bank of England for assistance. The Bank, already having discounted Ayr Bank notes in the amount of £150,000, was disinclined to go further. Douglas, Heron, and Company, kept afloat for a while by makeshifts, finally went down in August, 1773, when a general meeting of the partners resolved to cease doing business and appointed a committee for winding up its affairs. This event is said to have left "an amount of destruction in [its] wake such as Scotland had not experienced since the wreck of the Darien Expedition." The failure of the Ayr Bank forced into the market landed property worth about £750,000, including a high proportion of the land in Ayrshire. The shareholders continued paying for the rest of their lives. Indeed, some families did not close their accounts until the 1830's.[4]

The crisis of 1772 affected relations between Scotland and America in several ways. One of the most conspicuous was the impetus which it gave to emigration from the Lowlands. The bursting of the financial bubble threw thousands of weavers and other town-dwelling "mechanics" out of work. At the same time, the inflation of monetary values, by inducing the landlords to raise their rents, caused emigration from Lowland farms.[5] In the early 1770's, then, unemployment was the chief stimulant of emigration from the Lowland towns; high rents, of emigration from the Lowland countryside. The townsmen indented themselves in order to get to America, while the ruined small farmers joined together in associations and companies to finance and organize their removal to the New World.

The extent of the unemployment in the Lowlands must have been considerable. In the year following upon the bankruptcies of 1772, the exports of Scotland, the overwhelming bulk of which originated

[4] Sir William Forbes, *Memoirs of a Banking-House*, ed. by Robert Chambers (London, 1860), pp. 39–42; Andrew William Kerr, *History of Banking in Scotland*, 2nd ed. (London, 1902), pp. 96, 100–104, 107, 109; *Scots Magazine*, XXXV (1773), 443.

[5] *Scots Magazine*, XXXIV (1772), 587–588.

in the Lowlands, fell by nearly £300,000. The quantity of linen manufactured for the market fell from 13,000,000 yards in 1772 to 10,750,000 yards in 1773. In March of 1774 a gentleman in Glasgow, writing to a friend in Philadelphia, observed that the

distress of the common people here is deeper and more general than you can imagine. There is an almost total stagnation in our manufactures, and grain is dear; many hundreds of labourers and mechanics, especially weavers in this neighbourhood, have lately indented and gone to America. . . . If any of your colonies desire to set up manufactures of linen, of stamping, &c. they have now an opportunity as favourable as they could wish for.[6]

In February, 1774, the ship *Commerce* left Greenock for New York with seventy-seven weavers and their families from Paisley and thirty-three persons of various trades from Glasgow. They emigrated "for Poverty and to get Bread." Want of employment was the complaint of 147 Borderers and Galwegians, who sailed from Stranraer in May, 1774. The shipload comprised a mixture of farmers and tradesmen. Fifty-seven farmers and farm laborers of Galloway, who sailed from the same port for New York in May, 1775, gave as their reason for leaving high rents and the desire to improve their situation. Unemployment and high rents drove twenty-seven Lowlanders to New York in May of the previous year. In the same month sixty-six persons from the southwest of Scotland sailed from Kirkcudbright, the most common reason for departure being want of employment. Throughout the spring and early summer of 1774 about 250 emigrants were sailing every week from Greenock alone. But the total of some five thousand who departed from this Lowland port in the four months from April to July included many Highlanders, who marched south to the Clyde to take ship for America.[7]

[6] Chalmers, *Estimate*, pp. 202, 205 n.; *Virginia Gazette*, Rind, June 9, 1774, Supplement, p. 2.
    [7] Viola Root Cameron, comp., *Emigrants from Scotland to America 1774–1775: Copied from a Loose Bundle of Treasury Papers in the Public Record Office, London, England* (London, mimeographed, 1930), pp. 1–5, 28–33, 35–40; Newsome, "Records of Emigrants," pp. 49–50; *Virginia Gazette*, Purdie and Dixon, Oct. 6, 1774, p. 1, where "two and fifty" is clearly an error for "two hundred and fifty"; *ibid.*, Oct. 13, 1774, p. 1.

III

A number of associations were formed in the Lowlands to facilitate emigration. A high proportion—perhaps a majority—of those who invested their savings in such schemes to provide for cooperative settlement in America were small farmers. The first of these associations seems to have been formed at Wigtown in Galloway in 1773. Early in the following year a letter from that town asserted that between two and three hundred people were preparing to embark at Whithorn in a few weeks.[8]

Early in 1773, 139 persons, mostly farmers, formed themselves into the Scots-American Company of Farmers, for the purpose of purchasing and settling a large tract of land in America. The members who reached the company's settlement at Ryegate, New York (later in Vermont), called the association the "Inchinnan Company," because so many of them came from the neighborhood of this Renfrewshire town, because they subscribed the bond of copartnery there, and because they wished to distinguish their organization from another, formed shortly afterward in Stirlingshire. The agent for the Stirlingshire company was Colonel Alexander Harvey, who purchased and settled a large tract in the township of Barnet, a little farther up the Connecticut River from Ryegate. These Scottish settlements formed the nucleus of Caledonia County, Vermont, although they were in the province of New York at the time of their establishment. The Stirlingshire association should perhaps be identified with a group known as the "Arnpyrick Society of Emigrants," who, according to a correspondent in Cardross near Stirling, sent over their deputies in the spring of 1774 with powers to purchase land for them. They raised a sum of money to finance the scheme and lodged it in a Glasgow bank.[9]

Of these associations, the Inchinnan Company is best known today, on account of the journal kept by its remarkable agent, General James Whitelaw, who ultimately became surveyor-general of Ver-

[8] Charles McLean Andrews, ed., *Guide to the Materials for American History, to 1783, in the Public Record Office of Great Britain* (Washington, 1912, 1914), II, 185; *Virginia Gazette*, Purdie and Dixon, May 19, 1774, p. 3.

[9] James Whitelaw, "Journal of General James Whitelaw, Surveyor-General of Vermont," *Proceedings of the Vermont Historical Society*, 1905–06, p. 105; *Virginia Gazette*, Purdie and Dixon, Sept. 15, 1774, p. 1.

mont. The diary, which Whitelaw wrote with decreasing regularity between 1773 and 1794, demonstrates his extensive and accurate observation as well as his sound practical judgment.[10]

The Scots-American Company of Farmers chose James Whitelaw and David Allen to go to America and select a place of settlement, for which they were to pay out of the capital subscribed by the members. On the quay at Philadelphia, where they landed in May, 1773, they met a certain Alexander Semple, who conducted them to his brother's house. There, quite by chance, Whitelaw was introduced to Dr. John Witherspoon. This celebrated Scottish-American, a future signer of the Declaration of Independence, had been president of the College of New Jersey at Princeton since 1768. He was currently engaged in a project for settling Scots on a tract of land which he owned in Nova Scotia. Witherspoon's land speculations, however, were not confined to the Pictou colony. He informed Whitelaw that he owned a share in a township of about twenty-three thousand acres called Ryegate, in New York province, on the upper Connecticut River, which he was ready to sell if the agents found it suitable for their purposes. Whitelaw and Allen, after wide explorations through several colonies, decided to purchase one half of the township of Ryegate, then in the frontier county of Gloucester, New York. Witherspoon, whom they visited twice at Princeton during their travels, urged them repeatedly to conduct a thorough search before choosing a site for the settlement, "as he is very fond," recorded Whitelaw, "that our scheme should succeed." Pennsylvania land appealed to them, but all the unsettled portion within 150 miles of a landing cost over twenty shillings per acre. Witherspoon offered them half of Ryegate township at three York shillings per acre. The purchase was concluded on October 2, 1773, and the agents took possession in the following November.[11]

In April, 1774, the agents began to survey the town, and on May 23 the first party of immigrants arrived from Scotland. By the end of the year only about thirty people, men, women, and children, had reached Ryegate. More came in 1775, in the months before the British government prohibited emigration to America. Among the

---

[10] Whitelaw, "Journal," *passim.*

[11] *Ibid.;* "A Journal of the Managers of the Scotch American Company of Farmers," *Proceedings of the Vermont Historical Society,* 1926–28, pp. 181–182.

settlers were servants, laborers, quarriers, and a few skilled crafts-men. But most of them were, as the name of the company suggests, farmers. They came from various towns and parishes of the Clyde Valley which had been afflicted by the slump in business and manu-facturing—Glasgow, Paisley, Inchinnan, and other places.[12]

From its inception the Inchinnan Company possessed a democratic constitution. There was to be a general meeting of the company in Scotland in February and August of each year. At the February meeting members were to elect by simple majority a court of di-rectors consisting of "preces" and eleven managers. Meanwhile, at Ryegate, the members in America set a date in May for the annual town meeting, at which they would choose the town's civil officers. In May, 1776, they appointed three military officers for the town-ship and elected a treasurer, two assessors, two overseers of the high-way and two of the poor, a collector, and four constables. Early in 1793 the company's members in Ryegate met and elected three managers, to whom they ordered Whitelaw to turn over the deed to the company's lands, to be held thenceforward by these officers and their successors.[13]

The Inchinnan Company was a truly co-operative enterprise. It did not depend on outside capital. Every member brought to it at least as much as would pay for his own passage to America and his lot in the township of Ryegate. The poorest members were obliged to put up this minimum, but often could pay no more, so that they required assistance to get started in their new homes. For these the constitution of the company provided that credit should be avail-able for a period of ten years on the security of the borrower's lot.[14]

The Lowland land speculator was unable to exploit such a well-organized group as the Ryegate settlers. Elsewhere, however, work-ing usually as an individual, he sought great tracts of land on which to settle such Scots as he could induce to cross the ocean. The number of these ambitious Lowlanders was small and their achieve-ments as promoters of emigration and resettlement almost negli-gible. It was the Highland tacksmen, whose case will shortly be examined in detail, who took the lead in, and indeed monopolized,

---

12 Whitelaw, "Journal," pp. 147–148; "Journal of the Managers," pp. 181–187.
13 "Journal of the Managers," pp. 187–188; Whitelaw, "Journal," pp. 150, 154.
14 "Journal of the Managers," pp. 197–198.

this form of promotion. As will be demonstrated presently, the Highlander's aim was not, like the Lowlander's, to enjoy the profits of trafficking in land, but to uphold his waning prestige and social position by setting up a new clan system in America. The younger sons of the Lowland gentry, it is true, were not blind to opportunities that beckoned from the colonies. Many of them held prominent offices there. But few of them expected to set up new family estates in America. Those who did so aspire were sometimes a shade too optimistic. A few months after the outbreak of the American Revolutionary War a Scottish gentleman wrote to Norfolk in Virginia asking a friend there to buy him "a handsome Seat on James River which he expects may be had cheap [as] all the Lands will be forfeited to the Crown." [15]

Whatever the specific forces behind emigration from the Scottish Lowlands to the American colonies in the eighteenth century, they worked against a general background of widespread poverty, coupled with growing opportunities for seeking relief across the Atlantic. The apparently chronic tendency of population to outrun the means of subsistence affected Scotland more than England. In Scotland itself, the evil was more severely felt in the Highlands than in the Lowlands. But even in the most advanced parts of the Lowlands agriculture was very primitive and manufactures few until late in the century. At the best of times there was always a surplus of people who might be siphoned off into military service or emigration. In periods of scarcity the flight from farm and workbench increased in rough proportion to the extent of the crisis.

IV

In far greater measure even than the Lowlands the mountainous north suffered from a backward economy, grinding poverty, and overpopulation. Distinctive in its broad features and unique in its

[15] Among the Lowlanders who contemplated colonizing activity in America and who failed to carry out their plans was Adam Chrystie. In June, 1774, he petitioned the Privy Council for a grant of forty thousand acres of land in West Florida, claiming that he would induce a hundred families to go over from Scotland and settle there. His petition was postponed and apparently dropped. See Cecil Johnson, *British West Florida, 1763–1783* (New Haven, 1943), p. 144; J[ohn] H[atley] Norton, [Yorktown, Va.] to [John Norton, London, Oct. 16,

details, the migration from the Highlands sprang from the same basic cause as that from the Lowlands. Overpopulation, a growing burden to the whole country in the eighteenth century, was especially conspicuous in the Highlands. The barren and rocky soil of the north could never support the people who sought a living from it.

Crevecoeur's "Andrew, the Hebridean," who came to Pennsylvania in 1770 from Barra in the Outer Isles, declared the land he had left to be bad enough, having "no such trees as I see here, no wheat, no kyne, no apples." In spite of his admiration and loyalty for the McNeil of Barra, his hereditary chief and landlord, he had to admit that the island was cold, the land thin—and, he added, "there were too many of us, which are the reasons that some are come to seek their fortunes here." Although forced from home by the hardships of life in a poor but overpopulated region, the thrifty Andrew had brought with him the sum of eleven guineas and a half. Andrew was typical of hundreds, perhaps thousands, of his fellow immigrants from the Highlands in the years just before the American Revolution. Accustomed to a life of penury, which he bore with resignation, Andrew had acquired a fortune of nearly forty pounds, most of it a legacy from an uncle. Rather than see the money dribble away in tiding over bad times, he had decided to invest it in the great gamble of emigration. He did not divulge the manner in which he had spent over twenty-seven pounds, the difference between his original fortune and the sum he possessed upon landing at Philadelphia. Be that as it may, his investment was a good one, if Crevecoeur's figures mean anything. In four years, by his own labor and that of his son, he acquired property worth £240 Pennsylvanian, or $640.[16] Clearly a letter home from such an emigrant as Andrew might well induce many friends and relatives to follow his example.

What Andrew said of Barra, that "there were too many of us," might have been echoed by small farmers and peasants in many parts of the Highlands and islands. Most eighteenth-century writers agreed that the rapid increase of population which they observed

1775], in Frances Norton Mason, ed., *John Norton & Sons Merchants of London and Virginia: Being the Papers from Their Counting House for the Years 1750 to 1795* (Richmond, Va., 1937), p. 391.
[16] J. Hector St. John Crèvecoeur, *Letters from an American Farmer* (New York, 1904), pp. 101–102, 118.

was a comparatively new phenomenon, dating back to the 1690's. The decline of private war, improvements in the control of smallpox, and the introduction of the potato raised the average person's expectation of life. Ministers of the Church of Scotland, who realized that emigration arose from overpopulation, blamed the latter on too many early marriages. It is even possible that the contempt felt by the Highlanders for the puritanical Presbyterians, who introduced them to Lowland Protestantism and suppressed their old religion, may have contributed to the high rate of illegitimate births that prevailed. The breakdown of the Roman Catholic religion certainly made for a temporary instability in manners and morals. But such immorality accompanied poverty in the Lowlands as well as in the north.[17]

The Statistical Account of Scotland, which appeared in the 1790's, made it clear to contemporaries that the population of the country had grown rapidly in the previous forty years. Economists and statesmen saw in this fact the basic cause of poverty and realistically tried to create employment through the improvement of agriculture and the expansion of manufactures. "So much was the country over-peopled by the system of clanship," wrote Sir Walter Scott, "that in the islands, whole tribes were occasionally destroyed by famine; and even upon the continent it was usual to bleed the cattle once a year, that the blood thickened by oatmeal, and fried into a sort of cake, might nourish the people." [18]

The chiefs, whose power and prestige depended on the numbers of their followers, were content with these conditions. They reckoned their wealth in terms of men. The rents which they drew in cash were not large. Cameron of Lochiel, whose rents amounted to some seven hundred pounds, brought as many as fourteen hundred men to the army of Prince Charles Edward. Scarcely a single contemporary writer on agriculture failed to notice the dense crowding of the people. Even as late as 1794 one of them found the country

[17] Adam, "Highland Emigrations of 1783–1803," pp. 85, 87, 88.
[18] Sir John Sinclair, *The Statistical Account of Scotland Drawn Up from the Communications of the Ministers of the Different Parishes* (Edinburgh, 1791–99), *passim*; Margaret I. Adam, "Eighteenth Century Highland Landlords and the Poverty Problem," *Scottish Historical Review,* XIX (1921–22), 2–4; Sir Walter Scott, *Manners, Customs, and History of the Highlanders of Scotland* (Glasgow, 1893), p. 45.

"burdened with a load of tenantry which had hitherto been considered a bar, even under a change of circumstances, to the prosecution of any rational plan of management." [19]

The land became divided into minute holdings. On the Lochtayside estates of the Earl of Breadalbane less than five thousand acres of arable land supported about twenty-five hundred people. In 1770 a group of tenants petitioned the earl against a proposed rise in rents, arguing that their small officiary, or division of the estate, had to feed fifty-nine families averaging six persons in each besides servants. "How difficult it is," they concluded, "to maintain such a vast number of souls upon so small possessions." By this time it was clearly to the Highland landlord's interest, if he wished to improve his estates and to raise his rental, to increase the size of holdings and restrict the numbers farming them. In spite of this conclusion, and in spite even of a good deal of consolidation of farms in the latter half of the century, there grew up among the more conservative landlords, especially in the period of intense migration between 1765 and 1775, a strong movement of opposition to emigration. This protest found expression in the political world and was an important factor in bringing about the governmental prohibition of emigration in September, 1775.[20] The outcry against "depopulation," as it was called, in the period when mass migration began to empty whole districts, was by no means confined, as speculation might suggest, to the town employers who had an interest in cheap labor. In 1785, for example, John Campbell of Achallader, who managed the Earl of Breadalbane's estates, and Lord Stonefield, uncle of the earl and trustee for the estates during the latter's minority, exchanged some letters that demonstrate their fears regarding the current popularity of emigration to Nova Scotia. They were very much opposed to the government's offering financial assistance to prospective emigrants.[21]

V

In the Highlands, where normal times involved a great degree of hardship for the crowding population, especially in the Western

[19] Isabel Frances Grant, *Every-Day Life on an Old Highland Farm, 1769–1782* (London, 1924), pp. 98–99.

[20] McArthur, ed., *Lochtayside*, pp. xlvi, lxxii.   [21] *Ibid.*, pp. lxxiii–lxxiv.

Isles and Sutherland, the occurrence of periodical crop failures and cattle blights was truly calamitous. A period of abnormal dearth and suffering fell upon the Highlands in the decade or so before the American Revolution. Climatic conditions caused shortages of foodstuffs extending south of the Border and to the continent of Europe. The strenuous attempts to increase the yield of the land carried out by the improving landlords earlier in the century had made too little headway to mitigate the effects of the dearth, except in a very few places. The peasants and small farmers had resented bitterly all such efforts to improve their lot permanently at the cost of temporary sacrifices. They would not tolerate a break with the old, wasteful, inefficient methods of cultivation. Early in the century the mobs had thrown down new enclosing walls, torn up young trees, and shunned the alien turnip and potato. As late as 1775 agriculture, especially in the Highlands, was hopelessly backward, and much of the arable land went unplowed under the wasteful runrig system.[22]

The disasters of the terrible decade before the American war began toward the end of 1767, when there was a sudden fall in the price of black cattle, which "again damped the spirits of the farmers and ruined all the cattle-dealers." Prices continued to decline until 1770. Much of the Highlands depended upon the black cattle for a livelihood. Many districts imported their grain in exchange for beef on the hoof. In Skye the large numbers of animals constituted the island's main wealth. When murrain broke out among them in 1772, appalling human suffering resulted. Mull, too, lacked resources with which to meet the challenge of that black winter of 1771–1772. For eight continuous weeks the snow lay on the ground, reducing the island's people to helpless misery. Hundreds of emigrants poured out of Skye and Mull in the years 1772–1775. The exodus from the Macdonald lands in Skye, which will be described in more detail presently, was perhaps the most spectacular event of its kind down to that time.[23]

[22] William Graham, *The One Pound Note in the History of Banking in Great Britain*, 2nd ed. (Edinburgh, 1911), p. 105.

[23] [William Alexander], *Notes and Sketches Illustrative of Northern Rural Life in the Eighteenth Century* (Edinburgh, 1877), pp. 71–72; Roderick C. MacLeod, "The Western Highlands in the Eighteenth Century," *Scottish Historical Review*, XIX (1921–22), 45; Adam, "Highland Landlords," p. 162.

Other districts, though severely hit, were better able to weather the storm, sometimes through the generosity of an enlightened landlord. William Mackintosh of Balnespick was such a laird. This landed gentleman of Badenoch, or Upper Strathspey in Inverness-shire, met the crisis in the central Highlands by importing grain for his tenants at his own expense. In 1769 his farm of Dunachton produced 172 bolls of cereal crops, of which 89 were sold. No grain was brought in from elsewhere. In 1771 it produced 41 bolls, of which none could be sold. Seventy-seven bolls had to be imported. The production of 1772 was even less, and this worst of years saw the purchase of 170 bolls of grain to feed the people. Even in the comparatively good year, 1769, heavy rains prevented harvesting until the end of November. There was snow on the ground until the middle of the following April. In 1771 rain, snow, and frost delayed the harvest, while the freezing weather continued from December 23 to April 4. In 1774 the frost lasted until March 22, while the summer brought hardly a day without wind and rain. After an improvement in 1773 Balnespick had to import 54 bolls of grain in 1774. Moreover he was seldom able to collect from his subtenants a sum which would cover the rent he owed the Chief of Mackintosh.[24] Balnespick was a fairly wealthy man, who was able in the midst of the above expenditures to lend his friend, Lord Adam Gordon, the sum of a thousand pounds for the purpose of speculating in New York lands.[25] There were few lairds in such a good position, and even fewer who were willing, to take care of their helpless tenants in time of need. There was apparently no emigration from Balnespick's farms before 1775, but other parts of Badenoch lost people to America.

Bad as the early 'seventies were for the Highlands, and serious as was the emigration from this area to the American colonies, the harvests of 1782–1783 are said to have been worse than any-thing in the earlier period, and emigration appears to have sur-passed all previous records during the first decade after the recogni-tion of the United States. The first French war interrupted it again, when the surplus population could find employment in the army, but it rose to yet greater heights at the opening of the nineteenth

[24] Grant, *Old Highland Farm*, pp. 55–58, 83–84.
[25] *Ibid.*, pp. 27, 267, 270.

century.[26] These matters lie outside the scope of the present study. But the stress laid on the hardships and emigration of the early 1770's should not be allowed to distort the picture. The briefest examination of emigration from the Highlands in the century after 1783 will reveal still greater human misery and a growing number of voluntary and involuntary exiles. The scale of emigration in the early 1770's and the severity of the conditions that provoked it were remarkable by comparison with what had gone before, not with what was to come.

By a strange paradox, one of the conspicuous features of the migration of the 'seventies was the comparative affluence of some of the emigrants. If misery and want were the root causes of increasing emigration in the period, how is it possible to reconcile this conclusion with the fact that emigrants were removing considerable quantities of cash from the country? The explanation may be found by examining the economic classes among the emigrants.

VI

While the great mass of the people were extremely poor, a few had risen above the general level. These exceptional persons were best situated to afford the expenses of emigration. Not all the emigrants from Scotland, or even from the Highlands, were destitute. After 1750 some of them were suffering more from dissatisfaction arising out of the decaying clan system than from the pressure of poverty. Many of the six hundred clansmen whom Glengarry led at Culloden went to America, although, it has been said, most of them were in comfortable, and some in affluent, circumstances. Their action has been attributed to disgust at the conduct of the chief in the years after the '45 rebellion. There were still hundreds of Macdonalds left in the glen, however, and numbers of them volunteered for service in the 76th Macdonald Highlanders 1777.[27]

Nevertheless it remains true that the overwhelming bulk of the

---

[26] *Ibid.,* p. 108; Adam, "Highland Emigrations of 1783–1803," p. 73.

[27] Alexander Mackenzie, *The History of the Highland Clearances,* 2nd (Glasgow, 1914), pp. 170–171.

emigrants from Scotland between 1763, when the French and Indian War ended, and 1775, when war came to America once more, left primarily for economic reasons. Other motives were usually present, but economic pressures carried weight both with those who, having nothing, hoped to do better in the New World and with those who, having something to lose, wished to safeguard their savings or property during bad times by starting life afresh across the sea.

As to the fact of moneyed emigration there is no room for doubt. Contemporaries commented upon it. According to Josiah Tucker, a discriminating observer of economic and political matters, the emigrants who sailed from the north of Scotland in such multitudes about 1772–1773 "were far from being the most indigent, or the least capable of subsisting in their own Country. No; it was not Poverty or Necessity which compelled, but Ambition which enticed them to forsake their native Soil." Tucker put forward the interesting theory that avaricious speculators began to have success in inducing people to emigrate "after they began to taste the Sweets of Industry, and to partake of the comforts of life." In other words, the harpies who profited from emigration applied their persuasive powers to persons who had "gotten some little Substance together worth devouring." They told their prospective victims plausible stories. One such tale was intended to convince emigrants that, if they would go to North America, they might get estates for nothing and become gentlemen forever. Their dupes did not realize "that a Man may possess twenty Miles square in this glorious Country, and yet not be able to get a Dinner." [28]

As Tucker suggested, ambition was a constant spur to emigration from Scotland to America. People who had a little money saved, who inherited modest fortunes, or whose wealth and social position were being threatened by the social changes in the eighteenth-century Highlands, were often easy prey to the lure of America. Samuel Johnson observed, during his tour to the Inner Hebrides in 1773, that "many men of considerable wealth have

[28] Josiah Tucker, *The True Interest of Great-Britain Set Forth in Regard to the Colonies,* in Robert Livingston Schuyler, ed., *Josiah Tucker: A Selection from His Economic and Political Writings* (New York, 1931), pp. 364–365.

taken with them their train of labourers and dependants; and if they continue the feudal scheme of polity, may establish new clans in the other hemisphere." [29]

Johnson was referring to members of the tacksmen class, which embraced the great majority of the intermediate landlords in the Highlands. It was they who suffered most disturbance and loss of social position as a result of the measures taken after the '45 rebellion. An account of their misfortunes, their conduct toward their tenants, their relationships with the chiefs and superior landlords, and their remarkable efforts to transmit Highland civilization to America deserves a separate chapter. For the present it is enough to note that not all the persons of substance who emigrated in the 1770's were tacksmen. The great majority of them, indeed, seem to have been small farmers, peasants, or merchants, who had saved up sums ranging from ten to a hundred pounds. Such men desired to better their condition, but they had no thought of establishing "new clans in the other hemisphere."

According to William Gilpin, Prebendary of Salisbury, who toured the Highlands in 1776, the rage for emigration in the 'seventies aroused a discontented and restless spirit even in places where no oppression by landlords had occurred. He remarked with justice that the Earl of Breadalbane regarded the happiness of his tenants as a prerequisite of his own. Yet in March, 1775, some thirty families, making in all about three hundred people, agreed to a rendezvous at Killin in the following May with a view to emigration. One day that spring they formed a column and marched off to their port of embarkation. These were not the wretched emigrants of Goldsmith's "Deserted Village." Many of them possessed two or three hundred pounds, and few had less than thirty or forty. They were full of good cheer, carrying themselves, "not like people flying from the face of poverty; but like men, who were about to carry their health, their strength, and little property, to a better market." [30]

The lack of trade among the islands of the west, and the shortage

---

[29] Johnson, *Journey*, p. 90.

[30] William Gilpin, *Observations, Relative Chiefly to Picturesque Beauty, Made in the Year 1776, on Several Parts of Great Britain; Particularly the High-Lands of Scotland*, 2nd ed. (London, 1792), I, 169–171.

of cash there, impressed Johnson and Boswell during their journey of 1773. Even before the cattle blight there were many persons of substance who desired to improve their fortunes in America. A report of February, 1771, described a "large colony of the most wealthy and substantial people in Sky[e], making ready to follow [certain emigrants from Islay] in going to the fertile and cheap lands on the other side of the Atlantic ocean." In September, 370 persons embarked in Skye in order to settle in North Carolina. Several of them had money and intended to purchase land in America. Their reason for leaving the country was the recent sharp rise in rents. The raising of rents, it is clear, brought about emigration in many cases long before the tenants were reduced to starvation. People of some property would emigrate to avoid a mere threat to their resources, whether it came from the landlords or from the climate.[31]

In 1771 a group of Skye's tenuous middle class, including a minister, a merchant of Portree, and several tacksmen, began engaging servants and disposing of their property. In June they presented a petition to the Privy Council asking for forty thousand acres of land in North Carolina. The Council refused the request. The amount of land desired indicates the part played by ambition, reinforced by optimism, in encouraging plans for emigration among the possessors of a small property.[32]

There were many prosperous emigrants from Scotland, especially in the early 'seventies, but one cannot say how many. It is difficult enough to estimate the total numbers involved, without attempting the impossible task of counting them according to their economic classes. One can only draw somewhat vague and tentative conclusions from the records of the period as a whole. It is probably safe to say that most of the emigrants of the 1770's were poor—so poor as to be obliged to obtain a passage to America by indenting themselves—but that a higher proportion of them than ever before possessed some money with which to establish themselves in the colonies. A much smaller proportion, it appears, took with them substantial sums in cash, at the same time inducing their

[31] Johnson, *Journey*, p. 142; James Boswell, *Journal of a Tour to the Hebrides*, ed. by R. W. Chapman (London, 1924), p. 330; *Scots Magazine*, XXXIII (1771), 325, 500.

[32] *N.C. Recs.*, IX, 303–304.

tenantry from the old country to accompany them, with the intention of setting up new estates for themselves in America, from which they might collect rents, or quitrents, without having to pass on a large part of their incomes to a superior landlord. The tacksman, hitherto a middleman, had dreams of becoming a heritor in the plantations, with the position and privileges of a clan chief.

It is clear that the great governing cause of emigration from the Highlands in the middle fifty years of the eighteenth century was poverty—the kind of poverty that arises from a growing population pressing upon limited agricultural and industrial resources. This remains true in spite of the unusually large number of comparatively prosperous emigrants who left for America in the early 1770's. The poverty of the masses, especially in the Highlands, can hardly be overstressed. For most of the emigrants in and after 1772, the times were exceptionally difficult from an economic standpoint. Some of those who took a small capital with them were escaping from a depression in trade and agriculture that threatened to swallow up their meager savings. Although considerable sums in cash were removed from the country, most of this money seems to have been taken to America by a small number of men. Those chiefly responsible were the tacksmen, whose history and significance will be discussed in Chapter IV.

III

Forces behind Emigration: The Factor of Compulsion

BY 1763 the foundations of Highland settlement had been laid alongside the older Lowland settlements in America. Once the pioneer Highlanders had established themselves, they began writing home to urge their friends and relatives to join them. In time, emigration became, for the Highlanders left behind in Scotland, easy, tempting, fashionable, and infectious.

But before 1746, when the Jacobite cause went down forever, there were not more than a few hundred Highlanders in America. Powerful forces were necessary to persuade the home-loving Highlander to leave the glen or strath beyond which he had never wandered more than a few miles. During and after the period of the rebellions of 1715 and 1745, two of these forces involved compulsion —transportation for treason or felony and the drafting of troops to the colonies.

The severest form of compulsory emigration resulted from judicial decisions. In Scotland, during most of the seventeenth and eighteenth centuries, treason and crime were frequently punished with exile to the English colonies. According to Sir George Mackenzie, "the turning capital punishment into exile was an act of clemency not cruelty." The Stuart jurist's idea gave many generations of British Hanoverians a plausible excuse for referring to political banishment as "the King's Mercy." Much was heard of this phrase after the battle of Culloden.[1] Hundreds were sentenced to transportation after each of the major Jacobite rebellions.

Sir Thomas Johnson, a merchant of Liverpool, contracted with the government to remove the captured rebels of 1715. In the spring and summer of the following year he conveyed at least 639 of them to the Southern colonies and the West Indies. At Chester Castle some of them were told to sign indentures for seven years. Many complied, but "the gentlemen unanimously refused to do the same," alleging that they had been sentenced only to simple transportation. Their captors retorted by throwing them into a dungeon and feeding them on bread and water.[2]

In March, 1717, when Johnson received his payment, the Treasury recorded details of the shipments. Of the 173 prisoners who started for the West Indies, 30 mutinied and escaped, so that only 145 (less such as may have died on the voyage) reached the islands. Two-thirds of these were aboard a single ship, which took them to Antigua. Six shiploads, carrying altogether 451 prisoners, arrived in North America, where they were fairly evenly distributed among the colonies of South Carolina, Maryland, and Virginia. Thus the whole number which actually reached the plantations was not over 594.[3]

James Mackintosh of Balnespick in Strathspey was one of the landed gentlemen sentenced to transportation for his part in the '15. He indented himself for seven years to Henry Trafford of Liverpool, whom he agreed to serve in Virginia or any other colony. Trafford agreed to pay for his passage to America and to keep him supplied with necessaries, "according to the custom of the country." The contracting parties signed the document and the Mayor of Liverpool witnessed it. In spite of this written agreement, Mackintosh was said to have been abroad for only two years.[4]

If it is true that he returned to Scotland, he was far from the only one. Many of those deported in 1716 returned illegally to their homeland. In 1746, when the prisoners of the '45 were await-

---

[1] Sir Bruce Gordon Seton and Jean Gordon Arnot, eds., *The Prisoners of the '45* (Edinburgh, 1928), I, 24.

[2] Smith, *Colonists in Bondage*, pp. 197–198.   [3] *Ibid.*, pp. 198–199.

[4] Grant, *Old Highland Farm*, p. 18, n. 1.

ing disposal, the Crown solicitor pointed out this fact to the government of the day. To prevent the followers of the Young Pretender from doing likewise, he suggested branding them. But this was too much even for a British government of that time. Only some half dozen of the exiles of the later rebellion are known to have found their way home.[5]

After the Jacobite disaster at Culloden the British government held some 3,500 rebel prisoners. Of these, 936 were sentenced to exile for life in America. All but a few were to indent themselves, and those who refused to do so were to be compelled to enter service. Orders survive for the transference of 794 of the deportees from prison to the transportation contractors. The difference between the number so transferred and the number sentenced to exile (142) represents deaths in British prisons and possibly a few last-minute reprieves. Records exist of the sailing of only 610 persons, while a mere 407 are known to have arrived in the British colonies. Of these, 254 traveled in three ships to the West Indies (Barbados and Jamaica), while the remaining 153 went to Maryland in two ships. Another 150 bound for the Leeward Islands were captured by the French and taken to Martinique. Thus, out of 610 who sailed from Britain, only 557 reached the New World. The difference of 53 must be accounted for by deaths aboard ship. Among the prisoners transported were old men of seventy, boys of thirteen, and women.[6]

The total number of Jacobite prisoners who reached the British colonies in America, therefore, was almost surely less than one thousand. If a reasonable allowance is made for deaths on the voyages of 1716, the figure will be even smaller. Of the thousand or less who reached America only 604 went to the mainland colonies. It is surely an exaggeration to describe the Jacobite exiles as a "wave" of emigration.[7] The bulk of the Jacobite settlers were Highlanders. They did no more, numerically speaking, than lay a narrow foundation for the migration of the future. From the beginning, the Highland emigrant's letters home were a powerful influence in attracting others to America. But it is difficult to imagine that the

[5] Seton and Arnot, eds., *Prisoners of the '45*, I, 24–25.
[6] *Ibid.*, pp. 39–43, 45–47, 152; Smith, *Colonists in Bondage*, pp. 201–202.
[7] Pryde, "Scots in East New Jersey," pp. 6–7.

letters of the Jacobites alone would have drawn so many to America
in the 1770's.

II

By the 'sixties the supporters of the Pretender had been reinforced by a far more numerous group of their countrymen, the
discharged soldiers of the Seven Years' War. Endowed with wilderness farms by a grateful and prudent government, thousands of
Highland soldiers remained in America. It was their persuasions,
rather than those of the Jacobite exiles, which constituted the chief
attracting, or "pulling" force, from the American side on the eve
of the Revolution. This is not to say that there were not many
Jacobite sympathizers, and even veterans of the '45, among the
beneficiaries of the French and Indian War. They are classed here,
not according to their political affiliation, but according to the
manner in which they reached America. As soldiers drafted for
overseas service they came to the plantations by compulsion. They
may have volunteered for the army in the first place, but they did
not intend to emigrate. Once thoroughly uprooted from their old
homes and habituated to life in America, they remained there of
their own free will. Their actual transference to America was effected by government order.

The discharged veteran felt confident of a material future in the
colonies better than anything he could find in the overpopulated
glens of the Highlands. It was overpopulation that had driven him
into the army in the first place. In the decade after 1753 two Highland parishes were able to furnish four hundred recruits for regiments in America without interfering with the working of their
farms.[8] The outlet for surplus population provided by the army
and the colonies was clearly a blessing. It is significant that, throughout the Revolutionary War, Scotland continued to be the most fertile
field for recruits. England, more populous but also much better able
to support its people, was less productive of soldiers, while Ireland contributed very few.[9]

[8] H. G. Graham, *Social Life*, p. 225.
[9] Edward E. Curtis, *The Organization of the British Army in the American
Revolution* (New Haven, 1926), p. 53.

A Highland minister told Dr. Johnson that about twelve thousand Highlanders had enlisted in the Seven Years' War. Those who had gone to America, he added, "went to destruction." As evidence for this statement he pointed out that from one regiment, originally twelve hundred strong, only seventy-six men had returned to Scotland.[10] Perhaps the minister was disingenuous. It is difficult to believe that he did not know perfectly well what had happened to most of the Highlanders in America. Still very much alive, they had settled down on lands offered by the Royal Proclamation of October 7, 1763, on easy terms to officers and men who had served in the royal forces during the late war. Most of them found homes in New York province and Prince Edward (then St. John's) Island.

In 1765, Hugh Fraser, lately a lieutenant in Fraser's Regiment, brought over some Scots at his own expense and applied for one hundred acres of land for each in New York. He got Sir William Johnson to approach Governor Colden in his behalf. He told Johnson that he hoped the expense he had incurred in bringing in immigrants would entitle him to apply for land on their account, and "something more for himself." If properly treated, he promised to use his endeavors to bring over more of his countrymen.[11] It is odd that Fraser does not seem to have used the argument that he was entitled to land under the Proclamation of 1763. Perhaps he had fewer friends in high places than other former officers. Personal contacts and influence counted for much in obtaining large estates in America.

Another former lieutenant, James Macdonald, for example, must have had powerful interests working for him in London. In the same year that Hugh Fraser struggled to obtain land on the basis of "head right," Macdonald secured a royal Order in Council requiring Governor Colden to grant him ten thousand acres of Crown land in New York. Two local patriots opposed this claim on the grounds that the governor could not grant lands, even in pursuance of an Order in Council, without the consent of the Council of New

[10] Johnson, *Journey*, p. 89.
[11] Sir William Johnson to Lt. Gov. Cadwallader Colden, Aug. 15, 1765, in *Colden Papers*, VII, 50.

48   *Colonists from Scotland*

York. Colden, upon official advice, ruled that the governor did have
such power, and Macdonald obtained his land.[12]

Many Scots settled in New York province at this time. Among
them were Donald Campbell and his brothers, sons of Lachlan
Campbell, who had brought five hundred Scots to New York
in the years 1738–1740. The sons had all been in the war. Campbell
and his relatives got ten thousand acres of land, the so-called
"Campbell Patent" in Washington County, then part of Albany
County. At the same time, the province granted 47,450 acres in the
same district to those "whom his father had deluded from Scotland
into this province," or to their children. Governor Colden, himself
a Scottish Borderer, wrote that he did this with pleasure, for only
what he called the "fraudulent practices" of Lachlan Campbell
had prevented such a grant during the previous quarter of a century. No doubt the sons' war service facilitated the business, by
making it easier for the governor to offend the many enemies of the
older Campbell.[13]

The Argyle, or Scots, Patent, as this grant was called, received
reinforcements from the disbanded Highland regiments. The first
town was Argyle, later followed by Greenwich and Fort Edward.
Most of the near-by township of Hebron was granted to discharged
men of Montgomery's Highlanders.[14]

In 1773 the Board of Trade had before it a petition from Major
General Simon Fraser, on behalf of himself and sixteen other
officers, asking to be included in any grant made to Captains Campbell and Curry and their associates of lands in New York. The
petitioners asked for a share in conformity with the provisions of
the Proclamation of 1763. Another request, from Lieutenant Colonel
Stewart and seven associates, in behalf of themselves and several
others, all of whom had served in America during the French and
Indian War, asked for a grant of 250,000 acres in recognition of

[12] George S. Pryde, "Scottish Colonization in the Province of New York," *Proceedings of the New York Historical Association*, XXXIII (1935), 154; John Tabor Kempe to Lt. Gov. Cadwallader Colden, July 27, and July 30, 1765, in *Colden Papers*, VII, 48–49.
[13] Pryde, "Scottish Colonization," pp. 154–155. An account of Lachlan Camp-bell's enterprise and of the protracted controversy in New York to which it gave rise will be found in the following chapter.
[14] *Ibid.*, p. 155.

their services in sustaining the claim of the Crown to certain lands disputed with John van Rensselaer.[15]

The activities of the former Scottish officers in getting and settling New York lands contributed much to the expansion of the frontier of settlement in the Mohawk and upper Hudson Valleys in the decade before the Revolution. A strong connection was established between certain parts of the Highlands and Albany County. So rapid was the settlement of the northeast part of the county, where Scots-born people predominated, that in 1772 it was erected into the new county of Charlotte.

The other important area of settlement for discharged veterans of the French and Indian War was Canada. Most of the Highland settlers went to the Maritime Provinces, but some went to Quebec, which naturally attracted the Catholics among them. Three regiments contributed the bulk of the Canadian pioneers—the 42nd or Black Watch, Fraser's, and Montgomery's Highlanders. Disbanded in 1763, men of the last two regiments chose Murray Bay in Prince Edward Island as the site of their new homes. Two officers, Captain Malcolm Fraser and Major Nairn, secured large grants from the British government, which was then encouraging the settlement of the island. They led their men to the place. It was among these soldier settlers that, in 1775, Colonel Allan McLean raised the Royal Highland Emigrants, the unit which garrisoned Quebec during the American invasion.[16]

Scottish immigrants were foremost in capturing the fur trade from the French in newly conquered Canada. There were many Scots among the officers of regiments disbanded in Canada after 1763, and some of these became leading merchants in the northwest fur trade.[17]

Once the Highland veterans had taken up lands in the northeastern colonies, kinship and friendship became a powerful factor in drawing thousands of other Scots to North America. The military

[15] *Colden Papers,* VII, 275.
[16] W. J. Rattray, *The Scot in British North America* (Toronto, [1880–83]), I, 254–255, 262–263; Stanley C. Johnson, *A History of Emigration from the United Kingdom to North America, 1763–1912* (London, 1913), pp. 3–4; MacDougall, ed., *Scots in America,* p. 110.
[17] Wayne Edson Stevens, *The Northwest Fur Trade, 1763–1800* (Urbana, Ill.), 1928, p. 24, n. 30.

settlers invited emigration by letter. Some even went back to Scotland to persuade their relatives and friends to return with them to America. The parish ministers who contributed to the *Statistical Account of Scotland* in the 1790's repeatedly mentioned letters from America as one of the strongest inducements to further emigration. So effective was this form of persuasion that a consistent pattern of migration emerged from certain localities in Scotland to corresponding districts in America. From 1772 onward, South Uist and Barra in the Outer Hebrides had a continuous connection with Prince Edward Island. Other Hebrideans went in a steady stream to Cape Breton Island. The people of Argyll, Ross, Sutherland, and the Isle of Skye gave their preference to the Carolinas. Thus the clannish instinct helped to increase emigration once the initial Highland settlements had been made. The more Highlanders there were in America, the more those left at home desired to join them. By 1770 this force of attraction, exerted from America, had contributed much to the growth of an "epidemical fury of emigration," which characterized the years immediately preceding the American Revolution.[18]

In October, 1773, the people of Skye were so wrapped up in the general enthusiasm for emigration that James Boswell reported:

We had again a good dinner, and in the evening a great dance. . . . And then we performed . . . a dance which I suppose the emigration from Skye has occasioned. They call it "America." . . . It goes on till all are set a-going, setting and wheeling round each other. . . . It shows how emigration catches till all are set afloat. Mrs. Mackinnon told me that last year when the ship sailed from Portree for America, the people on shore were almost distracted when they saw their relations go off; they lay down on the ground and tumbled, and tore the grass with their teeth. This year there was not a tear shed. The people on shore seemed to think that they would soon follow.[19]

[18] H. G. Graham, *Social Life*, p. 227, n. 2; Adam, "Highland Emigrations of 1783–1803," pp. 75–76; S. Johnson, *Journey*, p. 53; "Scotus Americanus," *Informations Concerning the Province of North Carolina, Addressed to Emigrants from the Highlands and Western Isles of Scotland*, reprinted in William K. Boyd, ed., *Some Eighteenth Century Tracts Concerning North Carolina* (Raleigh, N.C., 1927), pp. 435–436.

[19] James Boswell, *Journal of a Tour to the Hebrides*, ed. by Frederick A. Pottle and Charles H. Bennett (New York, 1936), pp. 242–243.

By 1773, when Boswell wrote, many causes were operating together in certain localities to bring about serious depopulation. The mass exodus of the Macdonalds of Skye, which began with the departure of about seven hundred persons in the spring and summer of 1772, resulted from a hard winter, the cattle blight, and rising rents. To the stricken islanders of Skye and Mull the letters from prosperous military pioneers in America brought a promise of new hope. Thus the forces of repulsion and attraction, of "push" and "pull," worked together in a single direction. Together they were strong enough to overcome the Highland peasant's conservative instincts and deep attachment to his home and clan. As many a Highlander watched his kinfolk depart for America, this very attachment began to work in the cause of emigration.

III

As the prewar emigration rose to a climax, a new compulsive force began to swell the tide still further. The eviction of the peasantry from their holdings, it is true, did not compel them to emigrate. But where it occurred, it drove the victims into a life of poverty in the coastal towns and villages. For the Highlander the first step away from his ancestral farm was the long one. The decision to emigrate was comparatively easy.[20] In 1770 emigration was fashionable. The device of indenture was long established, so that lack of funds to pay for a passage usually presented no insuperable problem. Having been compelled to evacuate his croft to make way for his landlord's sheep, the Highlander tended to seize the first opportunity to emigrate.

The problem of the eighteenth-century Highland evictions is, paradoxically, inseparable from that of the agrarian improvements of the period. The agricultural revolution in Scotland caused considerable social dislocation, including outright evictions, which gave an impetus to emigration. By a strange irony, no permanent improvement in the economic condition of the Highlands could take place without the infliction of additional hardships on that section of the population which already suffered the most from the evils

[20] Adam, "Highland Landlords," *Scottish Historical Review*, XIX (1921–22), 171.

of poverty. Whether the price paid for Scottish agricultural advancement in this and the following centuries was too great remains one of the standing debates of Scottish historiography.

The whole subject of the Highland evictions, or "clearances," as they are called, is intensely controversial. The term "clearance" has generally been used to describe the enforced removal of cultivators from arable land which was about to be converted into sheep pasture. Of the many forms of enclosure this one did, in fact, cause the most social disturbance. But writing on the subject has been too greatly charged with emotion. In late Victorian Scotland, Alexander Mackenzie's lurid and loosely organized *History of the Highland Clearances* aroused the kind of unthinking indignation that had hitherto been associated with Foxe's *Martyrs*. No doubt terrible injustices occurred in parts of the Highlands from time to time during the course of the nineteenth century. But one cannot judge of the extent to which clearances for sheep pasture brought about depopulation and emigration until a dispassionate and scientific study of the subject is forthcoming.[21]

Mackenzie was a propagandist and agrarian reformer. His book was concerned primarily with the nineteenth century. It referred only incidentally to the age of George III. Yet some recent writers seem to have assumed that the clearances, which Mackenzie describes in harrowing detail, were as common before the American Revolution as they were during and after the Napoleonic War. How far, then, were the notorious evictions for sheep pasture, or other forms of enclosure, responsible for emigration before 1775? In order to answer this question one must return briefly to agricultural conditions, and the efforts made for their improvement, in the eighteenth-century Highlands.

The cultivation of intermixed strips in open fields was known in Scotland as the runrig system. Universal at the commencement of the century, this wasteful and inefficient method of cultivation was little affected even by all the efforts of the improving landlords of the Age of Reason. As late as 1783 the old practices pre-

---

[21] Alexander Mackenzie, *The History of the Highland Clearances*, 2nd ed. (Glasgow, 1914, reprinted 1946). Little of this book was actually written by Mackenzie himself. For the most part it consists of a somewhat unbalanced collection of documents and contemporary opinions concerning the nineteenth-century Highland clearances.

vailed on the Argyllshire estates of the Earl of Breadalbane, a vigorous practical exponent of agricultural reform. The earl's chamberlain in Argyll reported to his employer in scathing terms upon the condition of these lands:

Many farms have eight tenants. . . . These eight tenants labour the farm and carry on all their other works together. First they plow the whole land, then they divide every field or spot of ground which they judge to be of equal quality into eight parts or shares and cast lots for what each is to occupy for that crop. After this each sows his own share and reaps it again in harvest and so they go on year after year.[22]

Even where the tenants held the same strips or rigs perennially, as they did in Badenoch and Lochtayside, things were little better, for the crofter had little or no security of tenure. The crofter, so called because he farmed a croft (part of the "infield," or better land near the center of the whole farm), seldom had a lease of the heritor. He might be ordered at any time, by a process called "precept of warning," to remove himself and his family from his holding. In many places the crofters had nothing to do with the heritor, and might not even enjoy the protection of a benevolent aristocrat. In 1769 on Lochtayside, for example, the Earl of Breadalbane placed very few of the crofters who occupied his lands. Most of them paid rent to, and did agreed services for, the tenants or tacksmen of the earl. The most wretched class of cultivators, the cotters, were virtually agricultural laborers. They occupied cottages with tiny arable plots attached and worked as farm servants for the tacksmen over them. The tacksman might move the cotter to another holding at will, whereas the crofter generally was exempt from such interference.[23]

Scotland, unlike England, did not recognize customary rights in her law courts. While the landlord might theoretically move his tenants around at will, the force of prescribed usage usually sufficed to keep things very much as they were. Only during the period when a lease was in force, however, was there any legal restraint on the landlord. Leases were by no means common. Even where they existed they were usually drawn up for such short

[22] McArthur, ed., *Lochtayside*, pp. liv–lv.
[23] *Ibid.*, p. lvi; Hamilton, ed., *Monymusk Papers*, pp. xxv–xxvi; McArthur, ed., *Lochtayside*, pp. xxxvi–xxxviii.

terms that they provided little security, let alone inducement to improve the land.[24] Many landlords were slow to grant longer leases. Since the burden of making capital investments in the land was generally left to the tenant, the landlords laid themselves open to the charge of discouraging enterprise on the part of their tenants. On old-fashioned estates, where practically all the land was leased to tacksmen, the proprietors had no direct power of granting leases to the undertenants. The middlemen, of course, were no more ready to grant long leases than they were to forego the oppressive services which were their customary due. If a heritor wished to abolish the institution of tacksmen on his estate, he had to wait at least until the tacks expired. The heritor might plausibly argue that security of tenure for the undertenants would achieve nothing in the way of agricultural advance. For had not the tacksmen enjoyed such security for generations without the smallest improvements taking place?

Had the landlords done everything in their power to ameliorate the plight of the peasantry, it is probable that they would have achieved very little, unless over a very long period of time. For there remained the fundamental problem of the pressure of population upon the means of subsistence. The surplus population of wholly or partially unemployed persons would still have remained as the greatest single cause of poverty.[25]

The Crown Commissioners for the Forfeited Estates of the 1745 rebellion attempted an enlightened policy, hoping to lessen the likelihood of future rebellions by making the Highland peasant more independent. They gave long leases to the crofters. From 1737 on, the undertenants of the Duke of Argyll in Morven enjoyed the security of leases, which came to be standardized at a term of nineteen years. According to the English traveler Pennant, the policy of giving long leases kept the crofters on the forfeited estates contented and banished from their minds all thoughts of emigration.[26]

The Act of 1770, to encourage the improvement of lands in Scot-

[24] *Ibid.*, p. lxx; Adam, "Highland Landlords," pp. 15–16.

[25] *Ibid.*, pp. 15–17, 19–20.

[26] *Ibid.*, p. 15; Thomas Pennant, *A Tour in Scotland, and Voyage to the Hebrides; MDCCLXXII* (Chester, Eng., 1774–76), I, 314.

land held under entail, had three main provisions. The first was intended to facilitate the granting of long leases. The second provided encouragement for holders of such leases to undertake agricultural improvements. Thirdly, the prospective heirs of entailed estates had to pay a high proportion of the cost of such improvements. According to one clause, leases for two lifetimes had to contain a provision obliging the tenant or tenants to fence and enclose all lands leased within thirty years. No field of arable land was to comprise more than forty acres.[27]

Two years after this act was passed, the Duke of Argyll was encouraging enclosure by foregoing 10 per cent of the rent of those laying out money in such improvements. Meanwhile the Earl of Breadalbane, anticipating the act, had his lands in Lochtayside surveyed in 1769. In 1771 he began to grant improving leases, which obliged their holders to manure the land and prescribed a proper rotation of crops. The tenant was to enclose corn and meadow lands at the rate of twenty roods a year until all the land was enclosed. The enclosures were to be made with stone dykes of a certain height. In return for greater security and the opportunity to borrow capital at 7½ per cent, the tenant paid a higher rent.[28]

The Breadalbane leases guarded against fragmentation of holdings by forbidding the tenant to sublet without the permission of the earl. Hitherto it had been the practice on Lochtayside for the tenant to carve new crofts out of his farm to accommodate his younger sons. Once the croft was sublet, it continued as an entity even when the holders changed.[29] The aim of enclosure, therefore, was not only to consolidate and abolish the runrig strips, but also to prevent fragmentation of holdings beyond an economical point.

The difference in productive power between enclosed and unenclosed lands was often very great. Farms might bring thirty to forty times as much profit after enclosure as before. But the benefits of enclosure could not be achieved without the reduction of numbers of the peasantry to the status of day laborers. Since the people crowded the land, it was not possible for everyone to possess an im-

---

[27] McArthur, ed., *Lochtayside*, pp. xvii–xx.

[28] Pennant, *Tour in Scotland*, I, 194–196; McArthur, ed., *Lochtayside*, pp. lxiv–lxv, lxviii–lxix.

[29] McArthur, ed., *Lochtayside*, pp. lxix, xxxviii.

proving lease and a holding of optimum size. The Highlander's intense dislike of working as a day laborer militated against the abolition of runrig by enclosure and helped to close off the one possible means of reducing unemployment and poverty. What the crofter and cotter wanted was not so much work as land.[30]

If the Highland landlords refused to allow continuing subdivision of the "mailings," or small holdings, they were charged with tyranny and with compelling younger sons to emigrate; those who allowed it were blamed for the consequent wretchedness of their estates and tenants. Many landlords were prepared to forego substantial rent increases by refraining from all forms of enclosure. But their generosity could only perpetuate archaic methods of agriculture and continuing subdivision of holdings. Such conservatism on the part of landlords fended off evictions by aggravating the general problem of poverty.[31]

In England, if a landowner wished to abolish strip cultivation and common lands, he secured a private Act of Parliament, under which commissioners were appointed to visit the village and divide the common rights and intermixed holdings. In Scotland the procedure was quite different. Private acts were never required. The only common rights adhered to the royal burghs. Only a written title was good in law. The shortness, or absence, of leases made it comparatively easy for the Scottish landlord to abolish the runrig in his own way. There were few legal proceedings over the enclosure of open fields.[32]

During the eighteenth century, then, the innate conservatism of the Highland landlords and peasantry wrestled with the new enthusiasm for agricultural improvement—an enthusiasm to whose indulgence there were no legal barriers—in a struggle that was to decide the economic future of the region. Only a few of the landlords succumbed to the spirit of modernization, but those who did so carried their plans into practice with great vigor.

Sir Archibald Grant of Monymusk, for example, began his great work in Aberdeenshire in the year 1717. When reletting lands, Grant would throw holdings together so as to give the new tenants compact

[30] Adam, "Highland Landlords," pp. 165, 171.

[31] *Ibid.*, p. 177; Adam, "Highland Emigrations of 1783–1803," p. 89.

[32] Hamilton, ed., *Monymusk Papers*, pp. lxv–lxvi; Grant, *Old Highland Farm*, pp. 31–32.

and reasonably sized farms. He restricted the number of cotters and crofters and arranged for the removal of redundant undertenants to new land in outlying parts of the farm. These improvements had the effect of transforming the undertenant into a farm laborer. But it was a very gradual process, for there was much physical work to be done in building dykes and so on. The enclosing of the fields could not be accomplished without disturbance to the existing social order. Tenants and crofters were displaced. But at Monymusk, one of the earliest and most thoroughly modernized estates, there do not appear to have been any cases of hardship caused by eviction. The redistribution of the rural population was effected with a minimum of inconvenience to the peasantry.[33]

After 1750 it was not uncommon for the Monymusk tacksmen to renounce their tacks. It is unfortunately impossible to say what happened to those who did so. Many of the crofters became farm laborers. But on other estates there is ample evidence for the emigration of tacksmen, accompanied by numbers of their former crofter tenants. The chief proximate cause of the exodus of the tacksmen was rising rents, which sometimes, but by no means always, arose from the landlord's desire to profit from capital invested in agricultural improvements. But this subject must be reserved for the next chapter. Meanwhile, it remains to discuss briefly that class of enclosures and evictions which has been so universally condemned as a cause of depopulation in both the eighteenth and nineteenth centuries. The enclosure of arable lands for pasture necessarily involved wholesale evictions wherever it occurred. But how far were such clearances responsible for emigration before 1775? It is here suggested, in spite of many statements to the contrary in other works, that they were negligible as a cause of emigration before the 1790's.

IV

We have seen how the conservatism of many landlords prevented the displacement of crofters and cotters for the purpose of enclosing the runrig lands. It has been pointed out that even where such displacement and enclosure took place it probably caused little or no hardship. No doubt numbers of the surplus farming population, as

[33] Hamilton, ed., *Monymusk Papers*, pp. xxvi, lxix, lxxi.

in England, drifted into the towns in search of employment. But it
does not appear that this type of enclosure contributed directly to
emigration. The great majority of those Highlanders who went to
America in the 1770's, whether tacksmen or crofters, complained of
high rents but not of eviction.[34] Those few who did mention outright
eviction as the reason for their decision to emigrate always explained it as the result of the graziers' turning them out to make way
for sheep.

The history of evictions through the enclosure of arable land for
pasture goes back to the 1720's, when tenants were turned out of
their holdings to provide grazing for black cattle. In 1725 bands of
men and women threw down newly raised enclosures in Galloway.
Others maimed or destroyed the cattle of the larger tenants who
favored the enclosures. As a result of this violence the fencing in
of the land by hedge or dyke was checked for a generation.[35]

Opinions differ as to the date when large-scale sheep farming began, but most authorities agree that sheep were unimportant before
1770. In the middle of the century the stocking industry of Aberdeenshire was almost entirely dependent on wool imported from
the south. Even in 1784 Inverness exported little more than a ton
of wool. In the 1770's Mackintosh of Balnespick owned a flock of
about a hundred sheep. At this time the great wool trade with the
south had just begun. In 1785 there had still been no clearances
anywhere in that district of Strathspey. Evictions began soon afterward at the Belleville property of James Macpherson, author of the
poems of Ossian. But a visitor to Badenoch in that year found the
congregation at Raits church much thinned. He was informed "that
the spirit of emigration had seized the people of these parts, and
that many handicraftsmen . . . had actually left the country." [36]

Lowlanders were chiefly responsible, it would seem, for the introduction of sheep farming into the Highlands, but many Highland
tacksmen took a part in the business, especially in Lochaber and
Badenoch. In 1770 eighty people of Aberarder in Badenoch were

[34] *Ibid.*, p. lxxiii; Cameron, comp., *Emigrants from Scotland, passim; Scots
Magazine,* XXXII–XXXVII (1770–1775), *passim.*

[35] H. G. Graham, *Social Life,* pp. 169–170.

[36] Mackenzie, *Highland Clearances,* p. 260; Grant, *Old Highland Farm,* pp.
66–68, 116–117; H. G. Graham, *Social Life,* pp. 176–177.

forced out of their holdings. These crofters lived on the west bank of Loch Laggan, near the upper Spey, in Inverness-shire. The history of the affair went back to the '45 rebellion, when Ewen Macpherson forfeited the estate of Cluny, which included Aberarder, to the Crown. Lachlan Mackintosh of Mackintosh, whose family had once owned the estate, engaged in litigation for its return to himself. A decision of the House of Lords gave the estate into the hands of the Commissioners for the Forfeited Estates.

The Barons of the Exchequer appointed Henry Butter, an Englishman, as their factor for the estate of Cluny. Butter was clever and unscrupulous, interested only in feathering his own nest. A certain Reverend Macpherson, on half pay as chaplain of a regiment, applied for a lease of the Aberarder farms, with the object of clearing off all the Roman Catholic possessors and turning the land into a sheep walk. Butter collaborated with Macpherson in this scheme, the minister got his lease, and, in 1767, Butter obtained a special warrant from the Barons of the Exchequer for ejecting the eighty tenants from their holdings. Some of these, headed by Ronald and Alexander Macdonald, brought Butter into court and tried to prove that the Cluny estate had never been forfeited, but rather had escheated, to the Crown. In 1770, after years of litigation, the House of Lords ruled in favor of Butter and Macpherson. The eighty tenants were evicted.

In their appeal to the Lords, the crofters pleaded that they

were conscious of having given no occasion for such harsh treatment— they were not in arrear of rent, and could hardly persuade themselves that the mildness of Government would allow fourscore honest Highlanders to be turned adrift, without having anywhere to go to, and their bread to be eat by a bachelor clergyman, who was to pay no higher rent than they had done.

A century later an inquirer could obtain no information locally as to the fate of the eighty, other than the tradition that they had all gone to America.[37]

The story of evictions for sheep pasture as a cause of emigration, from this early instance down to the outbreak of the American war,

[37] Charles Fraser-Mackintosh, "The Depopulation of Aberarder in Badenoch, 1770," *Celtic Magazine*, II (1877), 418, 420–421, 425–426.

is soon told. In 1772 a party of two hundred persons from Sutherland passed through Edinburgh on its way to Greenock to embark for America. They gave as their reason for emigrating "want of the means of livelihood at home, through the opulent grasiers ingrossing the farms, and turning them into pasture." In September, 1775, a group of 136 farmers and laborers from Glenorchy and Appin, who were sailing for North Carolina, complained of being forced from their lands by high rents, or "to make room for Sheepherds." Those from Appin seem to have been particularly affected by enclosures for pasture, asserting "that out of one hundred Mark Land that formerly was occupied by Tennants who made their Rents by rearing Cattle and raising Grain, Thirty three Mark Land of it is now turned into Sheep Walks and they seem to think in a few years more, Two thirds of that Country, at least will be in the same State." Not all the members of the party, however, gave eviction as a reason for leaving the country. The laborers and tradesmen either could not support their families on their wages or hoped for better remuneration in the colonies. "It is not from any other motive but the dread of want," said the laborers, "that they quit a Country which above all others they would wish to live in." [38]

Even from Sutherland, where the conversion of arable land into sheep walks began and was carried farthest, there are no other accounts of emigration for this reason before the American war. Many shiploads of Sutherland people left for America between 1770 and 1775, but none of the emigrants seem to have been driven to depart by eviction. The party mentioned above was certainly an exception; it may have been unique. Out of some 1,650 emigrants who left Sutherland and the neighboring counties between 1773 and 1775 for North America, not one mentioned eviction as even a minor cause of the step. All manner of other reasons were given, both economic and personal, but not eviction and not sheep. [39]

After 1790 evictions to make room for sheep were more numerous. The year 1791, indeed, was long referred to in the Highlands as, "the year of the sheep." While it has been assumed—largely, it would

---

[38] *Scots Magazine*, XXXIV (1772), 395; Newsome, "Records of Emigrants," pp. 138–142.

[39] *Scots Magazine*, XXXV (1773), 557; Newsome, "Records of Emigrants," pp. 130–138; Andrews, *Guide to Materials*, II, 184–185.

appear, on the basis of Alexander Mackenzie's unsatisfactory book —that clearances for sheep were practically the sole cause of the wholesale depopulation of the Highlands in the nineteenth century, it would be safer to say that the whole question is open to debate and requires careful study before authoritative statements can be made about it. But there can hardly be any doubt that such clearances were negligible as a cause of emigration before 1775. Many writers, unfortunately, have accepted the assumption about the role of the clearances in the nineteenth century, while others, with much less evidence to support their contention, have transferred it to the eighteenth.

V

Henry Grey Graham, the Scottish social historian, denied that the Highland evictions of the eighteenth century aggravated the poverty of the area. These evictions were carried out in order to increase the productivity of the land. The poorest districts were the very places where no such improvements occurred. The districts where population diminished or emigrated were the very ones where sheep walks and consolidated farms were last introduced. The Caithness sheep pastures rose to six times their former value. The greatest destitution was on the lands where the old ways remained unchanged.[40]

Graham's argument is not entirely convincing, but it contains or implies one significant truth: there was no direct relationship in the eighteenth century between enclosures, evictions, and the spread of sheep pastures, on the one hand, and the volume of emigration on the other. Graham, however, in his anxiety to justify the gospel of scientific progress and all its works, avoided the whole question of the cost in suffering of the eighteenth-century improvements. It did not follow, as Graham implied, from the enhanced land values and productivity that accompanied modernization, that the landlord allowed a share of the benefits to his tenants. It certainly did not follow that the evicted or displaced tenants derived some form of compensation from the profits that later accrued to the landlord. Firm answers to this, as to so many other questions, must await an

[40] H. G. Graham, *Social Life*, p. 224.

exhaustive study of the eighteenth-century estate papers in the National Library of Scotland.

Margaret I. Adam has brought some powerful arguments together in support of the contention that sheep farming caused little emigration from the Highlands in the eighteenth century. The majority of the writers who blamed this innovation for Scots emigration based their case on likelihoods and on a priori argument rather than on definite examples that established the immediate causal relationship. The case they presented was very incomplete. Even in the eighteenth century some writers pointed out flaws in the argument. They said, for instance, that sheep farms seldom curtailed arable land, since much of the new sheep pasture had hitherto been wasteland. They denied that the displacement of one type of farming by another necessarily produced emigration, and they suggested alternative causes.

The charges of depopulation made by the enemies of sheep farming are not substantiated by population statistics. Between 1755 and 1800, for example, the combined population of Argyll, Inverness, and Ross increased considerably. Argyll, which took strongly to sheep farming, provided comparatively few of the Highland emigrants in the years after 1783. But the Hebrides, which were much less affected by sheep farming, provided many. Emigration of displaced tenants was not inevitable; sometimes it resulted from their unwillingness to adapt themselves to new conditions at or near home.[41]

Enclosure of runrig and the consolidation of farms caused little social disturbance beyond the sullen disapproval of the conservative peasantry. They were not directly responsible for emigration. The spread of sheep farming resulted in evictions only in those few localities where the arable land of the glen bottoms was enclosed to provide winter pasture for the sheep, which came down from the hill tops in the cold weather. These evictions did not necessarily bring about emigration, although they encouraged it. At the same time, all these enclosures fell into a general pattern of agrarian improvement which increased the yield of the land. The improving landlords, whether responsible and paternalistic aristocrats of the old school or grasping profiteers of the new, made immediate gains

[41] Adam, "Highland Emigrations of 1783–1803," pp. 80–83.

from the new agriculture by raising rents. The increments of rent were not always, and could not be, exactly proportional to the additional profits produced by the improvements. More important from the standpoint of emigration, the rises in rents tended to extend beyond the limited areas where improvements had taken place. It is probably safe to say that the great bulk of the emigrants from both Highlands and Lowlands in the years 1770–1775 were motivated at least in part by rising rents. Yet the great majority of them, likewise, came from districts that were unaffected by agricultural reform.

It follows that the indirect results of enclosure were more important for the history of emigration than the direct ones.

Among the causes of Highland migration, rising rents were bound up inextricably with the social system as it emerged from the generation after the '45 rebellion. It was the rent question that made of the tacksmen the great disaffected class of the period. It was these very tacksmen who gave to the Highland, and indeed the Scottish, emigration of the years 1763–1775 its special character. To understand the phenomenon of communal migration and its connection with the discontented tacksman's ambition to "establish new clans in the other hemisphere" it is necessary to look more closely at the landed oligarchy who owned most of Scotland before the American war. Who were these landlords, and how far were they responsible for forcing emigration upon the tacksmen, the crofters, and the cotters?

IV

Forces behind Emigration:
The Social Structure

THE most common complaint of the emigrants of the 1770's was rising rents, which were widely blamed by contemporary writers for the prevailing poverty. After 1763 rents rose all over Scotland, but at different rates in different areas. The increase varied, in the Highlands from 33⅓ to 300 per cent, in the Lowlands from 200 to 400 per cent.[1]

The Lowland areas most affected also experienced great advances in agriculture and a general improvement in the standard of life. Examples of very large rent rises can be found in Perthshire, Berwickshire, and Ayrshire. Yet the people of those Lowland areas, it is said, did not suffer from rack-renting; they were able to pay what was required out of the increased yield of the improved land. Some farmers were able to save money and buy the land they had formerly held on lease.[2]

In the Highlands, high rents did not necessarily produce poverty nor low rents prosperity. The rents paid on unimproved land were

---

[1] Adam, "Highland Landlords," p. 10; Cameron, comp., *Emigrants from Scotland, passim;* a letter from "VERITAS" in *Scots Magazine*, XXXIV (1772), 700, asserted that the rent of farms in the south of Scotland had advanced from eight to ten times, that in the Highlands from three to five times.

[2] Adam, "Highland Landlords," p. 10; H. G. Graham, *Social Life*, pp. 211–213.

sometimes so high as to be impossible of payment. But such rack-renting was not common. Tenants on well-managed cattle or arable farms could afford to pay higher rents than those who continued to use the old farming methods. As a consequence, those who paid more rent often presented a better appearance than those who paid less. Real hardship of a kind to encourage emigration arose mainly from sudden, unexpected, and arbitrary increases in rent, which were a by-product of the short leases or absence of leases mentioned in the previous chapter.[3]

The landowners of the 1770's were charged by contemporaries with "tyrannical oppression," for letting farms at excessive rents on restrictive terms. Thomas Miller, the Lord Justice Clerk, who was much interested in the growing emigration of the 1770's, believed its chief cause to be rising rents. Henry Dundas, the Lord Advocate, likewise blamed the "precipitant and injudicious rise of rents," but he saw this phenomenon as merely one symptom of the social and economic revolution in the Highlands that followed from the legislation passed after the '45. The sheriff of Argyll and Bute thought that rents had been raised too swiftly and that had this been done more gradually mass emigration might have been prevented. Robert Forbes observed that eight hundred people had left Argyll in 1770 and 1771. Others were preparing to leave, "which, if not timeously and wisely looked to, may terminate in depopulating Old Caledon! All, *all* this is owing to the exorbitant rents for land." In 1773, 176 tenants of the forfeited estate of Lovat petitioned for a reduction of rent, implying a threat of emigration unless their grievances were redressed.[4]

A man named McQueen, landlord of the inn at Glenmoriston,

[3] Adam, "Highland Landlords," pp. 11–12.
[4] Dalphy A. Fagerstrom, "The American Revolutionary Movement in Scottish Opinion, 1763–1783" (unpublished doctoral dissertation; University of Edinburgh, 1951), ch. iii, citing the Edinburgh *Caledonian Mercury*, March 12, 1774; *ibid.*, citing PRO SP54/45, Thomas Miller to Earl of Suffolk, April 25, 1774, Archibald Campbell to Thomas Miller, March 3, 1774, BM Add. MSS 34, 422, f. 352, Henry Dandas to William Eden, Sept. 5, 1775; Rev. Robert Forbes, Bishop of Ross and Caithness, to Bishop Gordon, May 9, 1771, in Rev. Robert Forbes, *The Lyon in Mourning: Or a Collection of Speeches Letters Journals etc. Relative to the Affairs of Prince Charles Edward Stuart* (Edinburgh, 1896), III, 259; A. H. Millar, ed., *A Selection of Scottish Forfeited Estates Papers 1715; 1745* (Edinburgh, 1909), pp. 120, 122.

told Dr. Johnson indignantly that no man left his native country willingly, but that he was about to try his fortune in some other place, for the rent of his farm had been raised in twenty-five years from five to twenty pounds, which he found himself unable to pay. But McQueen cannot have been so badly off as he indicated, for he remained in the same place for another fifteen years, then moved to a farm close by, where he lived until past ninety.[5]

The views of contemporaries are borne out by the evidence of the emigrants themselves. In August, 1774, ninety Highlanders from Glenorchy and Kintyre left Greenock for Wilmington, North Carolina, with the universal chant, repeated like a jingle from mouth to mouth, "High Rents & oppression." Another group, also from Kintyre, left "for High Rents & better Encouragement." Such reasons were commonly given to the customs officers who registered the departing emigrant ships during 1774 and 1775.[6]

There is no doubt that the landlords in certain areas were oppressive to the poorer classes of cultivators.

II

The Reverend Thomas Hepburn of Birsay blamed the poverty of the Orkneys in the 1750's upon the oppressive and luxurious lairds and heritors. This minister was perhaps not entirely impartial, for he was defending his patron, the fourteenth Earl of Morton, whom the heritors were suing for fraud in collecting feu duties. Hepburn found the lairds responsible for crushing out of the farmers all desire to improve their land, through short leases, unlimited services, and many other hardships. As a result the arable land lay runrig, and the pasture, held in common, was understocked. The lairds gave short tacks, collected grassums (quasi-feudal reliefs levied upon successors to farms), and exacted numerous and uncertain services. Hepburn was candid enough to admit that the heritors' resentment against Morton had some basis in that many of them paid as much as half their gross rent receipts in feu duties. Yet, of the great crowd of Orkney heritors, only sixteen had joined in prosecuting the earl,

[5] S. Johnson, *Journey*, p. 35; Boswell, *Tour* (Pottle ed.), p. 104.
[6] Newsome, "Records of Emigrants," pp. 51–54, 142–143.

and their leader had failed in his attempt to stir up the gentry of Shetland.[7]

The above episode was evidently part of a long-standing feud between the heritors and their superior landlord, for the former had joined with the Shetland lairds to publish an account of their grievances at Edinburgh in 1750. Although there was little or no emigration from Orkney before 1774, conditions there help to illuminate the social relationships in other areas from which emigration did take place, largely as a result of the social structure and its effects. The lack of emigration from Orkney itself seems to have been due rather to a dearth of shipping than to the absence of desire. When the first emigrant ship arrived it was unable to accommodate all those who wished to go to America aboard her. However that may be, the strained position of the upper levels of the landed hierarchy in Orkney and Shetland indicates that the crofters were far from the only class who had reason to distrust their immediate superiors. Orkney, it seems, was one of those areas where there existed four layers of landholders, the superior, titled landlords, like Morton, the heritors, or lairds, who inherited their land inalienably but paid feu duties (in lieu of feudal services), the tacksmen, who held land on lease, and the crofters, who were usually tenants at will. In the quarrel outlined above, the significant thing is the stress it lays upon the discontent of the class of landholders next to the top of the social ladder. As we shall see presently, a similar discontent in other areas was to be a potent factor in bringing about mass emigration from certain parts of the Highlands in the period between 1763 and 1775.

In the other group of northern islands, the Shetlands, emigrants were preparing to leave in 1775 "because the Landholders in Shetland have raised their rents so high that they could not live without sinking the little matter they had left." Unfair rental assessments were due to special circumstances in the islands. The Crown rents were farmed out to the highest bidder in each parish. The collectors continued to use old Norse weights and measures in measuring rents, which were paid in kind. The receivers of butter, for example, gradu-

---

[7] [Rev. Thomas Hepburn of Birsay], *A Letter to a Gentleman from His Friend in Orkney, (Written in 1757) Containing the True Causes of the Poverty of That Country* (Edinburgh, 1885), pp. 2–4, 16–17, 19, 27–33, 42, 52.

ally raised the unit of measurement, the "lispond," from eighteen to thirty pounds. Scandalous sums were being demanded in lieu of delivery in kind. The chamberlains of the Crown and the factors of the other landlords added new exactions whenever they could find an excuse. But the peasant's payments were far from done with when he had satisfied the landlord. The fishing industry was severely taxed to pay the ministers' stipends. The "fishteind," or tythe, was usually paid in kind, but here again the cash substitute was twice the value of the tax when paid in goods. By 1775 such was the poverty brought about in Shetland by these hardships that the inhabitants were willing to emigrate in droves, but had not the means to transport themselves. The young men went off to sea when they could find a ship.[8]

Buchanon, in his *Travels* (1793), a book which describes the Outer Hebrides as they were about 1783, says that the services exacted there sometimes came to five days' work per week. In Reay, Sutherland, they varied from twenty to one hundred and twenty days a year.[9]

In the areas mentioned, and in some other of the more remote parts of the Highlands and islands, the crofter and cotter suffered severely from unreasonable rents and arbitrary services. The oppressor was usually a tacksman. It was in the most remote and backward areas that agriculture was most primitive, that the tacksmen, or middlemen, survived longest, and that the oppression of the undertenants was worst. But what was the position of the tacksman? Was there anything in his relations with his own superior in the landed hierarchy which tended to elicit such heartless behavior?

III

In 1773, according to Dr. Johnson, the tacksman was next in dignity to the laird. This would be true, of course, whether or not the laird, or heritor, paid feu duties to a superior landlord. The tacksman would farm part of his tack and let the rest to undertenants.

---

[8] Newsome, "Records of Emigrants," p. 48; letter from "Zetlandicus," dated March 24, 1775, Edinburgh *Weekly Magazine*, June 1, 1775, reprinted in James Anderson, *Observations on the Means of Exciting a Spirit of National Industry* (Edinburgh, 1777), App. IV, pp. 521–524.

[9] Adam, "Highland Landlords," p. 12.

The tacksman was responsible to his superior for the payment of rent on the whole of his tack. So the more he got from the crofters the less he had to pay out of his own pocket. Few tacks were any longer hereditary, and strangers could now buy their way into the position of tacksmen. Many members of the class were now indifferent to the laird's honor and safety. There were many in the Highlands who argued that the tacksmen were unnecessary middlemen, parasites whose elimination would at once increase the rents of the laird and reduce those of the crofter. To the conservative doctor this was a dangerously radical argument. It is not true, however, that the cultivator everywhere found a tacksman intervening between himself and the laird. In the Lochtayside survey of 1769, for example, only one tack appears.

No doubt the complicated and minute joint holdings of the cultivators usually made some kind of organizer indispensable, so that the laird could collect his rents from one man rather than forty or fifty. Since the tacksmen were left over from the almost vanished age of feudal relationships, they might at least continue to make themselves useful in this way.[10]

There were, as might be expected, good and bad tacksmen. There were various reasons for the oppressive conduct of the bad ones. Buchanon, after detailing the cruelties of the Hebridean tacksmen, notices the great difference between "the mild treatment which is shown to subtenants . . . by the old lessees, descended of ancient and honourable families, and the outrageous rapacity shown by those necessitous strangers who have obtained leases from absent proprietors, who treat the natives as if they were a conquered and inferior race." Fortunately such conditions did not exist, and such outrages did not occur, in the central Highlands.[11]

In Badenoch, between 1769 and 1773, Mackintosh of Balnespick consistently spent more in paying the Chief of Mackintosh for his estate than he received from his undertenants. In the bad year, 1771, he received less than eight pounds and paid out over forty-eight. While the Macdonalds of Skye were emigrating in crowds, the Macleod of Dunvegan in that island relieved his tenants from their oppressive rents. The laird of the neighboring isle of Raasey had

[10] S. Johnson, *Journey*, p. 78; McArthur, ed., *Lochtayside*, pp. xxxii–xxxiii.
[11] Grant, *Old Highland Farm*, p. 149.

treated his people so well that not a man had emigrated from the estate. By 1773 many landlords were letting down their rents in order to prevent emigration from their estates. In June, 1774, a hundred emigrants from Lewis in the Outer Hebrides arrived at Philadelphia. They declared that all possible methods were being used to prevent further emigration, including the lowering of rents.[12] Apparently there was some locking of stables after the horses had bolted.

Dr. Johnson, with his usual keen observation, noticed that the chiefs, divested of their former honors and prerogatives, had turned their thoughts to the improvement of their revenues. They expected more rent, as they had less homage. Another writer in 1773, this one a champion of emigration and himself very probably a tacksman, traced the evils of the day to absentee landlords, and absenteeism itself to the spirit of the times. He commented on the relations between landlord and cultivators:

Formerly the proprietors resided mostly among them upon their estates, conversed freely, and were familiar with them, were tender of them, cherished, and patronized them; to them the tenants were devoted; to them they had recourse upon every emergency: they were happy, they grew up and prospered under them. The modern lairds, unlike their fore-fathers, live at a great distance from their estates. Whatever misfortunes may befal the tenants, whatever grievances they have to complain of, . . . they have no access to their masters.[13]

By 1770 many of the crofters had dealings only with tacksmen or factors, and neither of these classes was well disposed to them. The factor cared only about pleasing his absentee master. The tacksman had exploited and squeezed the crofter for centuries. After Culloden, as the restraints of the old social system broke down, this exploitation became even more severe. In the generation before 1775 it is unlikely that in most areas the crofter could have paid more rent than he was paying. As we have seen, when rents rose suddenly toward the close of this period, the crofter was practically forced to emigrate.

[12] *Ibid.*, p. 88; Pennant, *Tour in Scotland*, I, 293; Boswell, *Tour* (Pottle ed.), p. 132; S. Johnson, *Journey*, p. 90; Millar, ed., *Forfeited Estates Papers*, p. 120; *Virginia Gazette*, Purdie and Dixon, July 7, 1774, p. 2.
[13] S. Johnson, *Journey*, p. 85; "Scotus Americanus," in Boyd, ed., *Eighteenth Century Tracts*, p. 430.

Before 1745 the tacksmen were usually relatives of the chiefs, of high social standing, and paid a merely nominal rent to their landlords, for whom they also performed important military services. The cash or kind payment was in the nature of a quitrent rather than a rent reflecting the true value of the land held. One of the Jacobite'prisoners of 1716 petitioned the government for release on the ground that he had been compelled to join the Marquis of Huntly's forces because of his feudal obligations, which required him to follow his superior "in hunting and hosting." He enclosed his tack (lease) with the petition. Military service was a normal incident of land tenure before 1745. Strong measures might be taken to enforce such obligations, and occasionally a recalcitrant vassal would complain of having his house burned down and his horses carried off. The Act of 1716, "for the more effectual securing the Peace of the Highlands of Scotland," ordered the commutation of a long list of feudal services for cash rents. These included personal attendance, hosting, hunting, watching, and warding, whether due by charter, contract, custom, or agreement. The measure did not prevent the outbreak of a yet more serious rebellion in 1745, but it foreshadowed the vigorous enforcement of peace, and the proscription of the Highland dress and arms, after 1747.[14]

When the chiefs ceased to wage private war, they had no further need of lieutenants to raise and officer the clansmen in time of danger. The military function of the tacksman therefore disappeared. Constant attendance upon the chief, once the general practice among tacksmen, was no longer necessary. In time many tacks (leases to tacksmen) and wadsets (holdings mortgaged by the superior landlord to wadsetters) were liquidated, and the former undertenants secured leases directly from the heritor or great landlord. Such crofters were lucky, for they escaped the clutches of the tacksman, and, while they paid no more rent than before, they contributed three times as much to the income of the chief, through the elimination of the middleman. Such tacksmen as remained—and many of them hung on even into the nineteenth century—had to pay higher rents in lieu of their former military services. A commentator of 1772 summed up these far-reaching social and economic changes

---

[14] Adam, "Highland Emigration of 1770," *Scottish Historical Review*, XVI (1918–19), 285–286; Insh, *Jacobite Movement*, pp. 128, 148.

in the Highlands and pointed out their relationship to the prevailing migration, in a remarkable passage:

Such of those wadsetters and tacksmen as rather wish to be distinguished as leaders, than by industry [i.e., by status rather than by wealth], have not taken leases again, alledging that the rents are risen above what the land will bear; but, say they, in order to be revenged of our master for doing so, and what is worse, depriving us of our subordinate chieftain-ship, by abolishing our former privilege of subsetting, we will not only leave his lands, but by spiriting the lower class of people to emigrate, we shall carry a clan to America, and when they are there, they must work for us, or starve. The industrious set [of tacksmen], who act on different principles, by preferring their native country, find it their inter-est to encourage the emigration for two reasons; one is, that by a scarcity of tenants they may chance to get farms cheaper; the other, that by getting rid of the idle part of the lowest class, such will no longer operate among them like drones, who have been (especially after a bad harvest) a dead weight on the tenant, who has been obliged to purchase meal for the maintenance of many such incumbents on his tenement, almost to his total ruin. Some of the proprietors, sensible of the latter, will readily consent to the emigration taking place, and even wish it, from a belief, that in their room strangers from the south will succeed, much to the improvement of their estates, and the country in general.[15]

Since these three classes, although from different motives, agree on promoting emigration, the writer went on, it is not surprising that the poor crofters listen to the artful insinuations of the emigrant tacksmen, encouraging them to become their followers in the prom-ised land. But the greedy tacksman will either sell their labor for a term of years, ostensibly to get his expenses back but actually making three times the value of their passage money, or he will use their labor himself, possibly for life, in clearing and working lands which he gets for nothing from the colonial governor by virtue of head right.[16] It is unlikely that a modern writer could express the tacksman's role in the emigration of 1763–1775 more succinctly.[17]

[15] Letter from "VERITAS" to the *Edinburgh Advertiser*, Dec. 31, 1772, re-printed in *Scots Magazine*, XXXIV (1772), 697–700.

[16] *Ibid.*, p. 699.

[17] In "Highland Emigration of 1770," pp. 285–290, Margaret Adam formu-lates the outlines of what may be called the "tacksman thesis" regarding the causation of the Highland emigration of the 1770's. Although she quotes briefly from the letter of "VERITAS" (n. 15, above), she does not sufficiently

Herein lies the essential meaning and explanation of Dr. Johnson's prophecy that the tacksmen, if allowed to go on as they were doing in 1773, would "establish new clans in the other hemisphere."

The tacksmen differed one from another in wealth and social standing. Among the lesser tacksmen were the wadsetters already mentioned. A Skye man told James Boswell that the "gentlemen tacksmen" there were accustomed to flatter their chiefs with the prospect of higher rents than were fair or even possible, thus forcing emigration upon the lesser tacksmen. The latter took with them to America whatever capital they could reduce to a liquid form and so impoverished the island still further.[18]

IV

The more conservative and less industrious tacksmen were unwilling to adapt themselves to the conditions that prevailed in the Highlands after 1747. They resented having to pay larger rents in place of military service to the chiefs. They usually found it impossible to transfer the burden of the increase to the peasantry, who already suffered under a crushing load of exactions. In these circumstances they were ready listeners to tempting tales from other lands. In America, they believed, it might be possible to reconstitute the old clan system with themselves as chiefs. If this could be accomplished, they would again enjoy their former prestige and would probably augment their incomes by carving new estates out of the wilderness. To put such plans in execution it was necessary to collect a group of persons who would do the pioneering work of building an estate in America and who would thenceforward remain a docile and dependent tenantry. Naturally they turned to their own crofters, who already possessed the desired psychology.

But why should the crofters agree to go to America with the very tacksmen who had oppressed them in the Highlands? What induced them to continue voluntarily the dependent relationship which seems to have been so much to their disadvantage? There

acknowledge her indebtedness to him for the ideas contained in her article, practically all of which are foreshadowed in the letter. She writes only of the Scottish end of the tackmen's migration. The most significant word in the letter, "clan," is misprinted as "class" in Miss Adam's article.

[18] Boswell, *Tour* (Chapman, ed.), pp. 295–296.

was, of course, the ingrained habit of obedience. They were not always sophisticated enough to see what course of action was in their own best interest. If their tacksman was leaving, they could scarcely imagine what life would be like in his absence. He was not only their landlord and employer; his whole life was interwoven with theirs. Their animals grazed in common; they tilled the runrig fields jointly; they bought and sold largely through him.[19]

Even in the eastern Highlands, where ties with the Lowlands were much stronger than elsewhere, the influence of the Jacobite lairds over their tenantry was very great. Early in the century most of the Duke of Gordon's tenants, being then Roman Catholics, followed their landlord into the Episcopal church.[20] The prestige and power of the tacksman differed from those of the chief only in degree. As has been pointed out, the latter had his own reasons for failing to discourage the emigrating tacksman. The former eliminated himself as a middleman and so allowed the landlord to take the whole rent of his tack. He carried off the surplus population and so made it easier for the landlord to consolidate and improve the farms on his land.

During the French and Indian War, many members of the tacksman class served as officers in the British army. These were able to take full advantage of the offer of land contained in the Proclamation of 1763. A high proportion of the colonial land grants made in the ensuing years were made to Scots, and especially to Highlanders. The tacksman-officer could obtain a generous grant with the greater ease when he brought over Highland immigrants who enabled him to satisfy the requirement of settlement by white Protestants.[21] Those who had not served in the war, and who therefore had no claim under the proclamation, could secure lands in proportion to the number of persons they brought with them.

Even without encouragement from the tacksmen, whole neighborhoods in the Highlands formed parties for emigrating. The sense

---

[19] Adam, "Highland Emigration of 1770," p. 292; Grant, *Old Highland Farm*, p. 138.

[20] Insh, *Jacobite Movement*, pp. 128–129; Richard Pococke, Bishop of Meath, to his sister, July 28, 1760, in Richard Pococke, *Tours in Scotland, 1747, 1750, 1760*, ed. by Daniel William Kemp (Edinburgh, 1887), p. 193.

[21] Lewis B. Namier, *England in the Age of the American Revolution* (London, 1930), pp. 314–316.

of community and kinship operated powerfully in the pattern of migration even where the initiative came from below. Most of the Highlanders traveled in groups from the same locality, whether or not they followed the tacksmen. It was sometimes given, indeed, as a motive for emigration that there were no titled landlords in America to tyrannize over the farmer, that men were there more on one level and valued according to their abilities. By the 1770's the Highlander had come to look upon America as a veritable paradise of cheap land, low taxes, cheap provisions, and high wages, where beggary was unknown and the climate was healthy.[22]

Such a group, apparently without a tacksman to lead them, foregathered at Killin, in Perthshire, in May, 1775. Thirty families came together, making in all over three hundred people. They spent a night in barns and outhouses and early the next morning assembled to the sound of the bagpipes. Dressed in their best attire and some of them armed in the Highland fashion in spite of the law, they settled the order of march, bade farewell to their friends and relatives, and set off down the road. The first day carried them twenty-five miles to Loch Lomond. They traveled down the loch in boats for a further twenty-four miles, marched a few more miles to Dumbarton, sailed across the Clyde, and took ship at Greenock for the New World. About the same time, two hundred persons rendezvoused at Aviemore in Badenoch and marched off for Greenock to embark for America. Among them was a woman of eighty-three, on foot; her son preceded her playing "Tulluchgorum" on his bagpipes. Some of the emigrants took along children a month old, who were carried in baskets on their fathers' backs.[23]

V

One of the most striking examples of communal migration occurred in Skye in 1769 and the following years. In the eighteenth century 220,000 acres out of Skye's total of 409,000 belonged to the Macleods and were known as Macleod's country. The remaining 189,000 acres belonged to the Macdonalds and the Mackinnons. In 1751

[22] S. Johnson, *Journey*, pp. 86–87; Fagerstrom, "American Revolutionary Movement," ch. iii, citing the Edinburgh *Caledonian Mercury*, Jan. 3, 1774.

[23] Gilpin, *Observations*, I, 169–171; *Virginia Gazette*, Dixon and Hunter, Aug. 19, 1775, p. 2.

the Macdonald and Mackinnon lands were occupied by 64 tacksmen and proprietors holding 135 farms, and by 374 joint tenants holding 77 farms. The Macdonald tacksmen were required, in the 1760's, to pay rents which they considered exorbitant. In 1769 Sir Alexander Macdonald's tenants formed a sort of company to purchase 100,000 acres of land in South Carolina. The tacksmen, perhaps only the lesser ones, proposed to emigrate in a body taking some of their farm servants with them. Macleod's estates in Skye, Harris, and Glenelg were similarly threatened. In the end some of Macleod's tenants did emigrate, and all of Macdonald's went, so that he was obliged to bring in tenants from other parts of Scotland. In May, 1771, it was reported:

Two thousand emigrants are preparing for their departure from the Isle of Sky[e] to some one part of our foreign settlements, perhaps the Island of St. John. They are all of the estate of Sir Alexander Macdonald, who may chance to be a proprietor of land without tenants. That they may go as a formed colony, a parochial preacher and a thorough-bred surgeon are to go along with them. They have already subscribed £2000 sterling for the purpose.[24]

Some may have left previously, as seems probable from the report of preparations as early as 1769, while at least fifteen hundred more left in 1772–1773. Perhaps the whole number of emigrants from Skye between 1769 and 1773 amounted to four thousand. In 1773 the population of the island was estimated at about fifteen thousand; so the lesser tacksmen had seduced more than a fifth of the population. The destination of the Macdonalds of Skye was not South Carolina or Prince Edward Island, as some had anticipated, but the Cape Fear Valley of North Carolina, a district already well peopled with Highlanders. So numerous were the Macdonalds in Cumberland County, North Carolina, after the great immigration from Skye and Raasey in the 1770's that the Highlanders' attempted march to the sea in February, 1776, which ended disastrously at the battle of Moore's Creek Bridge, was known for generations afterward as the "Insurrection of the Clan Macdonald."[25]

[24] Lachlan Macdonald of Skaebost, "The Past and Present Position of the Skye Crofters," *Celtic Magazine*, XI (1886), 323–327; Boswell, *Tour* (Chapman ed.), pp. 295–296; MacLeod, "Western Highlands," pp. 33–34; Robert Forbes to Bishop Gordon, May 9, 1771, in R. Forbes, *Lyon in Mourning*, III, 259.

[25] *Virginia Gazette*, Purdie and Dixon, June 25, 1772, p. 2, and Sept. 23, 1773, p. 1; S. Johnson, *Journey*, p. 142; McLean, *Highlanders in America*, p. 114.

Gentry of various grades of wealth and standing took a part in leading the crofters to America. Early in 1771 "a gentleman of wealth and merit whose predecessors resided in Islay for many centuries past" was preparing to conduct over five hundred emigrants from this and neighboring isles to America.[26]

In 1767 the whole of Prince Edward Island was allotted to sixty-seven proprietors, chiefly Scots, on condition that they should settle Protestants on their lands. They met the condition by stocking the land almost exclusively with Highlanders, many of whom were Roman Catholics. Sir James Montgomery, who drew one lot in 1767 and acquired others by 1775, sent a number of settlers from Perthshire in 1770. He simply directed them to his own land and leased them unbroken soil at a shilling per acre. Commenting on this a few years later, a certain Dr. Macgregor observed: "They were decoyed out by one of the great proprietors to settle his land. They were to pay a shilling rent per acre, and they thought it cheap till they came out and saw it; but then they found it dear enough." Some of them escaped death from hunger only by getting away to Pictou in Nova Scotia. In 1771 Captain John Macdonald of Glenaladale purchased a lot in order to settle there the Roman Catholic tenants of Alexander Macdonald of Boisdale (South Uist), who was trying to convert them to Presbyterianism. Altogether he brought over about three hundred persons. Reverend James Macdonald settled among them as a secular missionary priest, while Dr. Roderick Macdonald became their physician. Montgomery and Glenaladale, members of the same class of Highland landed gentlemen, displayed contrasting views of the American landowner's responsibility to the immigrants brought over to settle his land.[27]

VI

New York, traditionally a colony of large estates, was a favorite target of the emigrant tacksmen. In 1734 Governor Cosby issued a proclamation offering 100,000 acres of land near Lake George to families of loyal Protestants who should transport themselves thither

[26] *Scots Magazine*, XXXIII (1771), 325.
[27] S. C. Johnson, *Emigration from the United Kingdom*, p. 4; D. C. Harvey, "Early Settlement and Social Conditions in Prince Edward Island," *Dalhousie Review*, XI (1931–32), 449–451.

to settle. This offer brought over Lachlan Campbell, a gentleman of Islay, in 1737. In each of the next three years he imported a shipload of Highland immigrants, the total number being around five hundred. His enterprise gave rise to one of the more acrimonious disputes in the history of the province.[28]

In 1757 William Smith published the first edition of his *History of the Province of New York*. Smith was among the outspoken sympathizers with Lachlan Campbell. According to his account of the transactions that took place some twenty years before, Campbell viewed and approved certain lands in 1737 and got Governor Clarke's promise of fifty thousand acres for himself and his associates on the terms stipulated in Cosby's proclamation. He then returned to Islay, sold his estate there, and brought eighty-three families of Highland Protestants to New York at his own expense. But Campbell was unable to obtain the lands promised him, and Smith described him as the victim of the cupidity and double-dealing of the colonial officials. Campbell failed to obtain any satisfaction from the provincial assembly or the Board of Trade and returned to Scotland to fight in the '45 for the Hanoverian cause. He died there not long after, leaving a widow and six children. His sons served as officers in the French and Indian War. Meanwhile some of the Islay emigrants obtained lands on their own initiative and settled on them. Down to 1762, however, the collective scheme had failed to materialize. According to Smith, this was regarded throughout the province as a flagrant injustice.[29]

Lieutenant-Governor Cadwallader Colden, himself an immigrant from the Scottish Borders, read Smith's account with some indignation. In two letters to Smith he gave his version of the Campbell affair. In Colden's view, Smith's account of the transactions between the government of New York and Captain Lachlan Campbell was "in every circumstance a misrepresentation of Facts . . . [and] in the principal part absolutely false & an egregious calumny of the persons, who at that time had the administration of Government in

[28] Pryde, "Scottish Colonization," p. 147; E. B. O'Callaghan, "Early Highland Immigration to New York," *Historical Magazine*, 1st ser., V (1861), 301–304.

[29] William Smith, *The History of the Late Province of New York, from Its Discovery, to the Appointment of Governor Colden, in 1762* (New York, 1830), *passim*. The first edition, to which Colden refers in his letters to Smith, was published in 1757; Pryde, "Scottish Colonization," pp. 147–148.

their hands." As far as Colden could recollect, a large number of the families imported by Campbell had paid their own passages and were not bound to Campbell in any way. The remainder were under contract by indenture to serve Campbell for a number of years as repayment for his expenses in transporting them to the colony. Campbell petitioned Lieutenant Governor Clarke in Council claiming a grant of some thirty thousand acres for himself and his heirs, on the ground that he had imported so many families to cultivate the land. Hearing of this petition, those who had paid their own way, and were under no obligation to Campbell, met in the streets and loudly exclaimed against it, saying, "They had left Scotland to free themselves from the vassalage they were under to their Lords there, & they would not become Vassals to Laughlin Campbel in America." The assembly, wrote Colden, "knowing the Aversion which the people who came over with Captn Campbel had to him, for it was notorious, did not enter on the consideration of his petition." Although all these things were discussed publicly, Colden never heard anyone blame Clarke at the time, or anyone else in the administration, because Campbell's petition was not granted. Campbell did not have the capacity to settle and improve such a huge grant as he demanded, and the transference of so much land to him would have been a lasting obstruction to the settlement of the frontier. Campbell might have had two thousand acres for himself and an additional area for his people in proportion to their ability to improve it. Colden concluded:

In short, Captn Campbel had conceived hopes of erecting a Lordship for himself in America. He imagined that the people whom he inticed with him would have become his Tenants on condition of being supported till they could maintain themselves & an easy rent afterwards. His disappointment came from these people obstinately refuseing to become his Tenants on any terms & from the Assemblies being unwilling to support them at the expense of the people of this province.

So far as Colden was aware, Smith's story was unheard of until after Campbell's death, when it began to be propagated by his family in order to gain sympathy, and perhaps financial benefits, for themselves.[30]

[30] Cadwallader Colden to William Smith, Jr., Jan. 15, 1759, in *Colden Papers*, V, 283–286.

Campbell's petitions and the answers and actions of the Council's subcommittee appointed to deal with the affair tend to confirm Colden's vindication of the colonial officials and his criticism of Campbell's motives. Apparently Campbell knew that the 100,000 acres mentioned in Cosby's proclamation had been allocated to others before he made his own application. What he was promised and agreed to was "sufficient land" for however many settlers he brought at three pounds per hundred acres and quitrent. Yet in his various petitions of the years 1738–1741 he repeatedly harped back to the 100,000 acres already allocated. At his examination before the Council's subcommittee, Campbell showed that he knew perfectly well that the usual terms for prospective settlers in the province were three pounds for a hundred acres and an annual quitrent of one shilling and ninepence farthing payable to the Crown. He admitted that he was offered nineteen thousand acres for charges of conveyance and quitrent only but refused them. He included in his list of settlers several people who were known to have been in the province before he ever arrived there. In the hearing on the second petition the subcommittee advised him to apply for fifty acres of land per person and give assurance of immediate settlement, when he would be helped to locate suitable lands for them. Only four days after this finding, Campbell submitted a third petition in which he continued to urge his claims, now utterly discredited and irrelevant, under Cosby's offer of 1734, and to demand extravagant amounts of land for each immigrant he had brought or induced to come over. The second petition in effect demanded a grant of 89,500 acres, the third, one of 91,500. Campbell might have obtained a generous amount of land without difficulty had it not been for his obstinate determination to make tenants of his people and to get a larger grant of land than that to which he was entitled or than the Council was willing to make. Only Campbell was disappointed; his prospective tenants, scattered through the province, were quite contented. William Smith might have learned all this from the contemporary records.[31]

The case of Lachlan Campbell shows how early the Highland landlords were attracted by the idea of transferring their feudal type of society to America. Campbell had many imitators in the

[31] Pryde, "Scottish Colonization," pp. 148–151.

next forty years. Several of them were likewise drawn to the province of New York.

VII

Shortly before his death in 1774, Sir William Johnson, the celebrated Indian Superintendent in the North, induced many Highlanders to settle on his lands in the Mohawk Valley. Here Johnson had built up a sort of private kingdom, where he ruled paternally, compelling his tenants, very much as the tacksmen did in the contemporary Highlands of Scotland, to have their grain ground at his mill. In 1773 he imported about three hundred Roman Catholics from Glengarry, Glenmoriston, Glenurquhart, and Strathglass, all in Inverness-shire. The bulk of these people were Macdonells of Glengarry. They were to form the backbone of loyalist resistance in New York and to find new homes in Glengarry County, Ontario, during the Revolutionary War.[32]

About the middle of September, 1773, three gentlemen named Macdonell and their families, accompanied by some three hundred fellow clansmen, sailed aboard the *Pearl* from Fort William bound for New York, where they arrived on the eighteenth of October. The party were all in good health and had money for each man to purchase a freehold. They settled on the Kingsborough estate of Sir William Johnson, now Gloversville. The place was about four miles north of Johnstown, and thus very close to the seat of the overlord of the domain.[33]

Allan Macdonell, who seems to have been one of the three gentlemen who arrived at this time, wrote to Sir William in the middle of November, saying that he and his associates had "a great desire of Settling under your Wing . . . in which we may have a mutual Interest. . . . You have large estates to make & we some influence over people tho' at a distance that may be of consequence in Subsequent years." Macdonell had already been to see Johnson at John-

[32] *Ibid.*, p. 152; MacDougall, ed., *Scots in America*, p. 25.

[33] *Scots Magazine*, XXXV (1773), 499; *Virginia Gazette*, Purdie and Dixon, Nov. 11, 1773, supplement, p. 2, and Dec. 23, 1773, p. 2; Ezra Stiles, *The Literary Diary of Ezra Stiles*, ed. by Franklin Bowditch Dexter (New York, 1901), I, 425; Pryde, "Scottish Colonization," p. 152; Sir William Johnson to Maj.-Gen. Frederick Haldimand, Sept. 30, 1773, in *Johnson Papers*, VIII, 898.

son Hall and had clearly made a journey of inspection through the valley looking for a likely site for a future estate. The tacksman was reconciled to continuing in the same situation relative to Johnson the overlord as he had known in Scotland relative to his chief, for he wanted to know, regarding a tract of thirteen thousand acres, "at what its Sett in fee Simple or if any advantages of Saw or Griss Mills fish or Food attend it." There is something delightfully medieval about this inquiry. But Johnson and he spoke the same language. Both had no doubt profited from the mills on their estates; one came from a land where the heritor of land paid quitrents, while the other was building up his backwoods empire and settling it with a view to collecting quitrents. There were other questions about eighteen thousand acres of land near Schoharie, which Macdonell had not yet visited, and about lands in the great Susquehanna tract which Johnson had purchased from the Indians in 1770. Macdonell believed that "the people here [i.e., at Albany]," very probably Highland immigrants, and possibly some of those who came in the *Pearl,* though still in a "fluctuating Situation . . . will adhere to us if Sir William gives the encouragement their Sobriety & Industry will Merit.—The principle [*sic*] of which is a years Mantinence to each family that will Settle upon his estate." For himself and his associates he desired enough room to accommodate any friends and countrymen who might wish to come and share their fortunes in the area. He had reason to hope that several Scotsmen would come to the new settlement. Finally he asked that "any of us calling ourselves Gentlemen" should be free, after a few years spent in improving their lands, to move elsewhere, and that in such an event Sir William should purchase their plantations "at the Appreseation or estimation of honest men Mutualy chosen." [34]

In all this the implications of a dependent tenantry are rather indirect. It is difficult to say just what relationship Macdonell anticipated setting up between himself and the settlers from Scotland whom he evidently intended to bring to some large tract whose location was about to be decided. But there is a strong suggestion in his words, especially where he writes of people "adhering" to him and his associates if properly encouraged, that he was endeavor-

[34] Allan Macdonell to Sir William Johnson, Nov. 14, 1773, in *Johnson Papers,* VIII, 915–917.

ing to maintain his status as a tacksman in the face of an environment where the small farmer could reasonably hope to own his own farm.

The Colden family owned lands in the province. The sons of the lieutenant governor, David and Cadwallader, Junior, had fifteen thousand acres, and they ordered their surveyor to complete the division of this tract into twenty-nine lots in August, 1773. They were interested in some Scottish immigrants who arrived earlier than summer but went to settle on Johnson's lands. These were possibly a party of seventy from Ross-shire, who arrived at New York on the *Britannia* about the middle of May. They were expected to go to Skenesborough, the estate of another Scottish speculator on Lake George, but instead went to Johnson's domain. The Coldens endeavored to direct the stream of immigrants from Great Britain and Ireland to their fifteen-thousand-acre grant and to another of twenty-nine thousand acres, called Skinner's Patent, which the father owned. On the former, they would give a lot of five hundred acres to any five families willing to settle it, on the latter a thousand acres, and after three years would convey the land in fee simple to these families, free of all charges except the ubiquitous quitrent.[35]

One of the most interesting of the Scottish land speculators in New York before the Revolution was Lord Adam Gordon. The fourth son of the second Duke of Gordon, Lord Adam entered the army about 1746. Later he was a Member of Parliament for Aberdeenshire, and he was still a member when asked to take the 66th Regiment of foot to Jamaica in 1762. He used this opportunity to travel widely in North America and to speculate in Florida and New York lands. He visited Sir William Johnson twice and chose a tract for himself in the Mohawk Valley. He traveled as far as Niagara Falls and Detroit. Johnson was favorably impressed by the somewhat penurious nobleman and entrusted his son to Lord Adam's care for the voyage to England.[36]

[35] David Colden to William Cockburn, Aug. 12, 1773, in *Colden Papers*, VII, 187–188; *Virginia Gazette*, Purdie and Dixon, May 27, 1773, p. 2, and July 1, 1773, p. 3.

[36] H. Manners Chichester on Lord Adam Gordon, *D.N.B.*, XXII (1890), 158; Mowat, *East Florida*, pp. 51, 184 n. 8; [Lord Adam Gordon], "Journal of an Officer's Travels in America and the West Indies 1764–1765," in Newton D.

In October, 1766, Johnson wrote to Gordon offering him a tract
of ten thousand acres in the famous "Royal Grant," a vast territory
of 200,000 acres above German Flats, and north of the present city
of Little Falls, which Johnson had recently purchased from the Indians and was to have confirmed to him by the Crown in 1769. A
year later John Watts, a prominent citizen of New York and Johnson's agent in that city, wrote to Sir William referring to the ambition of Lord Adam Gordon and other great people to colonize. By
that time Gordon had sent over some farmers from England to settle
in the Mohawk Valley, and he may have sent others from Scotland.
He certainly intended to recruit emigrants wherever he could find
them in Great Britain. In this enterprise he was apparently co-
operating with the Duke of Atholl, whose uncle's widow he had
recently married. The marriage was to distract his attention from
his American affairs to such an extent that as late as July, 1771 his
property in East Florida lay just as when he acquired it. At this time
he was having Watts credit Johnson with "the whole outlay, for
Patent, fees, & quitt rent to Feby 1771—and to charge Mr. Adam
Drummond with the same," and he had just asked Watts to pay his
future quitrent annually for the New York lands. He asked Johnson
for a survey of the tract, marking in his neighbors all around. Johnson did not send the deed of conveyance to Watts for forwarding
to Gordon until July, 1772. Watts could still write that he had "no
reckoning with Lord Adam," so that he had to charge certain expenses incidental to the conveyance to Sir William Johnson. Watts
did not draw a bill upon Gordon for the value of the land until
January, 1773. All this seems to indicate that Gordon was struggling
to make ends meet. It may well have been in order to meet his
obligations in New York that he borrowed, about September, 1772,
the sum of one thousand pounds at 5-per-cent interest from William
Mackintosh of Balnespick in Inverness-shire.[37]

Lord Adam Gordon was a younger son of a great Highland landlord. He himself enjoyed the possession of a mere 750 acres of landed
property in Scotland.[38] He clearly intended to make up any de-

---

Mereness, ed., *Travels in the American Colonies* (New York, 1916), p. 367;
Johnson Cal., pp. 275, 282, 285.

[37] *Johnson Cal.*, pp. 331, 375–376; *Johnson Papers*, VIII, 194–196, 536, 706;
Grant, *Old Highland Farm*, pp. 27, 267, 270.

[38] Lord Adam Gordon to Sir William Johnson, July 21, 1771, in *Johnson Papers*,
VIII, 194–196.

ficiency in his income from new estates in the American wilderness. It is certain that he never had any intention of emigrating himself. From the time of his first visit to Johnson he regarded the situation of the denizen of the frontier with aversion. "I passed some Days at Sir Wm. Johnson's," he wrote in his journal in 1765, "but no consideration Should tempt me to lead his life." He could think of no other man "equal to so disagreeable a Duty." [39] It is uncertain how many emigrants Gordon sent out or upon what terms they had farms of him. His tenants may have got their land, as those of Johnson's son did, rent free for five years and afterward at six pounds per hundred acres per annum, or a lesser rent if leased for a number of lives.[40] Gordon was far from a typical tacksman. His career illustrates the methods by which the younger sons of the Scots nobility and gentry might hope to build up a fortune in America through the promotion of emigration.

Highland gentlemen were constantly arriving in America just before the Revolution to inspect frontier lands. Late in 1773 the ship *Brunswick* arrived in the James River, bringing Godfrey McNeil, "a Gentleman of Fortune in Argyleshire," who intended to find a suitable place of settlement for a number of families from Argyll. These people were ready to emigrate to America as soon as McNeil returned to Scotland. In November, Daniel McLeod of Kilmorie landed at New York and set off for Albany, on his way to Beekman township on Lake Champlain, where he was to look at some land which he had just purchased. He would then return to Scotland immediately in order to bring over a number of emigrant families to settle on his land.[41]

VIII

A small number of Lowlanders also took an interest in American lands and the promotion of emigration to their purchases. Chief among these were Philip Wharton Skene, who brought over Lowlanders to his colony of Skenesborough on Lake George, and the celebrated John Witherspoon, president of the College of New Jersey,

[39] Gordon, "Journal," in Mereness, ed., *Travels in the American Colonies,* p. 418.

[40] *Johnson Papers,* VIII, 345.

[41] *Virginia Gazette,* Purdie and Dixon, Dec. 23, 1773, p. 2; *ibid.,* Rind, Nov. 25, 1773, p. 3.

himself an emigrant, who imported hundreds of Highlanders into Pictou, Nova Scotia, as a strictly business enterprise.

Philip Skene was a native of Fifeshire and the son of a Jacobite. He expiated his father's crime against the state by serving the Hanoverians for most of his life. His military career brought him to America as a captain in 1756, where he joined the expedition against Fort Ticonderoga two years later. In 1759, with General Amherst's support, he decided to found a settlement "near Crown Point, on the road leading to Number Four, on Connecticut River." He submitted a petition to the Board of Trade asking for a land grant but was refused. But he had not waited for official sanction before getting down to pioneering work. By 1760 he had induced thirty families to go to Skenesborough and had hired many indentured servants. Soon after the war he brought 270 discharged soldiers from the British army of conquest in Cuba to his estate. In 1765 he managed to obtain a patent embracing some twenty-nine thousand acres, sold his commission, and went to live at Skenesborough. There he built sawmills, a forge, a general store, a post office, several roads, and a large stone manor house. With the coming of the Revolutionary War, General Gage appointed him lieutenant governor of Crown Point and Ticonderoga. When the American patriots destroyed his estate, the manor ceased to exist.[42]

John Witherspoon's activities in Nova Scotia had more lasting effects. The British settlement of Nova Scotia began in earnest after the expulsion of the Acadians as a security measure during the French and Indian War. In the 1760's New Englanders poured into the province. British and American groups and individuals, especially Philadelphia men, speculated wildly in Nova Scotia lands. By July, 1765, there were sixteen "townships" reserved for as many companies. One of these, comprising some 200,000 acres, was known as Pictou or the Philadelphia Plantation, and it lay on the north coast opposite St. John's (later Prince Edward) Island. The fourteen original proprietors belonged to the Quaker City. On October 31, 1765, they obtained their grant, and they were henceforward known as the Philadelphia Company. In the spring of 1767 the first settlers left Philadelphia for Pictou, but the company's advertisements in Philadelphia produced little response. In the same year

[42] John Pell, "Philip Skene of Skenesborough," *Quarterly Journal of the New York State Historical Association*, IX (1928), 27, 29–30, 34–37.

Richard Stockton, one of the original proprietors and a future signer of the Declaration of Independence, went to Scotland at the behest of the trustees of the College of New Jersey to urge John Witherspoon to accept the presidency of that institution. Thus Witherspoon's first American connection brought him in contact with the Pictou project. Soon after reaching America, he associated himself with John Pagan of Greenock and acquired three shares in the company. The two began to encourage systematically the emigration of Highlanders to America. First of all, in 1770, they brought a party of them to New England aboard the *Hector*. Three years later they used the same ship to take the first cargo of Highlanders to Nova Scotia. The Scottish migration to Pictou inaugurated by Witherspoon and Pagan continued for a long time after their deaths.[43]

In September, 1772, John Witherspoon inserted an advertisement in the *Edinburgh Advertiser* inviting farmers and others to settle "upon easy terms" in Nova Scotia. To the first twenty families who volunteered to go, the partners offered 150 acres of land to each man and wife together with fifty acres for each child, relative or servant, at the rate of sixpence per acre. The second and third twenty families were to receive the same, but at a shilling and one and sixpence per acre respectively. John Pagan would provide the emigrants with their passages at £3 5s. for each full passenger, the money to be paid before leaving Scotland. The promoters named agents to whom application might be made in Inverary, Maryburgh, Portree, Fort Augustus, and Inverness, all Highland towns. Bailie Alexander Shaw of Inverness, however, inserted another advertisement stating that Pagan had taken the liberty of printing his name without his permission and that he was determined to take no concern in the matter. There were already twenty families settled at Pictou, with a school catering to about thirty children. Churches and more schools were planned, and the first minister to go out would get five hundred acres of land, the first schoolmaster one hundred acres, in fee simple to them and their heirs forever.[44]

These blandishments did not go uncriticized. Among a number

[43] William Otis Sawtelle, "Acadia: The Pre-Loyalist Migration and the Philadelphia Plantation," *Pennsylvania Magazine of History and Biography*, LI (1927), 257, 262–263, 269–270, 279–283; L. H. Butterfield, ed., *John Witherspoon Comes to America* (Princeton, N.J., 1953), p. x.

[44] Advertisement headed, "Lands to be settled in North America," in *Scots Magazine*, XXXIV (1772), 482–484.

of protesting letters which appeared in the Scottish press was one from "A *Wellwisher to Old Scotland*," who thought the scheme of Witherspoon and Pagan deceptively attractive. How were the emigrants to subsist on their unimproved lands during the first year? They would require a capital of at least two thousand pounds to clear two hundred acres of land. They would find no market for their surplus produce. The settlers would have to drudge for others in some other part of the country like banished felons. The mention of Dr. Witherspoon's name might induce some ignorant persons to think that he would be near enough to watch over their interests, but this was far from true. He would be a thousand miles away in New Jersey, and might not see them more than twice in his whole lifetime.[45]

In November a correspondent calling himself "A BYSTANDER" wrote to the *Caledonian Mercury* defending the climate of Nova Scotia from its detractors. He stressed the severe effects upon the Scottish economy of the prevailing depression in town and country. Many of the small farmers had been ruined and set adrift, and thousands of weavers, tanners, and other mechanics had lost their employment. If such persons wished to emigrate, how could it be prudent to hinder them? He closed with a warning that to cut off the safety-valve of emigration from the distressed would invite the sort of turbulence and disorder commonly seen in Ireland.[46]

The principal agent of Witherspoon and Pagan in these matters was John Ross, whom they sent to Scotland to bring back as many colonists as he was able. Apparently, and understandably, Ross did not restrain himself in describing the advantages of Nova Scotia. The Highlanders knew nothing of the difficulties awaiting them in a land covered with dense, unbroken forest. Ross induced three families and five single young men to board the *Hector* at Greenock and a further thirty-three families and twenty-five single men at Loch Broom in Ross-shire.[47]

[45] Letter from "A Wellwisher to Old Scotland" to the *Edinburgh Advertiser*, Oct. 1772, reprinted in *Scots Magazine*, XXXIV (1772), 483–484.

[46] Letter from "A BYSTANDER" to the *Caledonian Mercury*, Nov. 12, 1772, reprinted in *Scots Magazine*, XXXIV (1772), 587–588.

[47] Alexander Mackenzie, "First Highland Emigration to Nova Scotia: Arrival of the Ship 'Hector,'" *Celtic Magazine*, VIII (1883), 141.

IX

Organized migrations were common during the eighteenth century. They dominated the picture in the ten years before the American Revolution. The examples cited above serve to demonstrate the variety of the arrangements by which Scots were brought to America. They indicate how often the initiative in emigration came from above. Even where an emigrant ship carried no leaders drawn from the upper ranks of the social structure, its cargo of men, women, and children was likely to be bound together by ties formed in the old country. Among the leaders of emigration the commonest group consisted of Highland tacksmen, whose changing social and economic position led them to seek a conservative but unrealistic solution of their difficulties in America. The attempt to transfer the clan system to the New World was, of course, only one form of enterprise linking land speculation with settlement. Highland heritors, Lowland lairds, the younger sons of the great landlords, gentlemen of every rank and condition, besides the tacksmen themselves, saw in the colonies an opportunity for preserving the rudiments of feudal custom and tradition. Here and there we catch a glimpse of popular rebelliousness and independence, notably among the people brought to New York by Lachlan Campbell in 1738–1740. But on the whole the Highland peasant was almost as docile in America as he had been in Scotland. This fact alone is sufficient to explain his arming himself in the Hanoverian cause, under the leadership of tacksman and landlord, in both North Carolina and New York during the Revolutionary War.

Witherspoon's advertisement of 1772 appeared at a time when mass emigration from the Highlands was causing much alarm in certain quarters in Edinburgh and London. Hence the Pictou scheme figured prominently in various arguments put forward in the press. The British government took steps to inform itself about the true scale of emigration, but for various reasons it could not obtain accurate statistics. After several months of war in America they prohibited the clearance of emigrant ships by the customs authorities. There was no consistent policy, and the interests of the colonies and measures of their governments did not always harmonize with concurrent British official views on the topic of emigration.

V

Government and Emigration

DURING the colonial period there was not more than one un-
qualified prohibition of emigration. This was the order of the Scots
Privy Council, issued in 1698, warning those who aided emigration
that they would be treated as man-stealers. The measure does not
seem to have had much effect, though it called forth a pamphlet of
protest.[1]

The legislative restrictions of the Parliament of Great Britain
began with the law of 1719, which was intended to curtail the activities of certain persons who had lately "drawn away . . . several
artificers and manufacturers . . . out of His Majesty's dominions
into foreign countries, . . . by making them large promises and
using other arts to inveigle and draw them away." Skilled mechanics,
much in demand as indentured servants in the colonies, were forbidden to leave the country. An amendment of 1750 provided for more
severe punishment of "persons convicted of seducing artificers," and
in this form the law remained in force until 1824. It was never rigidly
enforced, and even after 1783, when the problem it was designed
to solve was very much the concern of government, it was to a
great extent ineffective.[2]

[1] A. E. Smith, *Colonists in Bondage*, p. 348, n. 3.
[2] Herbert Heaton, "The Industrial Immigrant in the United States, 1783–
1812," *Proceedings of the American Philosophical Society*, XCV (Oct., 1951),
pp. 524–525.

Criminals, vagabonds, and other undesirables might depart for America without causing the government any worry. Local authorities supplemented the royal courts in swelling the steady stream of deportees. In the spring of 1714, eight gypsies, prisoners in the tolbooth of Jedburgh, heard the Lords of Justiciary on circuit sentence them to be transported to the plantations. The judges ordered the magistrates of Jedburgh and Glasgow to see to their removal and shipment. When the gypsies had been in the Glasgow tolbooth for several days, the magistrates of that city discovered that there was no public fund from which to maintain them. Several merchants who owned ships going to Virginia, having been approached by the Glasgow magistrates, "upon no terms would condescend thereto, there being six of the eight women, . . . except they got money for taking them." Deciding it was cheaper to pay their fare than to keep the gypsies in the tolbooth, the magistrates settled with three merchants interested in a ship going to Virginia to transport the vagabonds at thirteen pounds the lot.[3] The judicial branch of the Scottish government might readily solve its problem of dealing with undesirables by ordering them to the colonies, but there was no proper administrative or financial arrangement whereby their instructions could be carried out. The local authorities did not have an easy task in handling these people. In July, 1737, for example, the magistrates of Elgin recorded that one, Alexander Nicol, had been under indenture to go to Georgia, "but having revolted was now absconding."[4] Convict servants were as difficult to control when they reached the other side of the ocean. In 1773 six Highlanders ran away from the ship *Donald*, lying at Four Mile Creek in Virginia. But they must have been easily caught, for three of them "were habited in their own Country Garb," and only one of them could speak English distinctly.[5] The export of riff-raff to the plantations was as popular with Scots judges as it was obnoxious to the Americans who had to receive them; it was the other way around with skilled mechanics and artisans.

[3] *Extracts from the Records of the Burgh of Glasgow A.D. 1691–1717* (Glasgow, 1908), pp. 529–530.
[4] *The Records of Elgin* (Aberdeen, 1903–08), II, 337.
[5] *Virginia Gazette*, Purdie and Dixon, April 15, 1773, p. 3.

II

The need to prevent the emigration of skilled workmen was one of the principal pleas advanced by the opponents of the exodus of the 1770's. Discussion of the matter began in the Scottish newspapers not long after the Peace of Paris, and persisted until the American Revolutionary War broke out. Advertisements called urgently for millwrights, house carpenters, coppersmiths, blacksmiths, bricklayers, and wrights and masons for the West Indies, New York, and other colonies.[6]

The Sugar Act of 1764 increased the demand for skilled workmen in the colonies. A writer in 1765 bemoaned the emigration of so many "manufacturers." He noticed that it had become more common since the passage of the new regulations for the American trade in the previous year and that the colonists' difficulty in buying needed manufactures, which stemmed from the regulations, forced them to expand their own manufactures.[7]

At this time indentured craftsmen were leaving for America in increasing numbers. In March, 1765, forty-seven young men engaged themselves for Pensacola and St. Augustine, while in June "a great number of sawyers" left for Nova Scotia. In the last four months of 1767, three hundred tradesmen of various skills indented themselves, at high wages, for East and West Florida. In January, 1768, Charles Carroll of Mount Clare, in Maryland, informed his agents in Bristol that "there come in Gardeners in every Branch from Scotland at Six pounds a year." In 1770 and 1771 hundreds of linen makers embarked in Scotland for North Carolina, where the trade was said, in March, 1771, to be "now in the utmost perfection." Then came the economic crisis of 1772, which threw thousands of skilled workers out of employment and raised the emigration of this class of people to a new level.[8]

There were those who argued that a crisis like that of 1772–1774 would cause great riots and disturbances were it not for the relief

[6] Fagerstrom, "American Revolutionary Movement," ch. iii, citing the *Edinburgh Evening Courant*, April 1, July 6, Sept. 2, 1765.

[7] *Ibid.*, Feb. 13, 1765.

[8] *Ibid.*, March 2, June 3, 1765; *Virginia Gazette*, Purdie and Dixon, April 23, 1767, p. 2; *Maryland Historical Magazine*, XLV (1950), 251; *Virginia Gazette*, Purdie and Dixon, May 16, 1771, p. 1.

afforded by the opportunity of emigration. Others found it incomprehensible that men should oppose the departure of distressed Highlanders whom the opposers themselves branded as lazy and shiftless. One champion of emigration asked:

Why are such low arts used to hinder the Highlanders from quitting their country? why so much ridicule thrown on America? why so many false representations, and discouraging accounts given of it, in the public papers? and, when these seem to be disregarded, . . . why is recourse had to the daring effrontery of some puny scribbler, to threaten the interferance [*sic*] of administration against depopulating the Highlands, and that a parliamentary inquiry was to be made, to prevent any more emigrations?

In 1774 another writer pointed out that many persons had gone to the larger towns, such as Glasgow, Edinburgh, and Greenock, only to starve. If the anticipated act to restrict emigration was passed, he declared, it would be a cruel measure indeed, for it would hinder free-born subjects who were starving from going wherever they could find food and clothing.[9]

Many of the opponents of emigration employed the old mercantilist arguments in favor of conserving population and currency. "Numbers of people," wrote one of them, "are the truest riches and real strength of a kingdom, so no country can have too many." Others lamented the amount of cash being removed from the country by the emigrants. In 1772 it was reported from the Hebrides that since 1768 they had taken out from those islands some ten thousand pounds in specie. In September, 1773, a party of 425 men, women, and children sailed from Maryburgh, carrying with them at least six thousand pounds sterling. In the summer of 1774 it was learned in New York "from very good authority" that two thousand people were preparing to leave Galloway, in the southwest of Scotland, destined chiefly for New York colony, and would bring with them at least twenty thousand guineas.[10] While pessimists warned that continual emigration would render the colonies independent of

[9] *Scots Magazine*, XXXIV (1772), 588; "Scotus Americanus," in Boyd, ed., *Eighteenth Century Tracts*, pp. 431–432; Fagerstrom, "American Revolutionary Movement," ch. iii, citing the Edinburgh *Caledonian Mercury*, Jan. 19, 1774.

[10] Fagerstrom, "American Revolutionary Movement," citing Edinburgh *Caledonian Mercury*, Sept. 5, 1772; *Scots Magazine*, XXXV (1773), 557; *Virginia Gazette*, Rind, July 14, 1774, p. 2.

the mother country and reduce the Highlands to a desolate waste, the authorities in the American provinces did nothing to ease their fears.

III

For a long time several of the colonies, especially in the South, had been offering various inducements to prospective immigrants from Britain. The New England colonies enacted few laws of this kind, and the Middle colonies did little but offer land and naturalization on easy terms. It was the Southern colonies which were most liberal and active in passing legislation which would enable the immigrant to establish himself in America. Virginia for example, one of the favorite targets of emigrants from Scotland and especially from the Lowlands, granted land on the basis of head right throughout the colonial period. It was in part the liberal policy of the North Carolina Assembly in remitting the taxes of Scottish immigrants for a number of years which brought so many of them to that colony.[11]

The proprietors and governors of the various colonies frequently assisted immigrants from Scotland both before and after their arrival in the New World. The proprietors of East Jersey, among whom were a number of prominent Scots, provided shipping, small farms, stock, and tools for some families in return for half their output for a certain number of years. But most of the Scots going to the Jerseys paid for their passages by indenting themselves. In 1741 the Georgia trustees, through their embarkation committee, arranged for a ship to bring forty-three Highlanders to that colony, where many others had already settled at Darien on the frontier against Spain. They allocated funds for the maintenance of the Scots during their first months in America. They paid to James Grey, the captain of the ship that brought them, the sum of £146 5s. for all his services and expenses down to the time of their embarkation for Georgia, and one pound per head for transporting them. In October, 1769, Governor Tryon of North Carolina advanced the sum of fifteen pounds to a party of one hundred Scottish immigrants who intended making their homes among the Highland settlers of Cumberland

---

[11] Erna Risch, "Encouragement of Immigration as Revealed in Colonial Legislation," *Virginia Magazine of History and Biography*, XLV (1937), 10, and p. 6, n. 25; Boyd, ed., *Eighteenth Century Tracts*, p. 419.

County. The money was intended to furnish them with immediate necessaries. The Assembly backed him up a month later by accepting liability for this expenditure.[12]

In November, 1767, fifty islanders from Jura landed at Brunswick, North Carolina. Governor Tryon granted them land in Cumberland and Mecklenburg Counties, clear of all fees, at the rate of one hundred acres per person, man, woman, or child. The largest family, a man, his wife, and four children, received a little more than their quota, a neat square mile, or 640 acres of land. One can imagine the effect of such bounty, even when bestowed in the form of virgin wilderness, upon the mind of a man who in all probability maintained his family in Scotland from the produce of a holding of ten or twelve acres. In November of 1775, when already in possession of instructions to discourage emigrants from Britain by withholding the Crown lands from settlement, Governor Josiah Martin of North Carolina allowed a group of recent Highland immigrants to take up vacant lands, after receiving their solemn assurances of loyalty to the throne. He excused himself to the Earl of Dartmouth on the ground that he had thought it better to grant freely what might otherwise have been seized by force. As he wrote to the secretary, another party of 130 Highlanders arrived in the colony. Martin told Dartmouth that he intended also to give this group permission to settle on the vacant lands of the Crown.[13]

The legislature of North Carolina supplied timely aid on a number of occasions to newly arrived Highlanders in distress. When war came, the American patriots resented the seeming ingratitude of the Highlanders of Cumberland County in refusing to support the Revolutionary government of the province and in taking arms against it.[14]

IV

Spurred on by rising rents, hard times, the urging of the tacksmen, and the blandishments of colonial authorities, emigration grew at

[12] Wertenbaker, *Early Scotch Contributions*, p. 8; Earl of Egmont's Journal, Aug. 28, 1741, in *Ga. Recs.*, V, 541; *ibid.*, pp. 545, 504; *N.C. Recs.*, VIII, 144.

[13] *N.C. Recs.*, VII, 543–544; Gov. Martin to Earl of Dartmouth, Nov. 12, 1775, in *ibid.*, X, 324, 327–328.

[14] J. P. MacLean, *An Historical Account of the Settlements of Scotch Highlanders in America* (Cleveland, 1900), p. 123.

an increasing rate after 1763. Official opposition grew with it, until, after 1770, it began to take the form of a series of concrete measures, culminating in the prohibition of September, 1775.

Official opposition to emigration sprang from regret at such possible consequences as the loss of agricultural and industrial producers, reduction in the number of army recruits available in the Highlands, and an increase in economic and military strength in the colonies at a time when they threatened war.[15] Gradually the British government embodied these fears in a series of orders intended to discourage emigration.

In January, 1771, the legislature of North Carolina passed an act for the benefit of about sixteen hundred recent Scottish immigrants to Cumberland County. The law specified that persons coming directly from Europe to settle the province should be exempt from all taxes for a period of four years after their arrival. The Board of Trade under Lord Hillsborough recommended to the king that His Majesty disallow the act. They reminded him of their recent disapproval of a Skye petition asking a huge land grant in North Carolina for some intending emigrants, and they warned him not for the first time of the danger to the landed and manufacturing interests of Great Britain presented by excessive emigration. The Skye petition of 1771 was signed by James Macdonald, merchant in Portree, and Norman Macdonald of Sleat. It informed the Board of Trade that the petitioners and six other persons of substance in Skye had for some time been disposing of their effects in Scotland and hiring servants. They were now ready to leave the country and requested a land grant of forty thousand acres in North Carolina, upon the usual terms or any other thought proper. On June 21, the Board of Trade reported to the Privy Council:

That the emigration of the inhabitants of Great Britain and Ireland to the American Colonies is a circumstance which in our opinion cannot fail to lessen the strength and security and to prejudice the landed Interest and Manufactures of these Kingdoms and the great extent to which this emigration hath of late years prevailed renders it an object well deserving the serious attention of government.

Upon the ground of this opinion We have thought it necessary in Cases where we have recommended Grants of Land in America, to be

15 Fagerstrom, "American Revolutionary Movement," ch. iii.

made to persons of substance and ability in this Kingdom, to propose amongst other conditions, that they should be settled by foreign Protestants; and therefore We can on no account recommend . . . a resolution taken by a number of considerable persons to abandon . . . this Kingdom . . . with their Families and Dependants in a large Body.

A year later the Privy Council confirmed the decision of the Board of Trade and dismissed the petition.[16]

The Earl of Dartmouth corresponded with his kinsman and protégé, Governor Legge of Nova Scotia, expressing alarm at the rate of emigration. An Order in Council, dated April 7, 1773, and entered in the Nova Scotia council minutes for July 20, prohibited all land grants except those made under the proclamation of 1763. The rule was relaxed in February, 1774, when a system began for making land grants by sale only. Even this scheme was ultimately suspended to make way for the incoming loyalist refugees.[17]

Thomas Miller, the Lord Justice Clerk of Scotland, made himself a leader in the agitation for restrictions upon emigration. In October, 1773, he reported to the Secretary of State, the Earl of Suffolk, that twelve Glasgow strikers had been prosecuted for riotous proceedings and interrupting work for several weeks. They had led a combination to raise wages and had involved with them some thousands of weavers who now replied to the prosecution by threatening to go off in a body to America. Miller found the trial of the leaders a delicate affair. He conducted it with the utmost care, counseled lenity, and mitigated the punishment of the seven convicted. He believed he had been successful in laying to rest all thoughts of emigration. But he was sorry to observe "that in this part of the Kingdom, Transportation to America begins to lose every characteristick of a punishment." [18]

In November of the same year the Earl of Suffolk requested Miller to ascertain the numbers of those who had emigrated from the Highlands during 1772 and 1773. Miller fulfilled this assignment by writing to the sheriffs of Moray and Nairn, Argyll and Bute, Sutherland

[16] Board of Trade to the King, Feb. 26, 1772, in *N.C. Recs.*, IX, 251–252; *N.C. Recs.*, VIII, 620–622; Order in Council, June 19, 1772, in *ibid.*, IX, 303–304.
[17] John Bartlet Brebner, *The Neutral Yankees of Nova Scotia* (New York, 1937), p. 120.
[18] Fagerstrom, "American Revolutionary Movement," ch. iii, citing Thomas Miller to the Earl of Suffolk, Oct. 25, 1773.

and Caithness, Inverness, and Ross, who in turn required the parish ministers in these eight shires to submit lists of emigrants for 1772–1773. The returns for Argyll, Ross, and Moray recorded the departures by parishes and distinguished men, women, and children. They were the first attempt at a systematic enumeration of emigrants. But the system was far from uniform. The lists were submitted by only eight out of thirty-three counties. The eight covered the whole of the Highlands and islands except those parts in the mainland counties of Aberdeen, Banff, Perth, and Dumbarton, and the island counties of Orkney and Zetland. The figures for Argyll did not conform with the others in that they covered the years from 1769 to 1773 inclusive. The total number of emigrants listed, 3,169, appears to be well under the true figure. A careful computation from a variety of contemporary sources indicates that about sixty-five hundred people left these eight counties for America within the period covered by Miller's investigation.[19]

At this time, also, the government decided to have all future emigrants from Scotland registered by the customs authorities at the ports of departure. A letter from John Robinson, Secretary to the Treasury, dated December 8, 1773, required the customs officials of England and Scotland to record the names, ages, qualities, occupations, former residences, and reasons for emigrating of all persons leaving the country. Names of vessels and their masters were also to be put down. These records were kept from the beginning of 1774 until September, 1775, when emigration came to a halt for several years.[20]

The total number of emigrants from Scotland listed in the customhouse returns was almost three thousand. This was very much less than the true number. The official records themselves indicate how easy it was for a ship to escape without registering her cargo

[19] *Ibid.*, citing letters between Miller and Suffolk, Oct. 25, Nov. 5, 12, 1773, April 25, 1774, and emigration lists (PRO, SP 54/45, f. 164 c, d, e, f); *Scots Magazine*, XXXV (1773), 667; *Virginia Gazette*, Rind, June 9, 1774, Supplement, p. 2, where it is stated that some of the Highland clergy were alarmed lest it was intended to make them tools of oppression, suggesting that they may have given conservative estimates of the numbers which had emigrated. For a full discussion of the number of emigrants from Scotland during the period covered by the present study, see Appendix.

[20] Newsome, "Records of Emigrants," pp. 39–40.

of emigrants. Only ships departing from the larger ports, where there were customhouses, were entered in the books at all. Dozens of vessels sailed from remote Highland sea lochs and island beaches. In December, 1774, for example, the brigantine *Carolina*, driven by a contrary wind, put into Campbelltown in Argyll. The customs officials found aboard her sixty-two unregistered emigrants from Islay bound for the Cape Fear River. The ship had sailed from Greenock with a cargo of wares for North Carolina. At Lochindale in Islay she picked up the sixty people from that island and Mull, and clearly never would have had them registered but for a contrary wind.[21]

In April, 1774, the ship *Bachelor* was forced into Lerwick in the Shetlands by bad weather. The customs officers found that she carried 120 emigrants from Sutherland and Caithness bound for Wilmington, North Carolina. These persons, whose names would be unknown but for the accident of a gale, gave exceptionally full and detailed reasons for their removal from Scotland.[22]

Official agitation over the mass migration of the 1770's culminated in the prohibition of 1775. The Lord Justice Clerk feared that the emigrating Highlanders would be infected (if they were not already so before leaving Scotland) with radical American principles. He was anxious lest they become at once a loss to the British army and a gain to the American. The possibility that the emigrants would contribute to the rebel soldiery was the immediate reason for the Lord Advocate's ordering the cessation of emigration. Henry Dundas, the Lord Advocate, feared that whatever their intentions the emigrants would be forced to join the rebels. Soon after the issuance of a royal proclamation for suppressing rebellion and sedition, he heard of hundreds of people embarking with money, arms, and ammunition which might be used against the home government.[23]

The security of the country was the final argument which tipped the scales. The coming of war in America made it possible for the opponents of emigration to have their way. On September 21, 1775, the Scottish Board of Customs Commissioners recorded in their

---

[21] *Ibid.*, p. 129.   [22] *Ibid.*, p. 130.

[23] Fagerstrom, "American Revolutionary Movement," ch. iii, citing Thomas Miller to Earl of Suffolk, Aug. 14, 1775, and Henry Dundas to Suffolk, Sept. 4, 1775.

minutes the British government's order to deny clearance to all ships carrying emigrants. The order remained in force until the end of the war.[24]

V

Before 1775 government made no effort to regulate the emigrant trade in the interests of safety and health. Conditions aboard Scottish emigrant ships were very uneven. Some of the human cargoes suffered terribly while others arrived in America in perfect health.

In 1767 fifty indentured servants aboard the ship *Pearl,* which had arrived at Charleston from Glasgow, began to voice "most violent complaints" over the ill usage they had received during the voyage at the hands of Captain Buchanan. They appealed to the governor and Council, to the Assembly, and to the local lawyers. Henry Laurens, the Charleston merchant, believed the master had done no more than strike some of them. Nevertheless he found himself insulted in the streets by some "Irish" (probably Scotch-Irish) among the immigrants. So harassed was Laurens that he returned the bounty money he had drawn on forty-eight of them as indentured servants, converted them into ordinary settlers, and drew the bounty to which he was entitled for importing Protestants.[25]

The first party of Highlanders who went to Pictou in Nova Scotia aboard the *Hector* experienced many hardships. According to Alexander Mackenzie, who seems to have relied entirely on the oral traditions of a century later, the ship was so rotten that the passengers could pick the wood out of her sides with their fingers.[26] They met with a severe gale off the Newfoundland coast and it took them fourteen days to recover the distance they had lost. The accommodations were wretched. Smallpox and dysentery broke out among the passengers, so that eighteen of the children died and were committed to the sea. Provisions ran out and the water became scarce and bad. The oatcake they carried became moldy, and much

[24] *Ibid.,* citing *Minutes of the Scottish Board of Customs Commissioners,* XIV, entry of Sept. 21, 1775; *Scots Magazine,* XXXVII (1775), 523.

[25] Leila Sellers, *Charleston Business on the Eve of the American Revolution* (Chapel Hill, N.C., 1934), pp. 119–120, citing Henry Laurens to Pagan, Brown & Co., March 16, 1768, and to Henry Cunningham, May 25, 1768.

[26] Rattray, *The Scot in British North America,* I, 274, says that the *Hector* was an old Dutch ship, seaworthy but inelegant.

of it was thrown away. But one passenger gathered the rejected scraps into a bag, and during the last few days of the voyage the others joined him in feasting upon what they had recently spurned.

John Ross, the agent of Witherspoon and Pagan, had led the emigrants to expect free land and adequate shelter upon their arrival. Instead they found the uncleared forest and no food or covering. Those who had a little money bought what they could from the agents. The rest determined to take what they needed by force and pay when they were able. They sent emissaries who tied up the agents and hid their guns. Then they distributed among themselves carefully weighed amounts of the supplies they had captured. When the authorities at Halifax ordered Captain Archibald at Truro to suppress this so-called "rebellion" he refused to march. Many of the disappointed immigrants left the settlement and bound themselves to service elsewhere in return for the means of subsistence.

Mackenzie's story must be accepted with reserve. "Even to this day," he wrote, in 1883, "the narration of the scenes and cruel hardships through which they had to pass, . . . beguiles many a winter's night." While these almost bardic recitals were without doubt based on authentic incidents, one can imagine that Mackenzie's informants were never at a loss for imaginative embellishments to sharpen the harrowing tale.[27]

On September 17, 1773, 280 men, women, and children embarked on the brig *Nancy*, George Smith master, at Dornoch in Sutherland. About the middle of December, two hundred of them landed at New York. Eighty-one had died during the voyage, owing to disgracefully overcrowded conditions. A lurid report of the following January stated that fifty of the victims were young children, and that they were starved and otherwise cruelly treated by Captain Smith. Doctor Witherspoon, who happened to be in the city, preached a special sermon in the Presbyterian church, after which eighty pounds were collected for the relief of the distressed Highlanders. On January 15, Smith sailed precipitately from New York at four in the morning bound for Charleston, apparently to avoid the consequences of what was believed to have been his inhuman behavior.[28]

[27] Mackenzie, "First Highland Emigration," pp. 141, 143.
[28] Stiles, *Diary*, I, 428; *Virginia Gazette*, Purdie and Dixon, Jan. 27, 1774, p. 3, and Feb. 10, 1774, p. 2.

Favorable reports of conditions aboard emigrant ships from Scotland are no less frequent. Donald Macpherson, one of the 1715 rebels sent to Maryland, wrote to a friend that he and his fellow exiles had been healthy during the voyage to America. Another source reveals that only one prisoner aboard the *Elizabeth and Anne,* which landed 112 rebels in Virginia in 1716, died at sea, in spite of the complaints of ill treatment which the passengers made after disembarking. When the *Favourite* arrived at New York, in August, 1773, with 140 immigrants from Scotland, after a voyage of nine weeks from Whitehaven, an observer declared them to be "mostly young, and all remarkably healthy, well looking people, having had neither sickness nor death on the voyage, except a young child, who was ill before it came aboard." [29]

In September, 1773, James Boswell inspected the emigrant ship *Nestor,* lying in Portree harbor. "The accommodation for the emigrants was very good," he recorded. "A long ward I may call it, with a row of beds on each side, every one of which was the same size every way, and fit to contain four people." [30]

VI

Some captains conscientiously looked after their passengers' welfare, while others were negligent to the point of homicide. Whether due for a pleasure cruise or a watery grave, the emigrant paid about the same in passage money. It was usual to charge half fare for children under eight years of age. Some of the emigrants paid cash, while others, probably a majority, made use of the well-known facilities of indenture and redemption.[31]

James Grey, who contracted to recruit Highland settlers for Georgia in 1741, estimated that it would cost one pound per head for their passage from Gravesend to Savannah and sixpence each per day to maintain them while awaiting the ship. The 280 or so emigrants from Dornoch in Sutherland, whose sufferings were described above, paid for their passage at the rate of £3 6s. per full

[29] *Virginia Magazine of History and Biography,* XXXVIII (1930), 336–342; *Virginia Gazette,* Rind, Sept. 9, 1773, p. 3.
[30] Boswell, *Tour* (Pottle ed.), p. 156.
[31] *Scots Magazine,* XXXVI (1774), 446; "Scotus Americanus," in Boyd, ed., *Eighteenth Century Tracts,* p. 447.

passenger. Counting children under ten years of age as halves, there were, according to the official reckoning, 188 full passengers. All paid for their transportation in cash. In addition there were thirty-five persons who had indented themselves for three years. A correspondent in Dornoch reported that the passage money totaled more than 650 guineas. In fact, if the captain received £3 6s. for each of 223 full passengers (188 plus 35), then the total passage money must have been 700 guineas, in return for which Captain Smith seems to have given little but the use of his ship for rather more than three months. Clearly the emigrant trade was not unprofitable.[32]

In September, 1773, a party of emigrants from Caithness sailed for America, having paid over seven hundred pounds to an Edinburgh merchant for their passage. The ship was forced into the Orkneys by storms and had to go to Leith for repairs. The emigrants were put ashore, where they soon exhausted their small store of ready cash and were obliged to beg, or work for miserable wages, to obtain a livelihood. They brought an action against the merchant for not fulfilling his contract and for the damages they had sustained in being so long prevented from sailing. Not until June, 1774, did the Court of Admiralty in Edinburgh hand down a decision. The verdict was happily favorable to the sufferers, to whom the defendant was ordered to repay the passage money with interest.[33]

The role of the British government in all these matters was negative. Policy with regard to the Crown lands in America varied in accordance with the political and administrative exigencies of the moment. Powerful elements in the "political nation" quickly became alarmed when mass migrations occurred. While unskilled laborers and beggars had never been missed, except possibly by the most pedantic of mercantilist thinkers, trained mechanics and craftsmen were another matter. Even the departure of the primitive farmers of the north of Scotland aroused the fears of the ruling classes, who had come, since the days of the elder Pitt, to look upon the overpopulated Highlands as an ideal field for the recruiting sergeant.

The colonial authorities, on the other hand, were inclined to en-

---

[32] Earl of Egmont, Journal, in *Ga. Recs.*, V, 504; *Virginia Gazette*, Rind, Dec. 16, 1773, p. 3; Stiles, *Diary*, I, 428.

[33] *Virginia Gazette*, Purdie and Dixon, Sept. 15, 1774, p. 2.

courage migration from Protestant Britain. Governors and assemblies were not averse to working together in order to ensure the orderly disposal of new arrivals. The Highlanders are said to have been attracted to America in part because there were no beggars there. Many of them, upon arrival in the New World, were saved the necessity of begging through the wisdom and generosity of the provincial administrations.

VI

The Scots in America:
Aspects of Social History

THE social and economic history of the eighteenth-century Scottish migration has been traced to the moment of setting foot in America. It has been necessary occasionally to glance forward in order to illuminate some point in the story. But nothing has been said of the amenability of the Scots to assimilation in their new environment. The Highlander tended to regard America as a land of freedom where he could wear the tartan of his clan unrestrained by British legislation. How long, then, did he continue to wear it? And how long did he retain the mental garb of the old country? What were his relationships with the people among whom he found himself? To what extent did Highlander and Lowlander continue to be distinct from one another as they so markedly were in eighteenth-century Scotland? The answers to these, and to many other similar questions, form part of the social history of the Scots-Americans.

The Scots, and especially the Highlanders, left home unwillingly. According to a writer in 1773, "they have ever shewn the utmost aversion at leaving their country, or removing to happier regions, and more indulgent climates. That this is true of the Highlanders in general, will be acknowledged by those who are in the least acquainted with them." [1]

[1] "Scotus Americanus," in Boyd, ed., *Eighteenth Century Tracts*, p. 429.

The Highlander's attachment to locale survived his journey to
America. Charles Augustus Murray, traveling in Virginia in 1835,
found the descendants of a band of Jacobite refugees still residing
in the place where their ancestors had settled some ninety years
before. This was his comment:

The American agriculturists seem to have little local attachment. A New
Englander or Virginian, though proud and vain of his state, will move
off to Missouri or Illinois, and leave the home of his childhood without
any visible effort or symptom of regret, if by so doing he can make ten
dollars where he before made eight. . . .

How different this is from the Scottish character may be gathered
from the fact that a band of highlanders [who] settled in Virginia [after
the '45] are as unwilling to quit that spot as they were to leave their
original country.[2]

It was generally, but by no means universally, true that the Highland immigrants remained in the neighborhood of their original
settlements. They tended strongly toward certain areas where they
would be among friends. The most important of these were the
Cape Fear Valley in North Carolina, the Mohawk and upper Hudson Valleys in New York, the Altamaha Valley in Georgia, Pictou
in Nova Scotia, and Prince Edward Island. Those who re-emigrated
from New York to Canada in 1777 were forced to do so after their
military defeat at the hands of the Americans. There was, however,
a certain amount of voluntary re-emigration from North Carolina.
Descendants of the Cumberland County Highlanders can be identified among the pioneer settlers of Tennessee and Mississippi.[3] This
movement westward across the Appalachians took place while hundreds were still pouring annually into North Carolina from the old
country.[4]

It is understandable that the Highlanders of the eighteenth cen-

[2] Charles Augustus Murray, *Travels in North America during the Years 1834,
1835, & 1836* (London, 1839), I, 148–149.

[3] John Haywood, *The Civil and Political History of the State of Tennessee*
(Knoxville, Tenn., 1825), p. 37; C. W. Grafton, "A Sketch of the Old Scotch
Settlement at Union Church," *Publications of the Mississippi Historical Society,*
IX (1906), 263.

[4] Professor Herbert Heaton of the University of Minnesota, who has made
a study of immigration into the United States in the period 1783–1812, informed
the author that the Highlanders continued to enter North Carolina in considerable numbers at least down to the War of 1812.

tury should have found it desirable to form distinctive communities in America. They were then as much a race apart as the Germans, less amenable to assimilation than the Lowland Scots, and far less so than the Scotch-Irish with their hostile attitude to the British government. Like the Germans they spoke a strange tongue, but unlike them they respected the authority of the Crown. Perhaps it would be more accurate to say that they were prepared to follow wheresoever their social superiors, who had come with them to America, might lead them, and as it happened these leaders gave their loyalty to the House of Hanover. They were clearly distinguished from other colonial peoples by their dress and demeanor.

In February, 1736, Governor Oglethorpe of Georgia paid a visit to the Highlanders at Darien and found them in their tartan plaids, armed after the fashion of their country with broad swords, small round shields, and muskets. Forbidden to carry these weapons in the country from which they came, they were expected to do so on the Georgia frontier, whither they had been brought to provide a defense against the Spaniard and Indian. In compliment to them, Oglethorpe, during the whole time he was with them, dressed himself in Highland costume. Though the Scots had provided him with a fine soft bed, with holland sheets and curtains, the tactful governor chose to lie upon the ground in the open air, between two other gentlemen, wrapped in his cloak, so that all the rest were obliged to follow his example.[5]

When Lachlan Campbell came to America in 1737, the Highland dress he wore "was then a Novelty in the Country." The Indians of the Saratoga region, where Campbell went to examine some lands, were so delighted by his unusual appearance that they pressed him and his friends to settle among them. It is said that a party of 350 Highlanders, who landed at Wilmington, North Carolina, threw such a fright into the town officials by their outlandish costume and language that the latter proposed imposing an oath upon the newcomers binding them to keep the peace.[6]

No Highlander was willing to give up without a struggle the

[5] *The Political State of Great Britain for the Month of July, 1736* (London, 1736), p. 38.
[6] William Smith, Jr., to Cadwallader Colden, in *Colden Papers*, V, 290; W. Smith, *History of New York*, I, 291; R. D. W. Connor, *Race Elements in the White Population of North Carolina* (Raleigh, N.C., 1920), p. 54.

newly restored freedom to wear his traditional dress. In June, 1775, a certain Donald McLeod petitioned the New York legislature, saying that some Highlanders recently arrived from Scotland would gladly serve under him in defense of the liberties of the colony, "with the Proviso of having Liberty to wear their own Country Dress Commonly called the Highland Habit." These men, it appears, had not allowed their proscribed weapons to rust during the forced pacification of the Highlands, for McLeod reported them as being "already furnished with Guns, Swords, Pistols and Highland Dirks which . . . is very necessary as all the above articles are at this Time very difficult to be had." Less than a year later, three Scottish merchants in Philadelphia, who took the American side in the war, "raised companies of their own countrymen of a hundred men each, who are equipped in the Scottish dress." [7]

The North Carolina settlers of the period 1740–1775 belonged to several clans, and they continued to wear their distinctive costume, including kilt, plaid, and sporran. When Allan Macdonald of Kingsburgh landed in the province in 1774, with his wife Flora, the famous preserver of Prince Charlie, he wore a tartan plaid over his shoulder, a large blue bonnet with a cockade of black ribbon, a tartan waistcoat with gold buttons, and tartan hose. When the *Hector* arrived at Pictou in Nova Scotia with its first cargo of Highland settlers, many of the younger men celebrated by donning their national dress, which some of them were able to round off with the dirk and claymore, while the only piper aboard prepared the way for disembarkation by clearing the neighboring forests of wild life. [8]

II

Few of the Highland immigrants spoke English. James Grey, who contracted to guide a party of Highlanders to Georgia in 1741, put a high price upon his services, which, he argued, were indispensable. They must have a Gaelic-speaking conductor to adjust their grievances, for they spoke no English. Reverend Hugh Mc-Adam, when preaching in English to the Cumberland County High-

[7] Margaret Wheeler Willard, ed., *Letters on the American Revolution 1774–1776* (Boston, 1925), p. 315.

[8] Mackenzie, "First Highland Emigration," pp. 141–142; MacLean, *Highlanders in America*, p. 114.

landers in 1756, found that many of them "scarcely knew one word" he spoke. For several years after the arrival in Virginia of a group of Jacobite refugees, their local court had to maintain a Gaelic interpreter. In August, 1746, John Mitchell of Fredericksburg advertised in the *Virginia Gazette* for a runaway servant boy named John Ross, whom he described as "a Scots-Highland Boy, about 16 Years of Age, . . . speaks broken *English,* and has his Hair cut: He carried with him . . . a Tartan Waistcoat." As late as 1805 Gaelic was spoken among a number of families who moved into Jefferson County, Mississippi, from North Carolina. They appear to have brought with them a Westminster Shorter Catechism in that language.[9]

In 1717 Donald Macpherson, a prisoner of the 1715 rebellion, wrote from exile in Maryland to his father, who lived at Culloden in Inverness-shire. He entrusted the work of penning this remarkable letter to a Scots friend at Portobago, Maryland. The latter had come from Glasgow as a servant. He composed (or perhaps took down syllable for syllable what Macpherson said to him) the message to Scotland in the broad Scots tongue of the Lowlands, but phonetically spelled and with a Highland accent! This letter has been printed in the *Maryland Historical Magazine*[10] without any attempt at translation into a more acceptable form of English. No wonder Macpherson's kindly master promised him a life of ease and supervision of the slaves if he would only learn to speak English like a Virginian, for Donald reported the promise in these words: "My Mestir says til me, Fan I kan speek lyk de Fouk hier, dat I sanna pi pidden di nating pat gar his Plackimors wurk: for desyt Fouk hier dinna ise te wurk pat de first Yeer after dey kum in te de Quintry: Tey speak a lyke de Sogers in Inerness."[11]

[9] *Ga. Recs.,* V, 504; Connor, *Race Elements,* p. 59, makes the statement, without documentary support, that English, the official and legal language, won an easy victory over Gaelic. He does not say when this happened. Murray, *Travels in North America,* I, 149; *Virginia Gazette,* Purdie and Dixon, Aug. 7, 1746, p. 4; Grafton, "Sketch."

[10] Donald Macpherson, Portobago [Port Tobacco], Md., to James Macpherson, June 2, 1717, in *Maryland Historical Magazine,* I (1906), 347.

[11] The literal translation of these words is: "My master says to me, when I can speak like the folk here, that I shall not be bidden do nothing but make his blackamoors work; for decent folk here do not use to work but the first year after they come into the country; they speak like the soldiers in Inverness."

Broad Scots could be as incomprehensible to the American as
Gaelic. According to the Marquis de Chastellux, who traveled
through Virginia in 1780–1782, a Scottish innkeeper in the upper
James Valley was "the most ridiculous person imaginable. He pro-
nounces English in so unintelligible a manner, that Mr. *Dillon* asked
him, very ingenuously, what language he was speaking." [12]

The Lowland Scots are far more difficult to trace after their
arrival in America than the Highlanders, because unlike the clansmen they usually dispersed themselves through various existing
communities. They were not very easily assimilable and tended to
retain their sense of Scottish nationality. This was especially true of
the Scottish mercantile community, which formed a significant if
small section of America's commercial class both before and after
the Revolution. Merchants and storekeepers often regarded their
stay in the colonies as a temporary exile to be endured for the sake
of pecuniary gain. There were few Lowlanders who regarded emigration as in any sense an escape to a better life. The Lowland
farmers are the most difficult of all to detect in America, for many
of them went to areas like western Pennsylvania where they mingled
with and became almost indistinguishable from the Scotch-Irish.[13]
Here the Lowland speech fell pleasantly on familiar ears. In aris-

[12] Marquis de Chastellux, *Travels in North-America in the Years 1780, 1781,
and 1782* (London, 1787), II, 119.

[13] Solon J. Buck and Elizabeth Hawthorn Buck, *The Planting of Civilization
in Western Pennsylvania* (Pittsburgh, 1939), pp. 152–154. The authors give
figures based on the census of 1790 for the racial origin of the people of western
Pennsylvania in that year. They purport to be able to distinguish Scots, Ulster
Scots, and Ulster Celts. But the survey is made from the surnames of the heads
of families, always an unsafe method, and it gives no clue to the birthplace of
the persons concerned. For what they are worth, here are their conclusions:

Of almost thirteen thousand white families in western Pennsylvania's five
counties (Allegheny, Washington, Fayette, Westmoreland, and Bedford), it appears that racial origins were in the following proportions:

English	37	per cent
Scottish	17	" "
Welsh	7	" "
Ulster Scottish	7.5	" "
Ulster Celtic	2.7	" "
Anglo-Irish	4.6	" "
Irish Celtic	4.6	" "
German	12	" "
Others	8	" "

tocratic Virginia, however, the countryman's tongue was regarded as somewhat uncouth. Like Boswell in London, many of the middle-class Scottish townsmen in Virginia were tempted to adapt themselves to the language and manners of a society they felt to be more polished than that which they had left behind in Glasgow or Greenock. Alexander Macaulay, for example, a Scottish merchant in Hanover Town, Virginia, recorded in his diary at Newcastle on February 22, 1763, with a good deal of native Scottish sarcasm, that he had "had a visit from the amiable accomplished, Delicate genteel Mrs. Riddock . . . ; a good specimen of Scotch Ladies in this Land. Why in the name of wonder," he asked himself, in fear for his good name as a Scot, "do such go abroad. She is much better calculated for the meridian of the Mull of Cantire or the Esquimaux, than the polished Circles of Virginia." [14] If Mrs. Riddock was really from Kintyre, she may have had a certain Highland way about her which would be enough in itself to account for Macaulay's sense of superiority.

There were Scottish-born merchants in all the coastal cities throughout the eighteenth century. With their clerks and storekeepers, usually imported from Scotland, they made up a very small but remarkably influential group among the immigrants. Their economic power had far-reaching effects in Virginia, and indeed throughout the tobacco country of this and neighboring colonies, where the rise of Glasgow to commercial dominance caused a growing antipathy between Scot and American. But Glasgow's trading enterprise was by no means confined to the South. Before 1718 Thomas Mackie of Langtounsyde, merchant in Glasgow, was in partnership with John McWilliams, merchant in Philadelphia. When the former died, McWilliams owed him money, and the dead man's estate, consisting largely of debts due him, amounted to over £660 sterling. In 1766 two Boston merchants wrote to George Kippen and Son of Glasgow, whose interests in Virginia were then extensive, and established a connection for trading purposes. They opened business by placing an eighty-pound order with Kippen, and also requested forty-six pounds' worth of dry goods from George Brown of Glasgow. Meanwhile many firms in America were formed and run by Scots.

[14] Alexander Macaulay's diary, quoted in Malcolm H. Harris, "The Port Towns of the Pamunkey," *William and Mary Quarterly*, 2nd ser., XXIII (1943), 509.

Though the chief of these were in Virginia and North Carolina, two Scots in New London, Connecticut, William Glenn and William Gregory, both of whom had emigrated from Kilmarnock, traded with the West Indies, sending out lumber, fish, horses, and cattle in exchange for rum, molasses, and sugar.[15]

III

The Highlanders, too, found commercial opportunities in America which were altogether greater than anything they had known in Scotland. From a period soon after its foundation, Campbelltown, or Cross Creek, twin villages in the Cape Fear Valley of North Carolina, grew at a great rate. This place was at the heart of a great region of Highland settlement, and it was also a commercial crossroads between the ports of the tidewater area and the Scotch-Irish and Germans of the back country. Many merchants established themselves there, and a brisk trade began up and down the river. With the development of the market at Cross Creek came the opening of direct roads leading from it to various parts of the piedmont. Since their construction was too great a task for the local authorities, it was undertaken by the provincial assembly, which passed a series of important measures to that end. From 1755 on, a number of acts created highways all over central North Carolina. The highways, laid out for the deliberate purpose of encouraging trade, converged on the Highland town of Cross Creek. Settlers far from the river sent their goods to Cross Creek in large wagons, forty or fifty of which might be seen there in the course of a single day. The Wilmington merchants had stores and agents there to buy and lay up the goods.

Wilmington commerce, incidentally, was dominated by Lowland Scots. They purchased large timber rafts on which they floated down the river for a hundred miles their cargoes of livestock, beef, pork, rawhides, corn, flour, and butter. The same convoy which brought

[15] *Virginia Magazine of History and Biography,* XII (1904–05), 86–87; Jackson and Bromfield, Newburyport, to George Kippen and Son, Glasgow, June 27, 1766, and Jackson and Bromfield invoice book, Jackson-Lee Papers, in Kenneth Wiggins Porter, ed., *The Jacksons and the Lees: Two Generations of Massachusetts Merchants 1765–1844* (Cambridge, Mass., 1937), I, 169; "William Gregory's Journal," *William and Mary Quarterly,* 1st ser., XII (1904–05), 225.

these things to Wilmington would carry back up the river the supplies obtained in exchange for the farm produce. Vessels of twenty
tons could go up to Cross Creek. Most of the area's produce found
its way from Wilmington to Charleston, but some went to the West
Indies, and a little to London, Bristol, and Glasgow directly. By
1767 there were fifty sawmills on the Cape Fear and its tributaries,
cutting 7,500,000 feet of lumber annually.[16]

More than one Highlander made a handsome fortune in North
Carolina trade. A certain Neil McArthur, who settled at Cross Creek
in 1764 with only a small amount of property, claimed eleven years
later that he was worth over forty-six hundred pounds.[17]

Perhaps the most lucrative branch of trade for the Cape Fear
Highlanders was cattle raising and marketing. This activity constituted one of the few industrial links between Scotland and America
in the eighteenth century. About 1785 a minor political economist
wrote:

Black cattle have long been a staple commodity in the country [Scotland].
Their carcases and their milk make a considerable part of the food of its
inhabitants; their hides are the material of one of its most necessary
manufactures; and the surplus cattle, after the home consumpt is supplied, form a fund for paying part of the debt incurred to England, for
goods bought from thence.[18]

During the eighteenth century, cattle raising was the Highland
farmer's biggest source of income. In some areas of the Highlands
and islands the payment of rents depended almost entirely on the
sale of black cattle. The Union of the Parliaments had stimulated
various branches of commerce, including the cattle trade. Cattle
then began to be sent to the south in larger numbers and from
greater distances than before. Attracted by the profits of the trade,
certain families, who hitherto had considered themselves above
vulgar commerce, began to deal in cattle. At first few animals were
raised except in Galloway. The Highland hill pastures were poor,

[16] Charles Christopher Crittenden, *The Commerce of North Carolina 1763–
1789* (New Haven, 1936), p. 94; "Scotus Americanus," in Boyd, ed., *Eighteenth
Century Tracts*, pp. 448–449; Sellers, *Charleston Business*, pp. 38–39.

[17] Crittenden, *Commerce of North Carolina*, p. 111.

[18] John Naismith, *Thoughts on Various Objects of Industry Pursued in Scotland* (Edinburgh, 1790), p. 75.

and there was no food for the beasts in winter. But by 1723 it is
said that thirty thousand head of cattle were sold at a great fair at
Crieff in a single season, most of them to English drovers, who paid
the Highlanders over thirty thousand guineas in cash for them.
About 1764 the Galloway dealers began to drive cattle regularly
all the way into England. About the end of 1767 there was a sudden
fall in the price of black cattle, which hit the farmers hard and
ruined many cattle dealers. Prices went on declining until 1770.[19]
Only two years later a terrible winter worked havoc among the
herds of the Inner Hebrides. But while the trade suffered setbacks
in Scotland, it was advancing without check in North Carolina and
Georgia, whither it had been transplanted with the Highland emigrants.

Many of the Cape Fear Valley settlers came from Argyllshire, some
of them from the neighborhood of Campbelltown in Kintyre, after
which place they named the town that is now Fayetteville, in Cumberland County, North Carolina. In 1742 the Scottish Campbelltown
was a small fishing village. Thirty years later it had become a
flourishing port and the center of an important fishing industry.
By 1772 the town's seventy-eight vessels employed about eight hundred men. When boats began to rendezvous there, Campbelltown
grew rapidly. In the vicinity the farmers raised black cattle and
salted them for the use of the fishing fleets. Campbelltown was an
island of modest prosperity in an otherwise poor countryside.[20]

The Highlanders who went from there to Campbelltown and
Cross Creek in North Carolina soon built up a notable ranching industry. Settlements spread up the riverbanks, while the vacant, uncleared land behind them was, according to a contemporary, like
the wasteland around a medieval English manor, "all a common."
Over these great open tracts the neighboring planters set their cattle
loose to wander and graze. Their numbers were unrestricted. Herds
of two or three hundred were common, while some reached over
a thousand. At the spring roundup the farmers gathered all the animals at one place, separated the calves from the cows, put them in
fenced pastures, and branded them with marks registered at the

[19] Grant, *Old Highland Farm*, p. 59; [Alexander], *Northern Rural Life*, pp. 62,
71–72; H. G. Graham, *Social Life*, pp. 175–176.
[20] Pennant, *Tour in Scotland*, I, 192, 194.

provincial capital. They made butter and cheese and then turned the herds loose for another year, except for a few milch cows.

In the 1760's, it is said, some thirty thousand head of black cattle were driven each year from North Carolina to Virginia. Others were sold to vessels at Wilmington or Brunswick, and some were exported to the Bahamas and the West Indies.[21]

In November, 1739, the Earl of Egmont, secretary to the Georgia trustees, learned with displeasure that the Scots of Darien, being unable to subsist by the cultivation of their land, had "turn'd them selves to the keeping of cattel," for which purpose Governor Oglethorpe had lent them two hundred pounds of the trustees' money. The Highlanders were already indebted to the trust and, though they had given security for their latest loan, experience had shown, thought Egmont, that one might as well give as lend money to the people of the province, no such debt having been repaid except that contracted by the Moravians. By July, 1740, the Darien people were supplying five or six beeves a week to troops in the vicinity. They also sold butter and milk in large quantities to the soldiers. The cattle had become almost their sole source of livelihood. Oglethorpe, in order to recover the two hundred pounds lent to the Highlanders for their initial stock, and alarmed at signs of their selling out apparently with a view to leaving the province, seized the money obtained from the sale of the cattle and used it to amortize the loan. This act constituted one of several grievances, both real and imagined, against Oglethorpe which many of the Scots used to justify their removal to South Carolina.[22]

IV

While the Scots of Georgia and the Cape Fear looked to Charleston as their commercial capital, those of Albemarle Sound, like those in Maryland, belonged to the Virginia sphere of interest. In the more southerly system of markets many of the merchants were Lowland Scots. They worked all the way from Charleston itself to the Cherokee frontier. It has been said that many of the present day

---

[21] "Scotus Americanus," in Boyd, ed., *Eighteenth Century Tracts*, pp. 444–445.

[22] Egmont, Journal, Nov. 5, 1739, July 2, 1740, Oct. 5, 1741, in *Ga. Recs.*, V, 247, 381, 556; see also *Ga. Recs.*, V, 502.

Cherokees trace their Scottish surnames to this period of frequent
contacts with Scots traders. Though Scots merchants were scattered
throughout the colonies, nowhere was their historical role more
conspicuous and interesting than in Virginia.

In 1766 Scotland imported from Virginia and Maryland goods to
the value of £334,000 and exported to those colonies other goods
worth £147,000. The first figure represents more than one-third
of Scotland's total imports for that year. By 1769 the imbalance of
the trade had been slightly rectified: Scotland imported £398,000
from the two colonies and exported to them £227,000. In this year,
the last when separate figures are available for England and Scotland, the latter country actually took more from Virginia and Maryland than the former, in spite of her great inferiority in population
and wealth. But England's exports to the colonies named were
worth more than twice as much as Scotland's. In this year Scottish
imports of tobacco amounted to 25,457 hogsheads from Virginia,
9,641 from Maryland, and 460 from North Carolina. Total imports
were, therefore, 35,558 hogsheads. By 1771 the total had risen to
49,016. Out of this number 38,000 hogsheads were re-exported, most
of it to France and Holland.[23] Scotland had acquired a special position in relation to the tobacco colonies, and Glasgow had become
the premier entrepôt of the transatlantic tobacco trade.

In the early eighteenth century the tidewater lands of Virginia
being largely occupied, the tobacco industry began to expand westward beyond the fall line of the Atlantic rivers. The western planters,
finding direct relations with the older firms more difficult and dis-
satisfied with the risks of the old "consignment system," became
willing to sell their crops outright to any merchant who would
purchase them. It was in the period just after the Union of the
Parliaments of England and Scotland, when Scotland ceased to be
regarded as a foreign country in relation to the Navigation Laws,
that Scottish merchants, already notorious as illicit traders with the

[23] David Macpherson, *Annals of Commerce* (London, 1805), III, 456, 495;
Pennant, *Tour in Scotland*, I, 131–132; in the five years, 1770–1774, according
to Lewis Cecil Gray, *History of Agriculture in the Southern United States to 1860*
(New York, 1941), I, 215, 255, Scotland imported an average of 43,500,000
pounds of tobacco, and re-exported 42,600,000. The Scots had captured more
than three-fourths of the trade to France and about half of that to Holland,
which took almost as much tobacco in all as France.

English colonies, began to capture a growing segment of the Virginia trade by new and aggressive tactics. The Scots developed the practice of purchasing tobacco direct from the planter, instead of transporting it to Great Britain before the commodity changed ownership, as had been the usual procedure with the London merchants. By 1775, when the Glasgow merchants controlled the lion's share of the tobacco trade, three-fourths of the colonial output was purchased in this way. At the same time the growth of the class of colonial merchant-planters, like the first William Byrd, was a further blow to the consignment system. Toward the end of the colonial period there had grown up a specialized group of merchants in the tobacco colonies, some of whom were junior partners in British firms, some their salaried representatives, and some independent merchants with British correspondents. This pattern applied particularly to the Lowland Scots mercantile community in Virginia, Maryland, and North Carolina's Albemarle Sound region. The London merchants lost business, but the Glasgow ones gained more than enough to compensate for this loss.[24]

The Scots managed to reduce the costs of their operations, which of course gave them a distinct competitive advantage. In August, 1768, William Nelson wrote from Virginia to the merchant John Norton in London: "[The Scots] sail their Ships so much cheaper than you can from London, & they have some other Advantages in the Trade, to which you & I are Strangers, that it is my Opinion, that in a few Years the London Market will be cheaply supply'd thro that Chanell." In 1769 the Scots were even credited with establishing a virtual monopoly, enabling them to keep up the price of tobacco. Since the "Glasgow people are become almost the sole Engrossers," wrote Roger Atkinson, an active Virginia businessman, "ye price will be kept up tolerably well both here and with you." [25]

The Scottish merchants, too, enjoyed certain advantages in the store trade. Ultimately they came to control the channels of dis-

[24] Lewis Cecil Gray, "The Market Surplus Problems of Colonial Tobacco," *William and Mary Quarterly*, 2nd ser., VIII (1928), 2–4.

[25] William Nelson, Virginia, to John Norton, [London], Aug. 27, 1768, in Mason, ed., *Norton Papers*, p. 66; Roger Atkinson, James River, Va., to Messrs. Lyonel and Samuel Lyde, [London], July 5, 1769, and to Messrs. Hyndman & Lancaster, [London], Aug. 25, 1769, in *Virginia Magazine of History and Biography*, XV (1907–08), 346.

tribution in Virginia and Maryland for imported goods. The London merchants concentrated on the consignment branch of the tobacco trade and engaged in the store trade only to a limited extent.

The Scots were able to oblige the ship captains to take proper care of their goods. William Beverley of Blandfield stated: "I find the Scotch, who are the principal Importers of Goods from London, insist that the Captains shall sign their Bills of Lading, deliverable at a particular Landing on the River, whereon they reside. . . . By this means they receive their Goods in due Time and proper order." As these words imply, the Scots merchants did more than sell Scottish manufactures; they bought up goods which they knew would sell well in Virginia, obtaining them in the cheapest market.[26]

Scottish textiles found an outlet in the mainland colonies. Scots osnaburgs were cheaper than the German ones. They were manufactured around Glasgow, and provided much of the summer clothing of the slaves. Glasgow also re-exported continental linen and various English manufactures.[27]

The business structure which stretched from Glasgow to the Southern frontier was a rather complicated one. In the five years before the Revolution more than two dozen Glasgow firms operated stores in Virginia and Maryland. The great firm of Spiers and Glassford owned twenty-four vessels and sometimes transported more than ten thousand hogsheads of tobacco to Scotland in a single year. The tobacco merchants of Glasgow regarded themselves as an aristocracy, wearing distinguishing scarlet cloaks and bushy wigs. One of them, Andrew Buchanan, built himself a fine mansion with a street leading up to it which he named Virginia Avenue.[28]

In the eighteenth century it was the practice of Scots merchants to send out to Virginia their sons and other relatives to act as their agents and factors. Some of these young men remained in the colonies, set up in business for themselves, and founded wealthy families. "I observe," wrote Philip Fithian, a Scottish immigrant, indentured servant, and tutor at Nomini Hall, in 1773, "that all the Merchants and shopkeepers in the Sphere of my acquaintance and I am told it is the Case through the Province, are young Scotch-Men . . . and

---

[26] Calvin Brewster Coulter, Jr., "The Import Trade of Colonial Virginia," *William and Mary Quarterly*, 3rd ser., II (1945), 299–302.
[27] *Ibid.*, p. 298.   [28] Wertenbaker, *Early Scotch Contributions*, p. 12.

it has been the custom heretofore to have all their Tutors, and School-masters from Scotland, tho' they begin to be willing to employ their own Countrymen." [29]

Before the middle of the century the incoming Scots traders, find-ing the business of tidewater Virginia largely controlled by the London merchants, pushed into the back country and established local stores at suitable points. Many of these stores belonged to large Scottish wholesale firms, some to independent Scots immigrant merchants, and a number to firms which had partners on both sides of the ocean. The westward advance of tobacco culture, and there-fore of trading, beyond the fall line of the rivers resulted in the growth of the existing fall-line towns and the founding of new ones. The Scottish mercantile immigrant played the leading role in this economic expansion. The chains of stores in the back country de-pended for their supplies and outlets upon the collecting and dis-tributing points set up at the fall line. According to Francis Jerdone, factor for Alexander Spiers and one of the leading Scots merchants in the colony at midcentury, the planters of Goochland, Albemarle, and Cumberland Counties were accustomed by 1756 to "roll their Tobacco to Warwick, Rockyridge and Shockoes," while those who lived in Augusta, Orange and Culpeper "rolled to Fredericksburg." The first three places were in the neighborhood of·Richmond, at the Falls of the James, while Fredericksburg is, of course, the fall-line town of the Rappahannock. To Fredericksburg, Petersburg, Rich-mond, Falmouth, Dumfries, and Alexandria came merchants, mostly Scots, to profit from the new trade. All these towns today lie along the main north-south highway, U.S. 1. Not only did storehouses cluster at these points, but the largest concentration of retail stores belonging to Scots (and few of them belonged to others) was also here. Out of some sixty such stores in Virginia, owned by Glasgow firms alone during the five years before the Revolution, twenty-nine lay within ten miles of a line connecting up these towns. The Scot-tish middlemen did not restrict themselves to the back country but took the business of many tidewater planters away from the London

[29] Fairfax Harrison, "Western Explorations in Virginia between Lederer and Spotswood," *Virginia Magazine of History and Biography*, XXX (1922), 323; Wertenbaker, *Early Scotch Contributions*, p. 12; Philip Fithian, "Journal of Philip Fithian, Kept at Nomini Hall, Virginia, 1773-1774," ed. by John Rogers Wil-liams, *American Historical Review*, V (1900) 294.

merchants. By 1775 they were well on the way toward establishing a new system of trade, in which middlemen played the most important role.[30]

By the end of 1758 the Scots merchants in Petersburg were trying to get a license for their hitherto unrecognized church. Regarding the Presbyterians as dissenters, although they belonged to the legally established Church of Scotland, Reverend George Trask of Chesterfield County wrote to Commissary Dawson at Williamsburg, asking him to deny the license.[31]

Records survive of a succession of Scottish mercantile firms operating out of Fredericksburg from as early as 1759 until well into the nineteenth century. The functions of these men included foreign exchange, wholesale and retail trade, banking, and agriculture.[32]

Scottish associations with Dumfries antedated the Union. In 1680, at a time when ships from Glasgow, Dumfries, and Leith, in Scotland, were ranging the Potomac to obtain what illegal trade they could, the Virginia assembly ordered a town to be laid out near the mouth of Acquia Creek. Before 1700 there were Scottish settlers in Westmoreland and Stafford Counties on the Potomac. From the 1690's Scottish interests dominated the area around Quantico Creek, where the town of Dumfries grew up, and they continued dominant until the early nineteenth century. Some miles further north the town of Alexandria was chartered in 1749, and, from then until 1800, most of its settlers came from Scotland.[33]

[30] Gray, *History of Agriculture*, I, 426; Gray, "Market Surplus Problems," p. 4; Francis Jerdone to Messrs. Alexander Speirs [*sic*] & Hugh Brown, May 15, 1756, in *William and Mary Quarterly*, 1st ser., XVI (1907–08), 127; Robert Walter Coakley, "The Two James Hunters of Fredericksburg: Patriots among the Virginia Scotch Merchants," *Virginia Magazine of History and Biography*, LVI (1948), 5; *Virginia Gazette*, 1770–75 (all editions), *passim*.

[31] Rev. George Trask to Rev. Commissary Dawson Dec. 9, 1758, in *William and Mary Quarterly*, 2nd ser., I (1921), 281.

[32] *Annual Reports of the Archivist University of Virginia Library* ([Charlottesville], Va., 1940), no. 6, p. 5. The details of these merchants' activities are to be found in various collections of private and business papers in Virginia libraries. They do not throw much light on the topic of the present study. For some years Jacob M. Price of Harvard University has been working on the Virginia tobacco trade in the eighteenth century. The results of his research should supplement, if they do not further illuminate, the subject matter of this chapter.

[33] Henry J. Berkley, "The Port of Dumfries, Prince William Co., Va.," *William and Mary Quarterly*, 2nd ser., IV (1924), 101–102; *William and Mary Quarterly*, 2nd ser., XVI (1936), 113–114.

From the fall-line bases the Scots expanded their interests toward the coast as well as into the piedmont. Shortly before the Revolution the Glasgow firms had at least ten retail stores in the tidewater area of Virginia, and others in Maryland and North Carolina. In addition much of the trade of the tidewater region was carried on by independent Scottish merchants. These men had their headquarters in the port of Norfolk. In 1765 a French traveler found Norfolk and Portsmouth "Chiefly Inhabited by scotch, all presbiterians and altho they are the most bigoted set of people in the world, they have no house of worship of their own." Each place, however, had a church of the English establishment. Not so long before, indeed, Norfolk had been an "English" town. The merchants there bore distinctly English names. Then came the Scots and with them an acute business rivalry, followed by political strife. They carried on a "Smart trade" with the West Indies. Their exports were numerous: pork, corn, butter, cheese, candles, tallow, bacon, ham, lumber, shingles, masts, yards, hemp, and other naval stores. Many of Norfolk's leading merchants came from Glasgow, arriving as agents for Glasgow firms or as clerks with letters of introduction to Norfolk traders and building up businesses of their own.[34]

Perhaps the most successful of the independent Scots merchants of Norfolk was Neil Jamieson, whose papers are now in the Library of Congress. He owned a network of stores and warehouses on the Virginia rivers, where he exchanged European goods for tobacco, carrying on the trade in his own vessels. In partnership with various Scottish merchants, he owned the ships which carried the tobacco of Virginia to Glasgow and the naval stores and foodstuffs of North Carolina to London and the West Indies. Jamieson was independent only in the sense that he was the possessor of considerable real property in Virginia on his own account. But in trade he was the fourth partner in the Glasgow firm of Glassford, Gordon, and Monteath. In this capacity he owned a quarter share in the company's property and stock in trade in the colony. He also possessed a partner's share in some warehouses at Richmond belonging to the Glas-

[34] The ten stores were at Mattox and Westmoreland on the Potomac, Tappahannock on the Rappahannock (2), Aylett's (2), Urbanna, Surrey, Smithfield, and Suffolk. See the various *Virginia Gazettes*. See also "Journal of a French Traveller in the Colonies, 1765," *American Historical Review*, XXVI (1921), 739–740; Thomas Jefferson Wertenbaker, *Norfolk: Historic Southern Port* (Durham, N.C., 1931), pp. 15, 49–50.

gow firm of Henderson, McCall, and Company. The value of his real estate in Virginia was reliably estimated at £7,069 sterling—a comfortable fortune when one considers that he acquired it in sixteen years. In 1776 he was able to cash a large sum in treasury bills for Lord Dunmore.[35]

Of the six partners in the Glasgow firm of John Wallace and Company, only one, Michael Wallace, resided in Virginia. The others never left Scotland. Michael went to the colony in 1771 and had to leave it at the outbreak of the Revolution. Many factors and agents of Scottish firms had similar experiences. One remarkable firm had headquarters in Glasgow and in Suffolk, Nansemond County, Virginia. John Hamilton and Company had two of its three partners, representing four-fifths of its capital, in America. Old John managed things in Glasgow while his son and nephew, young John and Archibald Hamilton, supervised one of the largest businesses in the Albemarle region of North Carolina, if not in the entire South. With their principal bases at Suffolk and at Elk Marsh near Halifax, North Carolina, the Hamiltons owned a chain of stores extending from the James to the Cape Fear and into the back country. Besides their stores and warehouses, they owned a hatter's, a tailor's, a blacksmith's, and a cooper's shop, a tavern, several plantations, and many wagons and river vessels.[36]

V

The Albemarle area of North Carolina, the chief seat of John Hamilton's operations, was a commercial appendage of Virginia. A large part of its trade, like that of Virginia, was in the hands of outsiders. Here too, the Glasgow merchants succeeded in absorbing the cream of the profits. In the twelve years before the Revolution they advanced steadily against the competition of South Carolina, New England, and independent Virginia merchants. The Cape Fear

[35] Wertenbaker, *Early Scotch Contributions*, pp. 12–13; testimony of Neil Jamieson before Commissioner Pemberton, Halifax, N.S., May 16, 1786, printed in *Canad. Claims*, pp. 630–633.

[36] *Canad. Claims*, p. 720; Crittenden, *Commerce of North Carolina*, pp. 97, 110. It was said that the John Hamilton firm was accustomed to sell in North Carolina at a wholesale advance of about 50 per cent, and at a retail advance of about 100 per cent, over the first cost in Great Britain (*ibid.*, p. 35).

Valley, as has been pointed out above, was commercially attached to Charleston rather than to the Chesapeake ports. Its commerce was less under the control of outsiders than in most other parts of the province. Many of the independent merchants, however, were Scottish immigrants. The storekeepers of the North Carolina piedmont were the agents of firms in the Cape Fear and Albemarle regions and in Virginia and Great Britain. Many of them were Scottish "store boys." [37]

In the period preceding the Revolution the trade of Maryland was passing from the old towns, created and fostered by a provincial act of 1683, to Annapolis and New Baltimore. British merchants, who had operated retail stores with varied inventories in the old river towns, began to center their businesses in the growing cities further up Chesapeake Bay. Early in the century Scots traders had come to Maryland, and they seem to have done their business exclusively, according to the familiar pattern, through their own stores and factors. After 1750 they became prominent in the Potomac and Patuxent area. The Glasgow firms of James Brown and Company, Jamieson, Johnstone and Company, and John Glassford, Shortridge and Gordon maintained stores at Bladensburg, Upper Marlborough, Leonardtown, Piscattaway, Port Tobacco, and Nottingham. As grain cultivation grew in the Eastern Shore, the independents flourished there, while the factors of the Glasgow firms entrenched themselves in the tobacco country across the bay. In June, 1774, Nicholas Cresswell could note in his diary, at Annapolis: "Great number of Scotch tradesmen here, but very few English." [38]

It is difficult to estimate the number of Scots engaged in trade in the tobacco colonies before the Revolution. It is still harder to say how many of these were bona fide immigrants. Some of them regarded their stay in America as a temporary exile. Some were forced to return home after 1775 by the war and their loyalist sympathies. Some yielded to coercion in swearing allegiance to the

[37] Crittenden, *Commerce of North Carolina*, pp. 111–112; *ibid.*, pp. 97–98; Haywood, *History of Tennessee*, p. 37.

[38] Henry J. Berkley, "Extinct River Towns of the Chesapeake Bay Region," *Maryland Historical Magazine*, XIX (1924), 129–130; Charles Albro Barker, *The Background of the Revolution in Maryland* (New Haven, 1940), pp. 74, 76–77; Nicholas Cresswell, *The Journal of Nicholas Cresswell 1774-1777*, 2nd ed. (New York, 1928), p. 22.

United States, and some became patriots through enthusiasm and conviction. Yet in a broad sense, they had all at one time or another been immigrants.

A writer in the *Virginia Gazette* for April 13, 1776, said that there were probably fifty foreign houses or companies and two thousand factors in charge of the trade of Virginia.[39] Since the few non-Scottish firms were unaccustomed to doing business indirectly through factors, it may be assumed that most of the two thousand (if the number was so large) were Scots. Indeed, little mention is to be found anywhere of storekeepers, agents, or factors in Virginia who were other than Scots. The figure given, however, may be an overestimate. The writer had an interest in exaggerating it, for he was attempting to present an alarmist account of the amount of specie being removed from the colony by the outsiders in the mercantile community.

During the five years before the Revolution (or at some time within that period) there were well over sixty retail stores in Virginia belonging to some two dozen Glasgow firms.[40] These must have employed at least 120 storekeepers and clerks, while the base storehouses at Norfolk and along the fall line supported many others. This leaves out of account altogether the many independent Scottish merchants and their employees, not to mention the frontier traders. To all these must be added the operators of some twenty Glasgow-owned stores in Maryland and the Albemarle, and the independents in those parts. But even if the total number of mercantile Scottish immigrants was as little as two thousand at the peak period, the significance of this group is not to be judged merely by its size. They held a key position in the economic life of the tobacco

---

[39] Arthur Meier Schlesinger, *The Colonial Merchants and the American Revolution 1763–1776* (New York, 1939), p. 601. Isaac S. Harrell, in his *Loyalism in Virginia* (Durham, N.C., 1926), cites the above reference for the statement: "At the beginning of the Revolution there were approximately two thousand merchants in Virginia, a majority of them of foreign birth." Schlesinger says nothing of the sort.

[40] *Virginia Gazette,* 1770–1775 (all editions), *passim.* The firm of James and Robert Donald & Co. had the largest number of stores in Virginia—nine. William Cuninghame & Co. had six. Donald, Scot, & Co., Alexander Spiers & Co., Buchanans, Hastie, & Co., and James Ritchie & Co. had four each. Three other firms had three each, five firms had two, and eleven had one store each.

colonies, and they played an important part in the sequence of events which fostered discontent among the planters and helped to put them on the side of the Revolution. These events do not properly form a part of this study, but the strained relationship between Scot and Virginian to which they gave rise will be discussed in some of its aspects in Chapter VIII.

VI

The Scottish merchants were by no means confined to the Southern colonies. There was a sizable group of them in each of the larger Northern ports. There were probably fewer of them in Boston than in New York and Philadelphia. Like the Southern Scots, most of them were loyalists when the war came. Few of the New York merchants were the relatives of Glasgow businessmen, but perhaps it was an advantage to be one. William Pagan, at any rate, who was the son of George Pagan, a prosperous Glasgow merchant, did well for himself in America, in spite of his loyalist conduct. Starting as the master of a sloop trading to St. Eustatia, he became in 1769 a freeman of the city of New York. With his three brothers, all to be loyalists too, he conducted a business in New York as merchant and shipping agent. With the surrender of New York to the United States he went north, arriving in St. John, New Brunswick, in 1783. Three years later he was a member of the New Brunswick General Assembly. After that he joined the Governor's Council, and in 1798 he became the first president of the St. John St. Andrew's society. He had been a member of the New York St. Andrew's Society, one of a number of such clubs in the seaport towns, the earliest of which was founded at Charleston in 1729. As will shortly appear, it was through these charitable and social societies in some measure that Scottish influence was exercised in the colonies. Another member of the New York society was Thomas Buchanan, son of a leading Glasgow merchant and a graduate of the University of Glasgow. Arriving in New York in 1762, he entered business with his cousin Walter as an importer of British wares. The firm of Thomas Buchanan and Son came to own many ships, and Thomas preserved his property through the Revolution by adroit diplomacy. He was one of a very few who were able to remain neutral in the conflict and at the same time retain the esteem of both sides.[41]

Further afield still, in Canada, the Scottish traders were exceedingly active from the conquest onward. Scottish officers entered the fur trade of the Northwest upon their discharge from the British army. The agents of British houses extended their businesses into the territory hitherto controlled by the French. As the years passed, the Scots, here as elsewhere, outstripped their rivals. By 1768 it had become clear to some that the Scots would sooner or later engross the trade of the province of Quebec and its dependent territories. Because of the well-disciplined group of Scottish members in the House of Commons, who always voted solidly for the administration, the fur traders in Canada wielded an influence on affairs quite out of proportion to their numbers. They led the opposition to the regulatory measures of Sir William Johnson. The colonial governors were accustomed to issue trading licenses at random, thus greatly increasing the number of traders in the fur regions. Because of the expense of an enlightened policy of regulation, the government in Britain was willing to support the governors in this action. The very center of the opposition to Johnson, according to a student of the fur trade in Michigan, lay in "that brilliant line of Scotch fur barons which is still in existence." No less a scholar than Clarence Alvord has declared, from his intimate knowledge of the fur trade in the Old Northwest, his conviction that the Scottish influence "was a very real factor in shaping British policy towards that region for over fifty years." By the end of the eighteenth century the Scots fur barons in Montreal had attained their full wealth and power. They stood at the head of a commercial hierarchy which descended through the merchants of Michillimackinac and Detroit, who were middlemen, to the wandering traders of the backwoods, who dealt with the Indians.[42]

The Scots, especially the Lowlanders, showed amazing energy and enthusiasm in taking advantage of that section of the Treaty of

[41] William M. MacBean, *Biographical Register of the Saint Andrew's Society of the State of New York* (New York, 1922), I, 96–97, 116.

[42] Clarence Walworth Alvord, *The Mississippi Valley in British Politics* (Cleveland, 1917), pp. 25 (and n. 27), 195; Nelson Vance Russell, *The British Regime in Michigan and the Old Northwest 1760–1796* (Northfield, Minn., 1939), ch. v, *passim*; Stevens, *Northwest Fur Trade*, p. 123.

Union which opened the colonies to their commercial enterprise. In the first seventy years thereafter, they developed a trading empire stretching from the West Indies and Florida to Quebec and Nova Scotia. Their shipping routes stretched out from Glasgow like the ribs of a fan. At some of the extremities of these ribs, the year 1775 found the Scots merchants in a dominating position. Such was the case in the tobacco country and in Canada. Elsewhere, as at Charleston, Savannah, Wilmington, Philadelphia, and New York, they formed a powerful element in the trading community. Trade and emigration went hand in hand. The settlement of emigrants was in itself a commercial enterprise. The Scottish trade was carried on by emigrant Scots. Acting closely together, supporting one another against all comers, forming their own (but not exclusive) Scottish clubs and societies, they acquired a reputation for clannishness which made things all the harder for them when the Revolution came. Yet these merchants and storekeepers formed only one element among the professional classes, born in Scotland, who provided leaders in various fields in the eighteenth-century colonies. There were also, conspicuously, the doctors, the schoolteachers, and the officials of all ranks. It is not to be expected that the Scots immigrants, occupying so many positions of influence as they did, should play no part in the politics of the colonies. In general their political activities do not fall into the patterns commonly traced by historians of the period. In the various struggles between colonial executives and legislatures they may be found now on one side now on the other. The single consistent link in their behavior at different times and at different places seems to be their acting as an interest-group on the basis of their nationality. Such a pattern of conduct and sentiment was unlikely to appeal to the growing nationalism of the American seaboard. A glance at the political activities of the Scot in eighteenth-century America will help to explain his widespread unpopularity among Americans in the period of the Revolution.

VII

"Too Much Scoticism!"

THE influence of the Scots in eighteenth-century America was by no means confined to the commercial sphere. It was exercised in certain other directions, equally or more distasteful to the native Americans. After 1761 the Scots acquired a stronger position in the colonies than ever before. With the Earl of Bute at the head of the British government, offices were more easily obtained by needy Scots, whose favored position provoked a self-righteous indignation in some Englishmen and Americans who never before had been known to find fault with the system of patronage. The Scots were intensely unpopular in London, to which city numbers of them went during and after Bute's ministry. One cartoonist pictured a "cloud" of kilted Highlanders descending upon the capital in the wake of the Earl of Bute.

Long after Bute's fall, the myth of Scots intrigue and power at Court continued to keep alight the fires of anti-Scottish feeling. A great number of Americans shared these emotions. "Your king," wrote a Boston correspondent in 1775, "seems to be infatuated with a parcel of Scotchmen and Jacobites. At least this is the best excuse that can be made for his conduct, and keeping them about him. If this was not the case, he would have removed his evil councillors long since, and thereby healed this unhappy quarrel." [1]

[1] Willard, ed., *Letters on the Revolution*, p. 143.

For many years, recorded John Wesley in his journal for 1778, he had heard "the King severely blamed for giving all places of trust and profit to Scotchmen; and this was so positively and continually affirmed that I had no doubt of it." But now, he went on, he had just read a pamphlet whose writer proved by figures from the Court Calendar that of 450-odd places at Court only eight were possessed by Scots, and that of the 151 places in the Royal Household no more than four were held by Scotsmen.[2]

While there was some exaggeration in the charges leveled at the Scots by Londoners and by Americans, there were substantial grounds for their envy. In America, for example, the Scottish middle classes officered not only their own countrymen, but even spilled over into English regiments. More Scottish officials and officers than English went to America, and more Scots of the upper class than English had relatives in America or were intermarried with American families. By the autumn of 1775 the English soldiers in Boston were complaining of "the advancement, insolence, and self-sufficiency of a number of Scotch officers." A Boston observer commented:

This very day several common soldiers were reprimanded . . . for swearing they ought to be commanded by Englishmen, and that they would not sacrifice their lives in an attempt to butcher their friends and fellow subjects for any interested North Briton upon earth. This is the first instance of the kind; but as there is a general murmur, and too much room for complaint, it is likely to be productive of very serious consequences.[3]

Between 1707 and 1775 Scotsmen took over a growing number of American offices. The trend was especially conspicuous after Bute's ministry. Its beneficiaries ranged all the way from great public servants like Robert Hunter, who governed four colonies in the early eighteenth century, to the Scottish customs clerk of whom it was learned in 1770 that he had "lately in a very singular manner been figuring away with his Bag-Pipes at Carolina and the Florida's [*sic*]; importantly contending with Governors and Magistrates, suspend-

---

[2] John Wesley, *The Journal of the Rev. John Wesley*, ed. by Nehemiah Curnock (London, 1909–16), VI, 210, entry for Sept. 7, 1778.

[3] Namier, *England in the Age of the American Revolution*, p. 309; "Letter received from an Officer at Boston, [dated] BOSTON, Aug. 18, 1775," *London Evening Post*, Oct. 7–10, 1775, reprinted in Willard, ed., *Letters on the Revolution*, p. 190.

ing or turning out old Custom Officers, and puting [*sic*] in their places, petty Scotch Laddy's, that had quitted their Estates at home, in order to better their fortunes abroad." An inquiry elicited the fact that this mighty disposer of patronage was no more than "a common copying Clerk from some of the Public Offices in Scotland, sent over to . . . some subordinate office of the Customs in New-England!" [4] No wonder a contemporary American satirist, comparing Irish with Scottish impudence, concluded that the Hibernian variety had been put in the shade.

By the time the Revolution broke out, the Scots as a whole had a very bad name in America. Indeed, their reputation amounted to a significant factor in the Revolutionary situation. When, in 1776, John Witherspoon appealed to his fellow countrymen to support the American cause, the fiery Ezra Stiles of Yale, far from welcoming the Scot's pamphlet, delivered one of the bitterest of all denunciations of everything Scottish. "Too much Scoticism!" exclaimed Stiles. "He wants to save his Countrymen, who have behaved most cruelly in this American conflict." A few months later came this:

The Policy of Scotland & all the governmental Ideas of the Body of that People, are abhorrent to all Ideas of civil Liberty & are full of rigorous tyrannical Superiorities & subordinations. But Dr With[erspoon] goes all lengths with Congress. . . . Because he had Discernment to see from the Beginning that America would be inevitably dismembered, & then acted as all Scotchmen would do under such a conviction, determined to rise & figure in the Dismemberment. . . . We . . . scorn to be awed by him into an ignominious Silence on the subject of Scots Perfidy & Tyranny and Enmity to America. Let us boldly say, for History will say it, that the whole of this War is so far chargeable to the Scotch Councils, & to the Scotch as a Nation (for they have nationally come into it) as that had it not been for them, this Quarrel had never happened.[5]

II

Any American of 1776 who feared and distrusted the Scots as fiercely as Stiles did, however exaggerated or misinformed his views, could find cause for alarm in the power and influence of that nation's American indwellers. That influence, commercial, political,

[4] *Boston Evening-Post,* July 16, 1770, p. 2.   [5] Stiles, *Diary,* II, 184–185.

and intellectual, was reinforced by a number of permanent, Scots-dominated organizations—the Scottish charitable societies, usually called St. Andrew's clubs, which existed in several of the larger cities. Their history may be traced back to the middle of the seventeenth century. Founded in the 1650's, the Scots Charitable Society of Boston took its form and inspiration from a similar association in London. It continued to exist throughout the colonial period. But the true model and fountainhead of the American St. Andrew's clubs was the society founded at Charleston, South Carolina, in 1729. The St. Andrew's Society of Philadelphia is said to have been established (1749) by a wandering member of the Charleston group. More definite is the connection between the Philadelphia club and the New York St. Andrew's Society (1756), successor of the older Scots Society of 1744. There was a St. Andrew's Society in permanent existence at Savannah, Georgia, after 1750. But this club had been preceded by a short-lived association of the same name, popularly called the "Scotch Club," which played an important role in the politics of the colony during its first years. George Neilson, a Jacobite, founded the celebrated Tuesday Club of Annapolis, Maryland, in 1745. Its satirical history came from the pen of another Scot, Alexander Hamilton, the physician, educator, and author of a book of travels in the Northern colonies. Neilson claimed to hold a commission from the original Tuesday Club in Scotland authorizing him to establish branches. The Annapolis club was predominantly, but not exclusively, Scottish.[6]

The forty-nine founding members of the Charleston society are said to have been chiefly Scottish by birth. The principal aim of the club, according to an entry in the minutes for 1732, was "to assist all People in Distress, of whatsoever Nation or Profession they may be." By this time, its third year of existence, the society had collected £700 and disbursed £460. Sassenachs were freely ad-

[6] [Dr. William Douglass], *Postscript, To a Discourse Concerning the Currencies of the British Plantations in America*, reprinted in Andrew McFarland Davis, ed., *Colonial Currency Reprints* (Boston, 1911), IV, 54–55; J. H. Easterby, *History of the St. Andrew's Society of Charleston, South Carolina 1729–1929* (Charleston, S.C., 1929), *passim*, esp. pp. 1–48 for the period 1729–1783; MacDougall, ed., *Scots in America*, p. 38; MacBean, *Saint Andrew's Society of New York*, I, *passim*, esp. p. 1 ff. for the period 1756–1783; Barker, *Revolution in Maryland*, pp. 56–59.

mitted to the club, but most of its members were Scots-born or descended. Altogether, between 1729 and 1776, the club admitted 537 members. The number seems small at first glance, but it included many men of standing and influence in the colony.

Among the early members were such men as Alexander Skene, a member of the provincial council who was prominent in the overthrow of the proprietors, John Fraser, who traded with the Yamasees and acquired a great fortune as a Charleston merchant, John Stuart, the Southern Superintendent of Indians, and five colonial governors.[7]

Among the papers of Oucconastotah, chief of the Cherokee Nation, in the Library of Congress, Professor P. M. Hamer of the University of Tennessee found a certificate, dated 1773, which admitted the Indian to membership in the St. Andrew's Society of Charleston. The club was far from narrow in its aims, membership, and activities. Its prestige was high in the colonial capital. Its annual dinners were attended not only by members, but also by the governor, chief justice, councillors, speaker of the commons house, and prominent visitors to the colony. In 1774 fifty people sat down to consume fifty pounds' worth of food and two hundred pounds' worth of liquor. Such celebrations were paid for by dividing the cost among the members, and nothing was taken from the charitable fund.[8]

The New York society was founded in 1756 "for the purpose of caring for and relieving . . . distressed fellow countrymen." The celebration of St. Andrew's Day was the chief event of the year in New York, until it was superseded by the Fourth of July. The notables of the city always attended the annual dinner. Among the club's members were many prominent Scots-born merchants, officials, and physicians. There was Archibald Kennedy, son of an Ayrshire justice of the peace, who came to New York in 1714 with letters to Governor Burnet. Later he became Collector of the Port, Receiver-General of the Province, and, in 1727, a member of the Council. His liberal views on colonial government were embodied in two pamphlets published in 1749 and 1754. "Liberty and encouragement," he wrote, "are the basis of colonies." Colonials, he

[7] Easterby, *St. Andrew's Society of Charleston*, pp. 30–31.
[8] *Ibid.*, pp. 43–44.

thought, would advance what they believed to be their own interest and would regard all restraining laws as oppression, "especially such laws as, according to the conceptions we have of English liberty, they have no hand in controverting or making." [9]

Another New York Scot was Adam Thomson, a graduate of the Edinburgh medical school. He emigrated to Maryland, moved to Philadelphia, where he helped to establish the St. Andrew's Society of that city, and, about 1755, proceeded to New York, where he arrived in time to become a founding member of the Scots club there. He originated the so-called American method of inoculation against smallpox. In 1750 Franklin published a tract by him on this subject. Like Thomson, Peter Middleton was an Edinburgh medical graduate. He settled in New York about 1730. With Dr. John Bard, he performed the first human dissection before students in America. In 1767 he established a medical school in New York. He was president of the New York society between 1767 and 1770. Later he was to be one of the loyalist refugees under General Howe's protection on Staten Island.[10]

Among the Charleston Scots who were physicians, Alexander Gordon studied medicine with Dr. John Gregory of Aberdeen, emigrated to South Carolina about 1750, took up the study of botany, corresponded with Linnaeus, and, in 1772, was elected a Fellow of the Royal Society. A loyalist, he lost his property in the Revolution and died in London in 1791. John Lining was born in Dundee in 1708, studied medicine at Edinburgh, emigrated to Charleston in 1730, and built a practice there. He experimented with electricity and sent meteorological observations to the Royal Society. In 1753 he published at Charleston his *History of the Yellow Fever*. David Olyphant was born near Perth in 1720, served the Jacobites as a surgeon at Culloden, and then escaped to South Carolina. During the Revolution he was Director-General of Southern Hospitals. He

[9] MacBean, *Saint Andrew's Society of New York*, pp. vi, 13–14. At page [405, unnumbered], MacBean reprints in facsimile the "Rules and Orders agreed upon By the Scots Society in New York," dated Dec. 27, 1744. This document declares in the preamble that the society of 1744 was modeled after the Scots Charitable Society of Boston.

[10] *Ibid.*, pp. 19, 26; MacDougall, ed., *Scots in America*, p. 74; Willard, ed., *Letters on the Revolution*, p. 351.

practiced medicine at Newport, Rhode Island, from 1785 until his death in 1804.[11] The list of colonial physicians of Scottish birth could be greatly extended. They undoubtedly formed one of the most important professional groups among the Scots-Americans. They were to be found in most of the colonies. Some of them were merchants as well as doctors. They figured prominently in the St. Andrew's Societies, which gave a social and political focus to the more prosperous Scottish immigrants.

III

The most openly and notoriously political of the St. Andrew's clubs was the first society of that name founded at Savannah, Georgia, soon after the establishment of the colony.

According to A. A. Ettinger, the biographer of James Edward Oglethorpe, personal hostility to the first governor of Georgia began to crystallize toward the close of 1739 and early in 1740 in a series of attacks by Thomas Stephens, son of Secretary William Stephens, who had a grudge against his father's superior. Ettinger goes on to state that other and stronger opposition to Oglethorpe arose in 1741, when Dr. Patrick Tailfer published his *True and Historical Narrative of the Colony of Georgia*. These attacks are said to have hurt Oglethorpe "intensely." In spite of the considerable amount of space which this author devotes to his account of the party called the "malcontents" in early Georgia, he does not even hint at the fact that, from 1738 to 1740, the leadership of the opposition to the colonial administration was provided by the St. Andrew's club of Savannah. He fails to mention that Tailfer, the most galling thorn in the governor's side, was ringleader of the "Scotch Club," which was to the malcontents very much what the Jacobin Club was to the radicals of the French Revolution. Nor does he seem to be aware that the opposition to Oglethorpe began, not with Stephens' departure for England in August, 1739, but with a petition to the Georgia trustees organized by Tailfer and several other Scots in December, 1738.[12]

[11] MacDougall, ed., *Scots in America*, pp. 72, 74.
[12] Amos Aschbach Ettinger, *James Edward Oglethorpe: Imperial Idealist* (Oxford, Eng., 1936), pp. 212–213.

On December 9, 1738, 117 persons signed at Savannah a petition to the trustees from the freeholders of Georgia. According to Tailfer, "only a very few of the General's favourites declined to subscribe the same." The signatures of Tailfer, and of his Scottish cronies, Hugh Anderson and David Douglas, were among the first fourteen names. The complaints included the lack of "a free title or fee-simple to our lands" and the prohibition of Negroes in the colony.[13]

Secretary Stephens informed the trustees that the "chief fabricators" of this memorial were Robert Williams and his brother-in-law, Patrick Tailfer. He criticized the latter for failing to cultivate his land, getting "more money than any one by his practice, and letting out the servants he brought with him for hire." [14]

Little is known of Tailfer, apart from his activities in Georgia at this time. Like his chief intimates, who included Hugh Anderson and David Douglas, he came from Scotland. The three of them went to Charleston in the late summer of 1740, where they conducted an unremitting campaign of vilification against Oglethorpe and Secretary Stephens. Together they wrote and published the *True and Historical Narrative* of 1741. Anderson ran his own school in Charleston and later became a master in the free school there. He died at the same place in 1748. Douglas was described as a member of the "Scotch club" or "Juntillo" and as a "somewhat influential demagogue." [15]

Tailfer claimed to speak for a large number of "gentlemen of some stock and fortune, [who] willingly expended part of the same, in purchasing servants, tools, commodities and other necessaries," in order to qualify for land grants in Georgia. Their attempts at colonization had failed, he wrote, because of restrictive governmental policies. The rights and titles given by royal charter had been circumscribed, and restrictions, services, and conditions had been attached to the occupancy of land. The services were impossible of performance. The annual quitrent of one pound sterling per hundred acres was excessive. The proprietors were burdened by a prohibition of all land transfers, an obligation to grow a thou-

[13] Patrick Tailfer, Hugh Anderson, and David Douglas, *A True and Historical Narrative of the Colony of Georgia*, reprinted in *Collections of the Georgia Historical Society*, II (1842), 217–222.
[14] Egmont, Journal, Jan. 2, 1738/9, in *Ga. Recs.*, V, 140.
[15] Tailfer *et al.*, in *Collections of the G.H.S.*, II, 164.

sand mulberry trees on every hundred acres of land, the automatic reversion of land grants to the trustees upon failure of the heirs male, and a requirement that the whole of each five-hundred-acre grant be under cultivation after eighteen years upon pain of forfeiture to the trustees. Among the "real causes of the ruin and desolation of the colony," Tailfer listed a false representation of the Georgia climate, exclusion of women from land inheritance, the smallness of holdings (fifty acres being inadequate for the support of a family), the persistent denial of the use of Negroes, the assigning of fixed tracts of land irrespective of their quality, and various acts of arbitrary government on the part of Oglethorpe.[16]

Most of the disaffected gentry whom Tailfer mentioned by name were Scots. In the summer of 1739, he wrote, David Douglas, William Stirling, Thomas Bailie, and Andrew Grant, who had ruined themselves by their attempts to settle the frontier, applied to Oglethorpe and the trustees for the grant of an island off the coast. The governor promised them one if they would publicly declare their support for the colonial constitution and apologize for signing the freeholders' petition. Upon their refusal to comply with these demands, the trustees denied their request for new lands. About thirty miles upriver from Savannah was Joseph's Town, settled by some Scots gentlemen with about thirty servants. But by 1741, most of their servants having died, they had left the settlement. On the Ogeechee were the Stirlings with twenty-five servants. When they went there, the place was the southernmost extension of the colony and they had to build a fort for their defense. After three years they were obliged to leave the place, "having exhausted their fortunes to no purpose in the experiment." Hugh Anderson was settled at the Hermitage near Savannah with a total of seventeen persons including his family and servants. About 1739 he had to leave the colony because of the hardships outlined above.[17]

This was the "Scottish" side of the story as recorded by Tailfer. The official version of events was considerably different. Benjamin Martyn, secretary to the trustees in 1742, avowed that the Saltzburghers of Ebenezer were in a thriving condition and that not a single person had abandoned the settlement. No one had complained

16 *Ibid.*, pp. 196–197, 262–263.   17 *Ibid.*, pp. 240–241, 255, 257–258.

to the trustees about tenures or the lack of Negroes. On the contrary, they petitioned in a body against their use.[18]

In May, 1739, the Georgia trustees in London heard a report that it would "be well for the Colony when the Scots & others that call themselves Gentlemen shall leave the Colony: for carrying over servants, they would not work themselves, nor employ their servants on their lands, but let them go out to hire at I. 5. O sterl P head P month, and lived idly in Savannah on the Incom: But they were now grown very poor, & must soon go away." The following month, Robert Howes, lately clerk of the Savannah church, told Egmont that "it was very unfortunate for Savannah that the Scotch left their Country Lotts to live in the town, where they set an example of extravagance, & brought in their servants to work, which lessen'd the employment of the natural townsmen." [19]

In July, Oglethorpe wrote to the trustees telling them that Tailfer and Williams had abandoned the cultivation of the soil to sell rum. They had put almost the whole town of Savannah in their debt either for medicine or for rum. They had aroused the people to demand the alienability of land, so that they could get hold of their lands in settlement of debts, monopolize the country, and work it with Negro labor. Such was the spirit, wrote Oglethorpe, which underlay the demand for easier tenures.[20]

Tailfer and Williams are said to have formed their club at the house of one Jenkins and there to have concocted schemes against Oglethorpe in revenge for the latter's opposition to their request for Negroes. The demagogues who composed it got up horse races in the town and indulged generally in idleness and dissipation.[21]

The agitation of the Lowland gentry in the Savannah "Scotch club" does not seem to have affected greatly their Highland compatriots of Darien. Tailfer accused Oglethorpe of bribing the Highlanders to support his policies. According to the doctor, a copy of the freeholders' petition of December, 1738, was sent to Darien.

[18] [Benjamin Martyn], *An Account Showing the Progress of the Colony of Georgia*, reprinted in *Collections of the G.H.S.*, II (1842), 308.
[19] Egmont, Journal, May 2, June 6, 1739, in *Ga. Recs.*, V, 164, 178.
[20] *Ibid.*, p. 209.
[21] Robert Wright, *A Memoir of General James Oglethorpe* (London, 1867), pp. 265–267.

John More Mackintosh, the Highlanders' leader, sent the document to the governor, who promised (and later delivered) cattle to the people in exchange for an agreement to oppose the malcontents at Savannah. Soon afterward Mackintosh found himself set up in a store and plentifully supplied with goods.[22]

Not long after the submission of the 1738 petition a number of freeholders in the Darien colony signed a counterpetition against the use of Negroes. Eighteen persons signed this protest. In May, 1740, an army officer told Egmont that only a few Scots at Darien desired the introduction of Negroes and that even these made their demands to this effect "only to pleasure their Countrymen in the Northern Division." [23] Tailfer evidently enjoyed a limited success in gathering recruits for his cause at Darien. Here in Georgia, the ties of a common nationality were insufficiently strong to overcome the ancient antipathy between Highlander and Lowlander.

The malcontents had more luck with the trustees. Egmont began to weaken and, in June, 1740, told the trustees that, while he opposed the introduction of free Negroes to Georgia because their lower wages would drive out the white servants, he saw no other inconvenience arising therefrom and hoped that this one objection might be removed by passing an act to regulate wages, so as to keep them at the same level for all workers. He urgently favored the alteration of tenures in order to prevent the withdrawal of settlers from the colony. The only aim behind restricted tenures was to keep people in the colony, and since they were having the opposite effect they should be changed. He would remove all restrictions except that upon the outright purchase of lands.[24]

On August 31, 1740, the St. Andrew's Club of Savannah broke up. Dr. Tailfer "& his crew" left the colony and went to Charleston. "Thus," wrote Secretary Stephens three weeks later, "we have got rid of that cursed club." But his troubles were by no means over because the core of the malcontents had moved to a distance. The Carolinians already condemned Oglethorpe for arousing Spanish and Indian hostility by his warlike actions. The malcontents for

[22] Tailfer *et al.*, in *Collections of the G.H.S.*, II, 223.

[23] Egmont, Journal, Jan. 3, March 16, 1738/9, May 9, 1740, in *Ga. Recs.*, V, 88, 138, 161, 348.

[24] Egmont, Journal, June 26, 1740, in *ibid.*, pp. 378–379.

some time had been fanning this hatred into a hotter flame. Their
propaganda passed for truth in Charleston, where the factious Scots
were eagerly received after their migration. Returning from England to Georgia in September, James Campbell, keeper of the prison
at Savannah, was detained by illness at Charleston. There the Tailfer
group tried to dissuade him from going back to Savannah on the
grounds that Georgia was doomed to starvation and depopulation.
Meanwhile one of the Savannah bailiffs wrote to the trustees giving
a very bad character to the Scots and stating that "they all kept
whores, and condemned Religion, and were not well affected to
the Government." [25]

On December 19, 1741, Egmont received "a very sawcy letter
from four of the St. Andrews Club viz. Tho. Baillie, Will. Sterling,
Andrew Grant, and David Douglass, vilifying Col. Oglethorpe, and
divers of the Trustees for not allowing them Negroes." This was
their parting shot, written three weeks before the flight to South
Carolina. From a letter dated on the last day of January, Egmont
learned that the Charleston cabal was preparing to publish a pamphlet against the trustees and Colonel Oglethorpe under the title
A True and Historical Narrative of the Colony of Georgia.[26]

In October, 1741, Egmont confided to his journal that although
the Darien people said they were satisfied one or two families, "such
as were in their own esteem Gentlemen, and never contented," had
deserted to Carolina. At the same time the trustees learned that
John McLeod, the minister at Darien, had gone to Charleston, "having left his flock out of discontent, and labour'd to induce the rest
also to desert." After he arrived in Carolina, he surpassed even the
Tailfer faction in asserting the barrenness of the Georgia soil. At a
Common Council held in March, 1742, Hugh Anderson, who had
gone to England, showed Egmont a copy of a letter sent by McLeod
to his sponsoring society in Edinburgh, in which he justified the
desertion of his flock at Darien and attacked Oglethorpe as the
worst of men. "The whole letter," wrote Egmont, "is a pack of lyes,
to excuse his leaving the Colony, and accepting a Presbiterian
Church in Carolina." The malcontents, he thought, and particularly
the St. Andrew's club in Charleston—Tailfer, Anderson, and Douglas—had put him up to it. They were perennial intriguers. A Cap-

[25] *Ga. Recs.,* V, 394–395, 398.   [26] *Ibid.,* pp. 413, 421.

tain William Thompson reported that he had seen Tailfer, Anderson, and Douglas at Charleston. Douglas was employed as a bookkeeper and Anderson as a schoolmaster. The latter was losing his pupils among the gentlemen's sons by engaging in politics with the other two. Tailfer was without patients and the merchant who employed Douglas was tired of him. All three were despised and ostracized by the gentlemen of Carolina. They consorted with two or three more "Runaways of their Country" at a public house established by Jenkins, another renegade from Georgia.[27]

On November 22, 1740, the remaining malcontents in Savannah, consisting of sixty-three property owners of the town and county, signed a new remonstrance demanding the use of Negroes, complete freedom to dispose of land, abolition of quitrents, and the annual election of bailiffs. They threatened to quit the colony unless these demands were met. At the same time thirteen freeholders, chiefly of the "Scotch club," who had gone to Charleston, signed a similar memorial. The trustees received both documents in May, 1741. It is uncertain what proportion of the rump of the malcontents at Savannah were Scottish. The ringleader was John Fallowfield. Others upon whom Egmont had his eye bore distinctively English names. Three names, Campbell, Ormston, and Ewen, may indicate Scots who had stayed behind. Certainly the Scottish leadership was gone, and the great bulk of the malcontents were Englishmen.[28]

In January, 1743, yet another petition for the use of Negroes in Georgia appeared, this time before the House of Commons. Perhaps it was a mere coincidence that among the three members who favored a reorganization of the colony before granting further subsidies was Neil Buchanan, the member for Glasgow. The House divided 136 to 60 in favor of granting a further twelve thousand pounds for the settlement of the colony, and the trustees gladly accepted what amounted to a vote of confidence in themselves by a margin of more than two to one.[29]

The role of the Scots in early Georgia was not very creditable, but neither was it typical of other colonies. It should be remem-

---

[27] Egmont, Journal, Oct. 5, 1741, March 3, 1742, in *ibid.*, pp. 556, 559, 600.
[28] *Ibid.*, pp. 407, 558, 593–594.
[29] Egmont, Journal, Jan. 11, 1742/3, in *ibid.*, pp. 678, 681–682.

bered that all the noise was issuing from a small number of Lowlanders of a lazy, greedy, and intriguing disposition. The malcontents of the "Scotch club" were petty but ambitious members of the middle class, who probably included both lairds' relatives and townsmen. There was little commotion at Darien, where the Highland peasants had settled in 1736. The only deserters from that colony were a few self-styled gentlemen. In this as in so many other episodes of colonial history events took their shape at least in part from the divisions of class and territorial origin among the immigrants from Scotland.

IV

From time to time Scottish factions appeared in various colonies. The merchants of early Norfolk bore distinctly English names until the pre-Revolutionary generation brought an influx of Scottish rivals. Between the English and the Scots there was not only keen competition in business, but political strife as well. On election day the Scottish party wore badges of orange, the English of blue. Both factions had their headquarters in Commercial Place, where the liquor flowed freely.[30]

At Charleston, John Stuart, the Indian superintendent, involved himself financially with the Scottish mercantile community. Well before the middle of the century, a clearly defined Scots faction existed in South Carolina. Peter Timothy, the printer, resented Stuart's favoring his Scots rival, Robert Wells, with exclusive reports on Indian affairs. As publisher of the *South Carolina and American General Gazette*, Wells enjoyed a good deal of influence. Timothy, in the year 1741, found himself in the curious position of accepting business from the runaway Georgia Scots of the Savannah St. Andrew's Society. He printed Tailfer's *True and Historical Narrative*. The anti-Scottish party to which Timothy belonged gained considerable strength in South Carolina as a result of the Cherokee War of 1760–1761, which made Stuart unpopular. South Carolinians objected to the strong Scottish influence on the Board of Trade, an influence which usually sided with the interests of the British administration. James Grant, who succeeded his brother as laird of

[30] Wertenbaker, *Norfolk*, p. 15.

Ballindalloch in Banffshire and served as a general in the Revolutionary War, had influential friends in South Carolina who helped
him to develop the province of East Florida after he became its
governor. Among these friends was John Moultrie, the Scottish
physician, a powerful figure in early Charleston. Two of Moultrie's
sons were members of Grant's Council in East Florida, a thoroughly
Scottish body, which also included in its number John Stuart himself and three other persons with Scottish names.[31]

Elsewhere it was common for Scottish parties to form about the
person of a Scottish governor. During the period under review
(1707–1783) there were some thirty governors and lieutenant governors of Scots birth in the American colonies. The encroachment
of the Scots upon these high offices began some years before the
Union of the Parliaments. In the 1690's those who interpreted the
Navigation Acts as excluding the Scots from the colonial trade believed, not without reason, that their purposes would be defeated
by collusion and connivance among Scots, were the latter to infil-
trate official positions in the colonies. The appointment of Andrew
Hamilton, a Scotsman, to the governorship of East New Jersey
provoked much opposition. For a brief period, from 1697 to 1699,
there was a prohibition on the elevation of Scots to offices in the
English colonies. In the latter year Sir Thomas Trevor, the attorney
general of England, ruled that "a Scotchman borne is by Law
capable of being appointed Governor of any of the Plantac'ons, he
being a natural born-Subject of England in Judgm^t and Construcc'on
of Law, as much as if he had been born in England." [32] This was
merely to uphold the rights of common citizenship recognized
already in an English judicial decision of 1608 and wrongfully
denied to the Scots after the Restoration.

The episode was the climax of a long factional struggle which
divided East Jersey between 1692 and 1702. The Scots proprietors
there, a powerful minority of the total of twenty-four, assumed the
role of a provincial aristocracy. They controlled land purchases and
transfers, which aroused no little jealousy among their less active

[31] John Richard Alden, *John Stuart and the Southern Colonial Frontier* (Ann
Arbor, Mich., 1944), pp. 161–162, 169–190; *Collections of the G.H.S.*, II, 163;
David Duncan Wallace, *The History of South Carolina* (New York, 1934), II,
103; Mowat, *East Florida*, pp. 13–15.

[32] *N.J. Archives*, 1st ser., II, 250–251.

English colleagues. The leaders of the Scots and English parties were, respectively, Andrew Hamilton and Jeremiah Basse. Hamilton's enemies accused him of showing special favor to the Scots, even to those engaged in smuggling. In 1697 they obtained his dismissal on the grounds that he was ineligible to office as a Scot. Trevor's ruling of 1699 and the desires of the Scots proprietors brought about his restoration. Apparently unaware of Trevor's decision, the anti-Scottish faction in East New Jersey sent a remonstrance to the king in 1700, in which they complained of the misgovernment of the proprietors and asked for the appointment of a competent governor. They wrongly considered Hamilton's reappointment illegal. They grumbled at the "illegality" of a Scottish secretary, attorney-general, and clerk of the Supreme Court. They reminded the king of the likelihood of infringement of the Navigation Acts, "to the great Hindrance of Your Ma[jes]tys Loyall Subjects (the Power of Government being Chiefly in the Hands of Natives of Scotland)." [33]

When Queen Anne, in 1701, appointed Edward Hyde, Lord Cornbury, governor of New Jersey, the colony had six factions consolidated into two opposing parties. As before, one of the factions consisted of the Scots proprietors and their followers, most of whom lived in and around the Scottish settlement of Perth Amboy. The leaders—Dr. John Johnstone, a former mayor of New York, George Willocks, a Jacobite, Thomas Gordon, a prolific officeholder, and Lewis Morris, probably the wealthiest man in the province—controlled East Jersey. They sold land a little at a time to keep the price up and made a handsome profit. The politics of the group was based on land speculation. Their chief opponents were called the "English proprietors," mainly because they tried to blacken the other faction or party in the eyes of the home authorities by stigmatizing them as "Scotch." The two groups wrestled for control of a majority of the twenty-four proprietary shares. The "English" party had wealthy friends in England, but no popular support in the colony.[34]

William Dockwra and Peter Sonmans, two Dutchmen among the

[33] Pryde, "Scots in East New Jersey," pp. 12–13, 24–25; *N.J. Archives,* 1st ser., II, 322–325.

[34] Donald L. Kemmerer, *Path to Freedom: The Struggle for Self-Government in Colonial New Jersey 1703–1776* (Princeton, 1940), pp. 48–49.

East Jersey proprietors, led the fight against Hamilton. In 1702 they petitioned the queen in behalf of themselves and other proprietors. They acquiesced in a Board of Trade scheme for turning the two provinces into a single royal colony and begged for the appointment of a governor above party spirit. They mentioned that Hamilton enjoyed the support of some of the proprietors, and others, in West Jersey. Dockwra accused Hamilton of protecting Scottish ships and encouraging their illegal trade. In the spring of the same year, "the greatest part of the Proprietors of the Province of Nova Caesaria or New Jersey" petitioned for the appointment of Andrew Hamilton as governor of the new royal colony.[35]

Dockwra and Sonmans set out their complaints against Hamilton in a memorial to the Board of Trade. He had caused strife in the Jerseys, they said, by setting up a Quaker faction to the great disturbance of the peace and distress of the loyal, English interest. He was arbitrary and unjust. He encouraged and protected pirates. He had diverted to his own use money appropriated by the Assembly for specified purposes.[36]

The first of these charges had some truth in it. The Scots proprietors had allied themselves with the popular Quaker majority in West Jersey and the West Jersey Society to form a "country" party. The "English" proprietors continued to lead the opposition. This alignment survived for two decades after the arrival of Cornbury. The factional leaders competed for the favor of this "impartial" governor. In May, 1703, Dr. Johnstone of the Scots party gave two hundred pounds to Cornbury as an inducement to a political alliance. But Cornbury filled vacant offices, as they occurred, with "English" partisans and Anglicans from West Jersey, who came to be known as "Cornbury's Ring." A battle royal ensued between the Ring and the Scots. The Ring determined to obtain control of the key offices of surveyor-general and registrar of East Jersey, positions of great power under the land-grabbing proprietary regime. In August, 1705, Peter Sonmans presented Cornbury with a commission from the English proprietors appointing him their agent and receiver of quitrents. The governor accepted the honor and announced the cessation of Scottish control of the receivership and record-keeping. The Scots disputed the action on the grounds that

they held a majority of the twenty-four proprietorships. Sonmans'
sisters, oddly enough, enlisted the queen's sympathy for the Scots,
and she issued an order which in effect restored power to them, but
Cornbury postponed putting it into effect until the arrival of Governor Lovelace in 1708. For two years or more he and his Ring
disposed of lands very much as they pleased. Cornbury is said to
have distributed half a million acres of land among his friends and
allies. The two largest sales involved 170,000 and 42,500 acres. In
spite of these activities, Cornbury's policies favored the mass of
small landholders in East Jersey, who responded by giving him their
support. When his party, under pressure from its enemies, tempo-
rarily gave up its liberal land legislation, the small landholders
abandoned him and turned to the Scots proprietors. Thus in 1708
the Scots had enough friends in the Assembly to force the removal
of Cornbury. They were fortunate in having the ardent support of
the New York Assembly. Neither legislature would vote any further
supplies for the support of its administration.[37]

In June, 1710, arrived the Scotsman Robert Hunter, to take up
the governorship. From the beginning he preferred the Scots proprietary party, but he did not openly back them at first. By 1716 he
had ousted all officials who were unsympathetic to his views. The
Scottish faction nominated a new secretary and entrusted the important office of surveyor-general to a capable Scot named James
Alexander. The Scottish Duke of Argyll exercised great influence on
behalf of both Hunter and Alexander, although the latter had been
out in the '15, a rebellion largely suppressed by the duke himself.
The friendship survived Alexander's treason and, through Argyll's
efforts, Hunter helped the exiled Alexander to begin life afresh in
New Jersey. He became surveyor-general of that colony and New
York, built up a law practice, and by the middle 1740's was said
to be worth £150,000. By 1750 the Scots proprietary party in East
Jersey had reverted to its usual role as the party of wealth and
reaction. The small farmers and squatters vigorously opposed them
as they had done fifty years before. Between 1747 and his death in
1756 Alexander was one of the most active and influential members
of the Scots faction, which controlled the governing council.[38]

[37] Kemmerer, *Path to Freedom*, pp. 53, 65–69, 71, 74–75.
[38] *Ibid.*, pp. 88, 91, 100, 187–188.

Hunter liked New Jersey so well that he contemplated spending the rest of his life there and built himself a fine home. The historian of eighteenth-century New Jersey described him as "the most nearly ideal governor colonial New Jersey ever had." He had few serious faults, added the same writer, but among these few "was the partiality he showed for the 'Scotch' proprietors." [39] Indulgence to their fellow countrymen was not an uncommon weakness among the Scottish colonial governors.

V

In North Carolina the political storms of the period 1734–1752 centered upon the person of Gabriel Johnstone.[40] Born in Dumfriesshire in 1699, Johnstone studied medicine and professed oriental languages at the University of St. Andrews. In London he acquired fame as a political writer and Lord Wilmington as a patron. These achievements resulted in his appointment as governor of North Carolina in 1734. Johnstone was a zealous if indiscreet servant of the Crown. His policy was to promote the interest of the British government and to magnify the royal prerogative. Although his enemies might well have belabored him for these aims, they chose paradoxically to paint him in the colors of treason. They accused him of lamenting the defeat of Prince Charles at Culloden and of dispossessing poor Palatines to make room for Scottish rebels. While his denial of these charges was justified, he unquestionably favored his Scottish fellow countrymen as a whole and encouraged them to emigrate to North Carolina. This form of favoritism, however, was as beneficial to the American province as it was to Scotland.[41]

In a council held at Newbern, capital of the colony, in February, 1739/40, five recent immigrants from Scotland were among fourteen justices of the peace appointed for Bladen County. Three others had Scottish names and may well have been Scots.[42] An event such

---

[39] *Ibid.*, pp. 110–112.

[40] The name is often spelled "Johnston," but since the governor was a scion of the Johnstones of Annandale in Dumfriesshire the usual Scottish spelling has been preserved here.

[41] William L. Saunders, "Prefatory Notes," *N.C. Recs.*, IV, pp. iii, v, viii, x.

[42] *N.C. Recs.*, IV, 447.

as this lent color to the charges of favoritism leveled at Governor Johnstone by his enemies.

In 1747 six hundred Palatine Germans complained in a petition that they had survived an Indian war of 1711 only to find themselves victimized by one Thomas Pollock, "who ruled both Governor and Country" and took everything from the Palatine settlements even to the very mill stones. Pollock had cheated them out of the lands in Virginia which Queen Anne had given them. His heir had come recently to the Palatine settlement in North Carolina and turned them off their lands "by virtue of Authority in order to settle the Rebels the Scots in our Possessions." [43] It is to be noted that the Palatines accused "Authority" of instigating the settlement of Scots rebels on their lands; they did not mention the governor by name.

In December, 1748, some of the inhabitants and proprietors of North Carolina sent a list of complaints against the governor to the Duke of Bedford, Secretary of State for the Southern Department. Johnstone, they wrote, had corresponded too little with the home government and thereby had evinced an intention to disown the superiority of the Crown. They went on to charge him with favoring Scottish Jacobites during the '45, "by placing them in Chief Offices of Trust and Power." Not long after this, a certain Henry McCulloh began to attack Johnstone. When the governor refuted McCulloh's "charges" of Jacobitism, the latter denied ever having made them "directly or indirectly." [44]

The jealousies and rivalries in North Carolina during Johnstone's administration seem to have arisen from the governor's partiality for Scots when distributing patronage. A loyal servant of the Crown, he was undoubtedly tactless and sometimes unscrupulous in his methods. So conspicuous was his sympathy for the Scottish Jacobites as individuals that he laid himself open to the charge of treasonable correspondence with their party. Baseless as these charges were, they served to give him a reputation among colonials as a broad-minded sympathizer with their political aims. The libels of his enemies, indeed, elicited for him the undeserved praise of generations of American historians. His aims appear to have been no

[43] Petition of the Palatines to George II, 1747, in *N.C. Recs.*, IV, 954–956. The petition bore forty-two signatures.

[44] *N.C. Recs.*, IV, 925–926, 1148.

higher than those of his detractors and certainly little different from those of many another royal governor. If he had motives above the higgling of the market place, they sprang from that generous but invidious love of country which years of self-imposed exile had been unable to efface.

When one considers the manifest ties of kinship and interest that bound the eighteenth-century Scots together from the Clyde to the Mississippi, when one remembers the mercantile, political, and cultural connections between the mother country and the Scottish colonies within colonies overseas, and when one reflects on the awareness displayed by Englishmen and Americans of certain consistent attitudes and activities on the part of the emigrant Scots, it is difficult to escape the conclusion that this poor and small country played a part in eighteenth-century history far beyond what might have been expected of her slender resources and population, and a part insufficiently recognized outside the pages of romantic historiography.

The coming of the American Revolution transformed Scotland's relations with America. The conservatism of the great majority of the Scots in the colonies, coupled with the envy inspired by their commercial success and political power, exposed them to mounting unpopularity and abuse from Americans. Although emigration and trade resumed after 1783, the Revolution had cut cleanly through the web of relationships between Scotland and North America. Had it not been for the Revolution the Scots might be regarded in the United States today with the same familiar intimacy as they are in Canada, and the kilt and glengarry might be as inconspicuous in Omaha as they are in Windsor, Ontario. Instead, these garments have become the freakish hobby of a handful of well-to-do enthusiasts in Philadelphia, while few persons in Omaha could name the capital of Scotland. The Revolution severed the numerous ties between the educated and prosperous classes on both sides of the Atlantic. Thousands of Scots in this category remained aggressively loyal to the Crown, while thousands more opposed the Revolution passively. The postwar migration was mainly restricted to the underprivileged and the dispossessed, people whose memories of Scotland rendered them more easily assimilable to the American democracy than their predecessors before the war.

After 1775 Scottish influence lost most of its force, a loss which was never made good. During the period of aristocratic politics in the eastern states, the aristocrats were American-born veterans of the Revolution. Only two men born in Scotland signed the Declaration of Independence. The downfall of the Scots was largely the result of their failure as a group to support, or even to tolerate, the American Revolution.

VIII

"A Distinct and Separate Body

from the People

Who Receive Them"

THE loyalty of the Highlander in America to the Crown was a logical extension of his unquestioning obedience to his immediate landlord. It is true that some of the Highland peasants became independent farmers and appreciated the advantages of their new status. But at Cross Creek and elsewhere in North Carolina, the chief center of active Highland loyalism, the overwhelming majority of the immigrants followed those who had been their leaders in Scotland and who had accompanied them to the American colony.

Governor Tryon used this traditional feeling of respect for birth and social standing among the Highlanders by appointing the influential men in their various communities to be captains and justices of the peace. During the War of the Regulation these local leaders were able to bring many soldiers to his standard.[1]

On the day after the skirmish at Moore's Creek Bridge, which crushed militant loyalism in North Carolina, nearly all the Highland officers fell into American hands. It was fully evident to the Americans that so long as the leaders were prisoners there was no danger of another Highland uprising. This conclusion was supported by the

[1] Bassett, "Regulators of North Carolina," p. 176.

experience of Lord Cornwallis, who, after the Battle of Guilford Courthouse, stopped at Cross Creek on his way to the coast, hoping to gather some recruits among the Highlanders. Few of them responded. In a letter to Sir Henry Clinton, dated at Wilmington in April, 1781, Cornwallis wrote that the inhabitants on both sides of the Cape Fear River were universally hostile.[2]

Many Americans denounced the Scots for their hostility to the American cause and rightly coupled it with the system of subordination among the Highlanders. In 1776 a Philadelphia gentleman wrote:

We will never submit till the bayonet is removed . . . and your tyrannical Acts of Parliament are repealed. . . . These are the sentiments of all degrees of men in British America, a few tattered Scotch Highlanders excepted, who have lately emigrated, and whose ignorance, feudal notions, and attachment *to names,* keeps them servile and wholly at the beck of their Chiefs. These, with a few Episcopalians from the same country, who are to a man Jacobites, are all that favour the cause of slavery and oppression.[3]

The Philadelphian was able to accept unquestioningly the fact of Jacobite support for the House of Hanover for two reasons: he had plenty of evidence of it before him in reports from the Southern colonies, and the paradox involved in such support dissolved in the knowledge of the Highlanders' unthinking obedience to their leaders. True, these leaders were upholding their former Hanoverian enemies, but they were consistent in following their conservative instincts. They backed the authority with the greatest prescriptive right and were largely unconcerned with the rights of man. It is interesting to observe this writer's assertion that *all* the loyalists were Scots. He would have been more nearly right had he said that all the Scots were loyalists. But no matter how great his self-deception in ignoring other manifestations of aversion to the American actions, he could not deny even to himself that the loyalism of the Highlanders was beyond question.

From a traveling Englishman of around 1780 we learn that, while the English and Scots were regarded with jealousy and distrust,

[2] MacLean, *Highlanders in America,* pp. 133, 141–142.
[3] Willard, ed., *Letters on the Revolution,* pp. 314–315.

even when openly in sympathy with the American cause, "a native of Ireland stood in need of no other certificate than his dialect." [4]

Even rural Americans recognized the importance of Scottish hostility to their aims and conduct. An officer of Fraser's Highlanders, taken prisoner while aboard a transport bound for Halifax, was marched sixty miles inland from the place of his enforced landing. "Through every village, town, and hamlet that we passed," he wrote, "the women and children, and indeed some men among them, came out and loaded us with the most rascally epithets, calling us 'rascally cut-throat dogs, murtherers, blood hounds, &c &c.' But what vexed me most was their continual slandering of our country (Scotland), on which they threw the most infamous invectives." [5]

Over and over again the words Tory and Scot were used as synonyms. In July, 1776, a New York correspondent, after mentioning a plot headed by the mayor of the city to seize George Washington and other American leaders, commented that this conspiracy was "the second edition of that which was executed in North-Carolina, by men of the same principles. It has given us such a horrible idea of the Scots and Tories among us, that for the future they will not meet with very different treatment from what they have hitherto experienced." [6] That treatment, as the writer implied, had not been good. His remarks give an accurate picture of New York and North Carolina as nests of Scottish Toryism.

Even the judicious Thomas Jefferson reflected the prevailing animus against the Scots when, in his original draft of the Declaration of Independence, he complained that the "British" (by which term he could only have meant the English) were permitting their chief magistrate "to send over not only soldiers of our common blood, but Scotch and foreign mercenaries to invade and destroy us." To Jefferson, the English were his "unfeeling brethren." But the Scots were to be classed with the hated Hessians. Curiously enough, it was John Witherspoon, whose American patriotism could not excuse his Scottish birth in the eyes of Ezra Stiles, who persuaded Congress to delete the unfortunate words from the Declara-

---

[4] Chastellux, *Travels in North-America*, II, 37.
[5] Willard, ed., *Letters on the Revolution*, p. 334.
[6] *Ibid.*, pp. 328–329.

tion. He was one of the few men of this time who were working
for better Scots-American relations. Had it not been for the president of Princeton, the ephemeral revulsion against the Scots might
have been enshrined forever in this famous document.[7]

In August, 1782, the Georgia House of Assembly embodied its
special distrust of the Scots in an act whose preamble declared that
"the People of Scotland have in General Manifested a decided in-
imicality to the Civil Liberties of America and have contributed
Principally to promote and Continue a Ruinous War, for the Purpose of Subjugating this and the other Confederated States." The
law forbade any native of Scotland to enter Georgia with intent
to settle or to carry on any trade, profession, or business. Any Scottish native found in Georgia was to be imprisoned without bail and
deported as soon as possible. Excepted from the act were those
Scots "who have exerted themselves in behalf of the freedom and
Independence of the United States of America, . . . and who are
now entitled to the Rights of Citizenship in any . . . of the United
States." The law was to remain in force for the duration of the war
with Great Britain.[8] It is a remarkable testimony to the strong impression made upon the Americans by Scottish loyalism that, in the
course of a war with the United Kingdom, the state of Georgia
should have passed an act discriminating against the inhabitants
of one only of the sister nations of the British Isles.

A generation after the Revolutionary War, Mrs. Anne McVicar
Grant of Laggan wrote to a friend that she had just received a
copy of Campbell's *Gertrude of Wyoming*. The conservative Highland lady reported her reactions in these words:

It is very provoking that Campbell's democratic hoof should invariably
and unnecessarily protrude itself through all the beautiful drapery in
which he knows so well [how] to clothe the children of his rich poetic
fancy. . . . Nothing . . . could make me forgive his flagrant violation
of truth and national character, when he introduces "poor Scotia's moun-
taineers" as arming in the *Provincial cause*. Glowing with the love of

[7] Adrienne Koch and William Peden, eds., *The Life and Selected Writings of
Thomas Jefferson* (New York, 1944), pp. 26–27; Varnum Lansing Collins, *President Witherspoon: A Biography* (Princeton, 1925), I, 219.

[8] "An Act For Preventing improper or Disafected Persons Emigrating from
other Places, and becoming Citizens of this State . . . ," Savannah, Aug. 5,
1782, in *Ga. Recs.*, XIX, pt. 2, pp. 163–164.

their native land, and full of ancient, venerable, perhaps useful prejudices, they all to a man armed in the cause of Britain, whether right or wrong. If taking the other side were a virtue, 'tis a virtue they have no claim to, and will not thank Campbell for bestowing on them.[9]

These not altogether dispassionate words came from a lady who lived for many years in the United States.

Even a slight acquaintance with the part played by the Scots in Revolutionary America tempts one to agree with the celebrated "Junius," who had been "convinced by experience, that the Scots, transplanted from their own country, are always a distinct and separate body from the people who receive them."[10]

II

The British government imagined that North Carolina was swarming with loyalists who were eager to aid the royal cause. This impression derived largely from the letters of Governor Josiah Martin which repeatedly stressed that a little encouragement from London would soon bring about the defeat of the rebels. In 1775 Martin estimated that he could raise 3,000 Highlanders for the king. The number of able-bodied men of military age was probably somewhat less. The more reliable estimates of the size of the Highland army at Moore's Creek Bridge average about 1,600. There were probably something like 15,000 Highland settlers, of all ages and both sexes, at this time in the province. The population had been greatly augmented by recent Highland immigration. In 1767 there were less than 900 taxable Scottish males in Cumberland County, the center of the Scots settlements. Of the 2,560 persons who filed claims for loss of property with the British Loyalist Commissioners after the war, only 139 gave North Carolina as their former place of residence. Out of these, 101 had their claims heard, and 68 of them said that they were born in Great Britain. Forty-five had emigrated since 1760.[11]

[9] Anne McVicar Grant, *Memoir and Correspondence of Mrs. Grant of Laggan,* ed. by J. P. Grant (London, 1844), I, 236–237.

[10] Dicey and Rait, *Thoughts on the Union,* p. 309.

[11] Connor, *Race Elements,* pp. 55–57; Isaac S. Harrell, "North Carolina Loyalists," *North Carolina Historical Review,* III (1926), 576; *N.C. Recs.,* VII, 539–540; Harrell, "North Carolina Loyalists," p. 580.

It is more than half a century since John Spencer Bassett advanced the thesis that the War of the Regulation was not the harbinger of the Revolution in North Carolina. The leaders of the one, he found, were almost entirely hostile to the leaders of the other. While the coastal population demonstrated against the Stamp Act, the back country organized itself against domination from the coast and ignored the Stamp Act. It is true, Bassett concluded, that some Regulators were in the Revolutionary armies, but the great majority of them were Tories.[12]

The Highland settlers formed the only group which was on the side of the royal governor in both conflicts. This is perhaps a slight exaggeration, for there were a number of Scots loyalists, mostly Lowlanders, in the coastal area who fell into the above category. But the Highlanders were aggressively loyal to the established government throughout the period. In June, 1771, the *Cape Fear Mercury* printed a letter from a committee representing the inhabitants of Cross Creek in which they offered to raise a reinforcement in support of the colonial government. Their stimulus was the news of the Battle of the Alamance. Governor Tryon knew he could count on the Highland aristocracy to "raise the clans" in behalf of the Crown.[13]

The trade of Wilmington, commercial capital of the province, was in the hands of British merchants, most of them Lowland Scots. Martin praised their "noble and honest dormant spirit," of which he hoped to make use if it became necessary. That was in June, 1775. Two months later the governor wrote to Dartmouth and told him that the Scots merchants in Wilmington, who had so long maintained their loyalty, were now being compelled to give ostensible approval to sedition. The patriots' committees were holding musters and forcing the Scots to appear under arms, "although they are still at heart as well affected as ever." The small, compact group of merchants obeyed the Association only so far as their interests were served by doing so. In March, 1775, the Wilmington committee adopted the Virginia device of requiring all friends of the Association to sign the agreement. Only eleven persons refused to do so and seven of them were Scots merchants. Five of the latter had

---

[12] Bassett, "Regulators of North Carolina," p. 211.
[13] *Boston Evening-Post,* July 1, 1771, p. 2.

hitherto co-operated with the Association by permitting their imports to be sold under its terms. When General John Ashe arrived at the town in July, 1777, he found that the merchants had been reinforced by Scottish Tories from Cumberland and Bladen Counties. In fact so many of the town's inhabitants were hostile to the United States, so many loyalists from various parts of the state had crowded, and continued to crowd, into Wilmington, that Ashe feared a plot to seize the magazine. He therefore ordered out "the well-affected part of the militia" of the county and pessimistically anticipated a muster of no more than three hundred men. At this time the Highlanders at Cross Creek were once more in a rebellious mood and threatened to advance on Wilmington, in spite of their promises of good behavior, on the pretext of needing to get salt.[14]

Although a few of the loyal merchants of North Carolina took their leave in the early months of the war, most of them stayed until 1777. In April of that year the legislature decreed that any person convicted in the courts of the state for taking a commission from the king was guilty of treason and liable to the death penalty. Not content with taking away his life, the state also deprived him of his property. In addition, the law declared that all persons who had "traded directly to Great Britain or Ireland" were to take an oath of allegiance to the patriot government or immediately leave the state. Departing merchants had three months in which to dispose of their property, after which it was forfeit to the state. A number of merchants left during the summer. They lost heavily from the brevity of the period of grace and they had no opportunity to collect most of the debts due to them.[15]

The Cross Creek and Wilmington stores of James Gammell of Greenock were owed not less than fifteen thousand pounds, while the great firm of John and Archibald Hamilton, four-fifths of whose capital belonged to the partners in Virginia and North Carolina, lost nearly £200,000.[16]

Most of those who left as a result of the act of 1777 were High-

[14] Gov. Martin to Earl of Dartmouth, June 30, Aug. 28, 1775, in *N.C. Recs.*, X, 48, 236; Schlesinger, *Colonial Merchants*, pp. 520–522; Gen. Ashe to Gov. Caswell, July 28, 1777, in *N.C. Recs.*, XI, 546.
[15] Harrell, "North Carolina Loyalists," pp. 580–581; Crittenden, *Commerce of North Carolina*, p. 141.
[16] *Ibid.*, pp. 103–104.

landers from the back country. In October the *North Carolina Gazette* reported that "great numbers of these infatuated and over-loyal People returned from America to their own Country." Among them was the heroine of the Highlanders on both sides of the ocean, Flora Macdonald, who had emigrated with her husband only two years before. Others of the Carolina Highlanders made their way to new homes in Nova Scotia, which had received its own prewar influx of Scots immigrants.[17]

In July two-thirds of the population of Cumberland County are said to have been preparing to leave the state. They had become insolent and threatened trouble. The local American patriots requested Colonel David Smith to station an armed company in the county until the loyalists had departed. Toward the end of the month a large vessel left the coast carrying "a great number of Tories . . . chiefly Scotch Gentlemen who have refused to take the Oaths of Government to this State." They were mostly persons of considerable property which they had acquired in America. They had converted much of it into liquid or movable form and had taken it aboard with them. About the end of October, "a second Scotch Transport, having on Board a Number of Gentlemen of that Nation," sailed from North Carolina. Aboard were Archibald and John Hamilton, the merchants, who had long resided in America and built up a great fortune. Between August, 1777, and January, 1778, more than 150 refugees arrived in New York from North Carolina. They were mostly merchants and natives of Scotland. One of them, a Presbyterian clergyman named John McLeod, had emigrated from Scotland to Cross Creek in 1770. Having arrived in New York, he proposed a plan for bringing the Highlanders out of North Carolina. He claimed to have received the most solemn promises from some 270 men to join together when summoned.[18]

The military history of Scots loyalism in North Carolina may be said to have begun in June, 1775, when Governor Martin asserted in a letter to Dartmouth that, with a little help from General Gage, for which he had asked already, he could quickly collect a powerful

[17] Connor, *Race Elements*, pp. 66–67.
[18] Col. Smith to Gov. Caswell, July 26, 1777, in *N.C. Recs.*, XI, 534; *N.C. Recs.*, XI, 743, 790; XIII, 368; V, 1198; X, 577; MacLean, *Highlanders in America*, pp. 116–117.

force among the emigrants from the Highlands of Scotland. Martin optimistically hoped to raise three thousand men and thus to arm or neutralize two-thirds of the men of military age in the province. At the same time, he offered to organize without help a battalion of one thousand Highlanders if the king would restore him to his former rank of lieutenant colonel. Martin recommended Allan Macdonald of Kingsburgh, the husband of Flora, to be major of this unit and Alexander McLeod of the marines to be first captain, because, as he wrote, they "have most extensive influence over the Highlanders here, great part of which are of their own names and familys." [19] Not for nothing was the campaign of the ensuing year known for long in North Carolina as the "Insurrection of the Clan Macdonald."

By October, 1775, the situation in the province had deteriorated from Martin's point of view. It was seven months since he had requested arms and ammunition, but no help had been forthcoming. Meanwhile the patriots had been organizing themselves thoroughly and some of the Highlanders had been seduced by a fair-weather, Scots-born patriot called Farquhard Campbell. Writing to Dartmouth on October 16, the governor asked for two battalions from troops then being recruited in the Highlands of Scotland. These units would form an effective nucleus for a locally organized Highland army.[20]

Both Macdonald and McLeod, Martin's candidates for army office, were recent immigrants from Scotland. Neither had been in America for more than a year. Alexander McLeod was the son-in-law of Allan and Flora Macdonald. Without waiting for official permission, each of the men had raised by November, 1775, a company of Highlanders. But General Gage had ideas of his own. He sent a Major Macdonald from Boston to raise a battalion of Highlanders in North Carolina and he intended to place all the troops there under the command of Lieutenant Colonel Allan McLean. Martin feared that Gage intended to remove his "valuable officers" from the province and so "dissolve the union of the Highlanders in it now held together by their influence." McLeod revealed the exaggerated pride of the Highland tacksman and laird when he specu-

[19] Martin to Earl of Dartmouth, June 30, 1775, in *N.C. Recs.*, X, 45–47.
[20] Gov. Martin to Earl of Dartmouth, Oct. 16, 1775, in *ibid.*, pp. 267–268.

lated that Farquhard Campbell's defection had "proceeded as much from jealousy of the Superior consequence of [himself] and his Father in law with the Highlanders here as from any other motive."[21]

Allan McLean arrived in Cumberland County with a commission dated January 10, 1776, which authorized twenty-six people in central North Carolina to array all the king's loyal subjects and march them to Brunswick by February 15. Martin promised Dartmouth to do his best to aid McLean in his task of recruiting among the Scottish immigrants. Many of the Highlanders are said to have avoided service by hiding in the forests and swamps. On February 18, the Highland army set out for the coast.[22]

Meanwhile the British government had arranged to send regulars to the Cape Fear in order to effect a junction with the local levies. Sir Peter Parker took command of a fleet loaded with soldiers under the command of Lord Cornwallis. The British ministry promised their arrival at Wilmington in January, but they failed to get there until April. Martin had the Highlanders, under Brigadier Donald Macdonald, begin their journey far too early. Colonel James Moore, with one thousand Americans, opposed Macdonald's force at the bridge over Moore's Creek, whose decking he had removed. On February 27, as the Highlanders advanced in single file across the partially dismantled span, the Americans picked off about seventy of them without effort. The rest surrendered or fled to the woods. The Americans took about 800 prisoners, 1,500 rifles, 350 guns, 13 sets of wagons, and £15,000 in cash. Of the prisoners, the privates were soon released on parole and the officers sent to Halifax for exchange. Many of the latter settled in the Maritime Provinces after the war.[23]

Immediately after the battle many of the merchants of the upper Cape Fear were taken into custody and all but three of the stores at Cross Creek had to close. But by March 25 the imprisoned shop-

[21] Gov. Martin to Earl of Dartmouth, Nov. 12, 1775, in *ibid.*, pp. 325–326.

[22] Gov. Martin to Earl of Dartmouth, Jan. 12, 1776, in *ibid.*, p. 409; MacLean, *Highlanders in America*, pp. 125, 127, 132–133.

[23] Claude H. Van Tyne, *The War of Independence: American Phase* (Cambridge, Mass., 1929), pp. 190–193; Saunders, "Prefatory Notes," *N.C. Recs.*, X, xii–xiii; MacDougall, ed., *Scots in America*, p. 22; MacLean, *Highlanders in America*, pp. 123–124.

keepers had been let out on bond and were again running their businesses. Nearly all the Cross Creek stores were open and everything was quiet and peaceful. Soon after this some of the Highlanders entered the American service, but the bulk of the Cumberland County people were still regarded with suspicion. According to the testimony of an American patriot at Cross Creek, Cumberland County suffered, after Moore's Creek Bridge, from the selfish and oppressive conduct of local administrators, especially militia officers and justices. The chief villain was one William Rand, "scarcely known in the County," who had been "plundering the poor ignorant Scotch people after their defeat at Moore's Creek." Rand got himself and some friends elected to Congress, and then arranged for members of his faction to obtain the appointments to local offices in the county.[24]

The Battle of King's Mountain was essentially a battle between a revived Highland army in North Carolina and a force of Scotch-Irish patriots. It nipped in the bud Lord Cornwallis' attempt to organize a new regiment of North Carolina Highlanders.[25] It illustrated succinctly the divergent roles of the Highland Scots and of the Ulster Scots in the American Revolution.

Highland opposition to the American cause did not begin in earnest until the start of the agitation for independence. So far as the Highlanders showed any interest in the Stamp Act, their feelings were hostile to the ministry. The inhabitants of Cross Creek imagined Lord Bute to be the instigator of the new tax and burned him in effigy. They called upon the patriots of Wilmington in the name of "dear liberty" to resist any attempt to land the stamps in North Carolina. In 1775 and 1776 the Highlanders sent representatives to the provincial congresses and set up their own committees of safety. Only when they saw that these congresses and committees were drifting toward open rebellion and war did they refuse to go further with the Americans. About that time, the provincial congress began to angle for their continued support. In August, 1775, the congress, meeting at Hillsborough, resolved that eleven gentlemen form a

---

[24] Adelaide L. Fries, ed., *Records of the Moravians in North Carolina* (Raleigh, N.C., 1922–43), III, 1055, 1058; MacLean, *Highlanders in America*, p. 142; Robert Rowan to Gov. Caswell, Sept. 18, 1777, in *N.C. Recs.*, XI, 626–627.

[25] Wertenbaker, *Early Scotch Contributions*, p. 24.

committee to confer with the recent immigrants from the Scottish Highlands in order to urge them "to unite with the other Inhabitants of America in defence of those rights which they derive from God and the Constitution." Among the eleven names were those of a Maclaine, a McAlister, Alexander McKay, and Farquhard Campbell. No Gaelic-speaking minister—and no other could influence the Highlanders—was found to undertake their conversion to the cause of independence. Their own minister, John McLeod, did much to keep them faithful to the conservative side.[26]

It is said that a large part of the coastal merchants sooner or later joined the rebellion. The leading authority on prewar commerce in the province lists thirteen names of persons who took part in the movement for independence. The same author criticizes the well-known work of A. M. Schlesinger on the colonial merchants for not showing in his discussion of North Carolina what a large proportion of the merchants of that state joined the rebellion.[27] If this criticism is justified, it does not follow, of course, that a majority, or even a large proportion, of the *Scottish* merchants behaved in this way. The names of the thirteen, indeed, seem to argue against it, for only two of them have anything of a Scottish flavor. There is no doubt that the wealthiest among the Scots merchants, those who had most to lose, chose to sacrifice, or at least to risk the loss of, their property in America rather than countenance the independence movement.

III

The story of Scottish loyalism in Virginia is thoroughly woven into the fabric of her colonial history. There is some difference of opinion among historians as to the importance of trading activities in the lives of the great planters. Louis B. Wright has cited the letters of Robert Carter of Corotoman as further evidence of "the preoccupation of the Virginia cavaliers with trade." Far from being "silken aristocrats," according to Wright, the Virginia planters were working gentlemen, busy with the supervision of their estates and "occupied with the commerce which resulted from the sale of plantation prod-

---

[26] Connor, *Race Elements*, p. 61; Journal of the Provincial Congress of North Carolina, in *N.C. Recs.*, X, 173–174; MacLean, *Highlanders in America*, p. 116.
[27] Crittenden, *Commerce of North Carolina*, p. 142.

ucts and the importation of manufactured goods from overseas."
Proud and class-conscious as they were, they would have dismissed
as nonsense any talk of the "taint" of trade. Contrast this view with
that of John Spencer Bassett, who argued more than half a century
ago that Virginia's planter-traders "never got beyond the stage of
neighborhood storekeepers." They bought goods for their own estates
and those of their neighbors and, if the prospects seemed good, they
purchased the tobacco of the surrounding country and shipped it to
England. The planter-merchants of the colony, concluded Bassett,
"so far as they existed at all, were not a distinct feature of colonial life." While Bassett's emphasis is considerably different from
Wright's, he agrees with the latter in discounting the existence of a
social prejudice against trade "in the formative period of Virginia
life." This formative period, however, he does not consider to have
ended until the Revolution.[28] It is perhaps not too much to say that
the prejudices of a fairly settled society had begun to make themselves felt some years before the Revolution.

"The Virginians," wrote William Wiatt of Fredericksburg in 1772
to his brother in Liverpool, "[have] no idea of bringing up their
children to business. If a person has two or three negroes and a few
acres of land, let him have what quantity of children he may, they
must all be brought up genteely to preserve the dignity of the family,
although he spends twice his annual income." [29]

A few of the larger planters might fit Wright's picture of the "working gentleman," but the lesser gentry were perhaps not above dis-
dain for the taint of trade. Furthermore, as William Wiatt suggested,
they were living beyond their income. The enactment of Governor
Gooch's tobacco inspection law of 1730, according to one authority,
"inaugurated in the colony an era of prosperity and consequent
extravagance, the like of which had never been known before." It
was the period when fine horses and carriages became matters of
competition among the planters. The Scottish merchants made the

[28] Louis B. Wright, ed., *Letters of Robert Carter 1720–1727* (San Marino,
Calif., 1940), Introduction, pp. vi–vii; John Spencer Bassett, "The Relation
between the Virginia Planter and the London Merchant," *Annual Report of the
American Historical Association for the Year 1901* (Washington, D.C., 1902),
I, 557–560.

[29] William Wiatt to Francis Wiatt, July 21, 1772, in *William and Mary Quarterly*, 1st ser., XII (1903–04), 113.

most of this propensity among the landowners to spend their tobacco as fast as they made it—or faster.[30] They might not have enjoyed such a clear field had the planters been as forward in trade as is sometimes supposed.

As for the planters' extravagance, it is not infrequently admitted that their indebtedness encouraged them to favor independence of the mother country. That indebtedness was often more than seasonal. Sometimes it was chronic. Accumulating debts represented far more than advances against expected tobacco crops. They indicated a growing tendency among the planters to live beyond their means.

Both Beard and Schlesinger have quoted with emphasis the following words from the pen of an American writer of the early nineteenth century: "It is a firmly established opinion of men well versed in the history of our revolution that the *whiggism* of Virginia was chiefly owing to the *debts of the planters*." [31]

Now, in November of 1777, Ezra Stiles, while riding through Connecticut, met a Scottish merchant who told him that the Scots "had got *Two Thirds of Virginia & Maryld.* mortgaged or otherwise engaged to them [including what] was *owned in Scotland.*" The continent, said the man, owed Britain six millions sterling, most of it to the Scots. Scottish merchants and factors had often told Stiles, if his diary may be trusted, that the Scots "would in a few years have all the Property in Virginia if not in gen. of No[rth] America." [32]

Such exaggerated statements had a firm foundation in fact. The Scots in Virginia were extremely unpopular with the native-born population during the five years before the Revolution. Their invidious position as moneychangers in the temple of American liberty gave rise to many scurrilous attacks on them in the Virginia press.

In 1771 the Virginia assembly passed a bill to regulate the jurisdiction of the Court of Hustings. An attorney of the court, whose practice would suffer by the measure, joined with an insignificant

[30] Fairfax Harrison, "The Equine F.F.Vs: A Study of the Evidence for the English Horses Imported into Virginia before the Revolution," *Virginia Magazine of History and Biography*, XXXV (1927), 334, 367, n. 20.

[31] Schlesinger, *Colonial Merchants*, pp. 38–39; Charles A. Beard, *Economic Origins of Jeffersonian Democracy* (New York, 1915), pp. 297–298.

[32] Stiles, *Diary*, II, 227–228.

shopkeeper and wrote to a small merchant in London with the request that he stir up the tobacco merchants there to prevent the bill's receiving the royal assent. A certain "Junius Americanus" wrote to the *Virginia Gazette* with the complaint that those who undertook the business were "a junto of North Britons, whom the favour of the Virginians had raised from beggary to affluence." The tobacco merchants, he grumbled, "or, to be more humiliating, the Scotch part of them, are regarded as better judges of the municipal laws and internal regulations of Virginia, than the legislature of the province." After this occurrence, it seemed to the American Junius that there remained only one step to complete the disgrace of the province, namely the appointment of a "committee of Scotch store boys, to report to the Board of Trade on every bill that passes the two Houses of Assembly." [83]

In 1773 some of the inhabitants of Bedford County entered into an association not to pay their debts unless they were guaranteed previously agreed prices for their commodities. They put out a broadside, which circulated in the county. It condemned "the destructive total Combination of the Merchants against the People and Interest of this Colony." The tract advocated colonial manufactures, and its dominant theme was opposition to the trading monopoly in Virginia built up by the Glasgow mercantile firms. This document declared:

The Scotch Nation about fifty Years ago, being informed of this valuable Country, and of the weak and blind Side of its Inhabitants, chose, some of them, to quit their Packs, and leave their poor Fare, and Barren Country, and make an Experiment in the Tobacco Trade; which, by a little Industry, and the mechanick Turn of Mind and the artful Craftiness and Cunning natural to that Nation, they soon not only raised great Estates for themselves, but found a Plan to enrich their Country, and raise Glasgow, from being a poor, small, petty Port, to one of the richest Towns and trading Ports in his Majesty's Dominions, and all by Fawning, Flattery, and outwitting the indolent and thoughtless Planters.

"Let us BEDFORDMEN," wrote Guy Smith to the *Virginia Gazette*, "lead the Van to Liberty and Renown, and turn the Channel from centring in Glasgow (richly overflowing all Scotland, and aggrandising all Scotchmen) to centre in Virginia; which may be done very easily, by dealing with none that don't choose to reside here and

[83] *Virginia Gazette*, Rind, Oct. 17, 1771, pp. 11–12.

spend their Riches here, instead of in Glasgow." There might be a few American traders and tradesmen, added Smith, who charged extortionate prices, but this was only because they had "imbibed Scotch Principles." [34]

This version of history is interesting not only because it is so typical of the attitude reserved by Virginians for the Scottish immigrant and transient, but also because of its far-from-typical admission that the commercial success of the Scots in Virginia was at least partially due to the "blind Side," the indolence, and the thoughtlessness of the planters.

The blindness of the planter to the practical side of business was nowhere better seen than in a plan for a consumers' co-operative, which the landowners of Virginia's Northern Neck conceived in January, 1771. A number of planters in Westmoreland, Northumberland, Richmond, and Lancaster Counties, headed by John Tayloe, Landon Carter, Richard Henry Lee, Francis Lightfoot Lee, and Richard Parker, solicited funds for the foundation of "a patriotic store." The self-declared aim of the promoters was to assist people in avoiding the indebtedness said to have been forced upon them "through the excessive price at which goods have for many years been sold." They wanted to raise six thousand pounds sterling by subscription from any persons of reasonable property and fixed residence in the colony, who were not factors for any British merchant. The stockholders were to elect seven trustees who should purchase goods for cash to the full value of the capital. These were to be sold in the colony "with no other charge upon the real and *bona fide* first cost of them, than the necessary charges of importation, the expence of store keeping, the difference of exchange, making an allowance for its fluctuation," and 10-per-cent profit to the investors. Surplus profits from the sale of the goods beyond 10 per cent were to be "added to the original stock for the enlargement of the trade." The actual price of the goods, then, would depend upon how fast the directors decided to enlarge the trade. But the plan made no provision in this respect. There was certainly no more than a vaguely implied guarantee that the co-operative's prices would undercut those of the British merchants.

Then came this remarkable piece of logic:

[34] *Virginia Gazette,* Purdie and Dixon, Nov. 25, 1773, p. 2.

And as the extensive credits given by the sellers of goods in this colony have, according to their delusive intentions, accomplished the two mischievous purposes of forcing customers to deal with them, and inducing them to overlook the enormous . . . advance which such sellers have laid on their goods, . . . it is therefore agreed, that the goods imported under this plan, shall be sold only for ready money or tobacco.[35]

It was perhaps not the merchant's intentions which were "delusive." The planter rather deluded himself into believing that his own extravagance, facilitated by easy credit, was really the fault of the storekeeper. The promoters of this rather naïve scheme decided to save their brethren from themselves by refusing to sell them goods on credit.

The scheme became rather ludicrous in its provision that no person should be allowed to purchase in one year from the store or stores to be erected more goods than the managers decided he needed for the support of his family. Even in his cash purchases the small planter was to be protected from his spendthrift tendencies by the kindly paternalism of the larger landowners, who knew from experience where injudicious spending could lead. The gentlemen who advertised this plan proclaimed it twice in their prospectus as a "patriotic scheme." Clearly the emotional impetus behind the idea was less the ostensible resentment at economic exploitation than the purity of patriotism which helped them to find the cause of every misfortune, public and private, in the conduct of the "foreign" merchant.

The gentlemen who put forward these proposals were members of a class as tightly knit and clearly distinguished as the Scots merchants themselves. Richard Henry Lee presented the Westmoreland Resolutions against the Stamp Act to the patriots at Leedstown in February, 1766. This episode has been called the first formal defiance of the British in the troubles that preceded the Revolution. Francis Lightfoot Lee was one of the subscribers of the subsequent Westmoreland Association. As for the horror of these men at the prevailing credit system, early in 1773 the *Virginia Gazette* reported that fifteen hundred acres of land belonging to Thomas Poole, together with Poole's twelve slaves and all his horses, hogs, and house and kitchen furniture, had been sold off "to satisfy a Debt to the

[35] *Virginia Gazette,* Rind, Jan. 31, 1771, pp. 1–2.

Honourable John Tayloe, Esquire." Nor was Tayloe averse to accepting, along with the Scots merchant, Archibald Ritchie, a power
of attorney from the governor of the Bank of England and other
trustees of the bankrupt business of Bogle and Scott, of London, em-
powering him to collect the Virginia debts of the firm for distribu-
tion among its British creditors. It is worth noting that Tayloe was
a member of the Ohio Company, that Landon Carter and Francis
Lightfoot Lee were on the committee of the Mississippi Company
in 1768, that Richard Parker was a member of this company, and
that Richard Henry Lee was a member of both the Ohio and the
Mississippi Companies.[36]

Evidently the planters of the Northern Neck were more familiar
with the business of land speculation than with the intricacies of
overseas trade. Those whose interests were confined to the profits
of agriculture could feel free to criticize those who profited from
trade.

Meanwhile events in the Scots mercantile world beyond the control of the Virginia merchants added real to questionable grievances,
by inflicting on the planter a sudden contraction of credit. The
financial crisis of 1772, whose storm center was Glasgow, brought
a run on the Scots banks. "The withdrawals," wrote George F. Norton
from London to his representative in Virginia, "have very near broke
up many of the most substantial Bankers, the Scotch have not met
with so fatal a stroak since the Memory of Man." The late bankruptcies, wrote William Wiatt of Fredericksburg in June, 1773, had
made great changes in the past nine months. The factors for the
Glasgow merchants were forbidden to draw bills of credit on Glasgow. The merchant in Virginia who wished to support his credit
in Britain had to ship large quantities of gold and silver. According
to Wiatt, £100,000 had been so transferred during the previous
nine months. Thus the circulation of specie in Virginia was greatly
curtailed pending the receipt of a supply from other colonies or
the mother country. Robert Carter Nicholas, treasurer of Virginia,
put the matter succinctly:

[36] *Virginia Gazette*, Purdie and Dixon, Jan. 7, 1773, p. 3; *ibid.*, Rind, Oct. 8,
1772, p. 3; Kenneth P. Bailey, *The Ohio Company of Virginia and the Westward
Movement 1748–1792* (Glendale, Calif., 1939), pp. 35, 38, 229 n.; *Virginia
Gazette*, Rind, April 14, 1768, Supplement, p. 12.

It is notorious that a large Proportion, if not much the greatest Number of Bills had been, for several Years past, drawn by the Scotch Factors; these Gentlemen's Drafts have, of late, been restrained to narrow Limits, and, I believe very few of those, who used to deal most considerably in Exchange, now draw any Bills at all. Our Exchange has fluctuated for a considerable Time and generally under Par; . . . and, I think, last July [1772], when the Misfortunes, which had happened in Great Britain, began first to be felt here, it rose. . . . This Rise put the Remitters upon collecting all the Specie they could, and hence arose a Dislike in some to Paper Money.[37]

In these circumstances, it is not difficult to understand the planters' dislike of the Scots merchants, at least in the years 1772–1774, when the specie problem was at its most acute stage and when the prudent contraction of credit was interpreted inevitably as just one more evidence of Scots selfishness.

As the Revolution approached, however, the patriotic element in the South discovered another and more substantial reason for distrusting the Scots. They were left in no doubt as to the incipient loyalism of that group. When Patrick Henry's resolutions were read in the Virginia House of Burgesses in May, 1765, "the Scotch gentlemen in the House cried out treason." [38]

The consequent aggressiveness of the patriots against the Scottish settlers sometimes met with more than mere passive resistance. In 1774 James Gilchrist wrote that he was "lately in Mecklenburg [County], in Virginia, where one Malachi Macalle was carrying about a paper for expelling out of the country all *Scotchmen*, to which he had got 300 names. However, for his ill-bred invections against that country in general & against some individuals in particular, the Parson of the Parish (one Cameron from the Highlands) followed him & gave him a good & most complete caning." [39]

In Virginia, the chief dissent to the Association for the boycott of

[37] George F. Norton to John Hatley Norton, July 8, 1772, in Mason, ed., *Norton Papers*, p. 254; William Wiatt to Francis Wiatt, June 26, 1773, in *William and Mary Quarterly*, 1st ser., XII (1903–04), 113–114; Robert Carter Nicholas to Messrs. Purdie and Dixon to the *Virginia Gazette*, July 16, 1773, in *William and Mary Quarterly*, 1st ser., XX (1911–12), 235–236.

[38] "Journal of a French Traveller," p. 727.

[39] James Gilchrist to Capt. James Parker, Dec. 22, 1774, in *William and Mary Quarterly*, 1st ser., XIII (1904–05), 69.

British goods came from the merchants and factors, who, as Schlesinger pointed out, were "largely Scotch by nativity." The opposition of the Scots was clandestine but determined. The radicals were suspicious of the Scots merchants and did not accept their statements at face value. When the policy of nonimportation went into effect, the Scots as a class proved to be the most numerous offenders. The climax came when Purdie's *Virginia Gazette* for December 22 and 29, 1775, published a number of intercepted letters, which showed that the leading Scottish merchants were as deceitful as the most skeptical radicals had believed. The letters of Andrew Sprowle of Williamsburg and Robert Shedden of Portsmouth urged Scottish correspondents to send various commodities to the colony. Meanwhile the Scots traders hastened with businesslike prudence to press their debtors for payment while there was still time to collect. This brought hardship to many planters, some of whom had to sell lands to meet their obligations. In March, 1775, the colony's courts closed and the merchants were thenceforth powerless to enforce payment.[40]

By November, the Virginians had turned completely against the Scots and were even "Threating to Extirpate them." The people of Norfolk and Portsmouth were struck with panic by the approach of the provincial troops and had started to move into the country with their effects. On November 16, Lord Dunmore entered Norfolk, where he administered the oath of allegiance to the Scots merchants and their clerks and formed them into the "Queen's Own Loyal Virginians." The local Negroes he organized as the "Etheopean Corps." He then threw up earthworks around the town. In December, though the Norfolk Scots were "to a man . . . well-affected to the government," they suffered defeat and expulsion from the town at the hands of the patriots. General Lee ordered his men to burn down the house of Neil Jamieson, the wealthiest of the Norfolk Scottish merchants, who had acted as Dunmore's supply agent, as an example to any who might be thinking of giving aid to the royal governor. The following year, Jamieson supplied Dunmore with thirty thousand pounds in exchange for treasury bills and got ½ per cent interest for the favor. He went to Staten Island with the

[40] Schlesinger, *Colonial Merchants*, pp. 509–512.

governor in August and soon concerned himself in privateering against the rebels.[41]

Most of the Scots merchants wished only to be left in peace to continue business as usual. But the radicals were inclined, with some justification in the case of the Scots, to regard neutral sentiments as akin to treachery. A certain Colonel Pollock, a Scotsman, was traveling through the colony in the fall of 1775, when he made the mistake of saying in public that he had heard a gentleman in Annapolis tell a friend that his brother, in a letter from London, had remarked in a joking way that "he thought matters might be easily settled by hanging a half Dousen on each side the Question." For this piece of very indirect reporting, Pollock was exposed to the wrath of the local populace of Suffolk and came within a hair's breadth of being tarred and feathered. Spurred on by "a narrow Soul'd wretch one Major Smith," the mob locked up the colonel and denounced him, with the usual juxtaposition of epithets, as "a Scotchman and an Enemy to America." Only by distributing largesse to the patriots did Pollock get away unharmed.[42]

The fire-eating radicals of Robert Munford's comedy, *The Patriots*, written in 1776 or 1777, were held up to ridicule for their officiousness, ignorance, and tendency to impute guilt by association. There was little exaggeration in Munford's picture of a member of a committee of safety excoriating the Scots for being Scots. "The nature of their offense, gentlemen," said the committeeman, "is, that they are Scotchmen." [43]

While these things were going forward, and some months after the British government had forbidden further emigration to America, Highlanders were still arriving in the country. Late in 1775 a ship carrying 250 Highlanders, men, women, and children, bound for Newbern in North Carolina, was forced to put into Norfolk by bad weather. Dunmore, just defeated at the Battle of Great Bridge, had the Highlanders put ashore and seized their ship for the accom-

[41] *Virginia Magazine of History and Biography*, XIV (1906–07), 388; Wertenbaker, *Norfolk*, pp. 56, 60–61, 63–64; Harrell, *Loyalism in Virginia*, p. 47; *Canad. Claims*, p. 630.

[42] Mrs. Pollock to Joseph Hewes, Dec. 23, 1775, in *N.C. Recs.*, X, 1027–1031.

[43] Courtlandt Canby, "Robert Munford's *The Patriots*," *William and Mary Quarterly*, 3rd ser., VI (1949), 436–439.

modation of Tory refugees. He took about 160 of the immigrants into
his service. The rest, being in a wretched condition, petitioned
Colonel Woodford for his protection. The latter obtained authority
from the Williamsburg convention to supply their wants and to
conduct them to North Carolina. Hearing of these arrangements,
those who had been forced into Dunmore's service deserted and
rejoined their wives and families, "except two maidens, who were
detained as bedmakers to his lordship." [44]

While these Scots were arriving, others were planning to depart
with all speed. So insistent was the demand for shipping space that,
in February, 1776, John Harvey, master of the schooner *Rebecca*,
lying near the mouth of the Potomac, advertised his willingness to
take passengers to any part of Britain for twenty guineas a head,
each to find his own bedding. This was about seven times the prevailing fare for emigrants traveling in the opposite direction.[45]

On December 18, 1776, the House of Delegates, in a committee
of the whole, passed a resolution instructing the governor to require the departure within forty days of all "natives of Great Britain
who were partners with, agents, storekeepers, assistant storekeepers,
or clerks for any merchant in Great Britain," except those who had
proved themselves loyal to America. On January 1, Governor Patrick
Henry ordered the issuance of a proclamation to this effect. A greatly
accelerated exodus of Scots from Virginia ensued.[46] Some of them,
however, remained in Richmond and Petersburg throughout the war.
A number of Scottish store boys chose to demonstrate their "friend-
liness" to the American cause. In the very month of Patrick Henry's
proclamation, the Chesterfield County court examined a number
of British factors to ascertain their feelings toward the new commonwealth of Virginia. All of these appear to have been Scots. One
of them, Robert Donald, Jr., was in partnership with Patrick Hunter
of Scotland. When the state confiscated Hunter's share of the stock,
which was in Donald's hands, the latter decided wisely to look upon
himself "as not further concerned with the said Patrick Hunter."

[44] *Virginia Gazette*, Purdie, Dec. 30, 1775, p. 4.
[45] *Ibid.*, Dixon and Hunter, Feb. 24, 1776, p. 3.
[46] Harrell, *Loyalism in Virginia*, p. 76; H. R. McIlwaine, ed., *Official Letters of the Governors of the State of Virginia* (Richmond, 1926), I, 87.

Out of seven persons brought before it (all of them having distinctly Scots Lowland names) the court assured itself of the friendly
feelings of four. The three others desired to return to Britain. The
people friendly to the commonwealth were exempted from the
terms of the expulsion order.[47]

At the end of April, 1777, Nicholas Cresswell, the Tory diarist,
interviewed Governor Henry at the palace in Williamsburg. He obtained a permit to board the ship *Albion* then expected from North
Carolina. She was on her way to the Nansemond River to pick up
"135 Scotch Gentlemen" who were waiting there for her. The term
"gentlemen" here may not be very significant, since Cresswell probably applied it to shopkeepers and tradesmen as well as to landowners and professional men. The story was taken up a few weeks
later by Governor Henry himself in a letter to George Wythe, Speaker
of the House of Delegates. Henry was finding great difficulty in
ridding the state of loyalists in the spirit of the House resolution
of December. The *Albion* lost time in fitting out, sailed around into
the James River, and fell into the hands of the enemy. American
ships could not get away with the loyalists at this time, so Henry
asked, in view of their sincere endeavors to leave, that they not be
treated as prisoners of war. A large number of loyalists continued
to wait at Sleepy Hole in Nansemond County.[48]

Not long after Howe's occupation of Philadelphia, 120 new stores
were said to have been opened in that city, 118 of them by "Scotchmen or Tories from Virginia." [49]

In the late summer of 1779 the French took a Glasgow ship with
eight Scots merchants aboard, all refugees from North Carolina and
Virginia. They had embarked optimistically with valuable cargoes
.and had actually entertained the hope of purchasing confiscated
estates in South Carolina and Georgia. Persistence and optimism,
indeed, were characteristic of the Scots in Virginia. In 1783 three
or four Scottish merchants appeared in Petersburg on a debt-
collecting mission. The inhabitants of the town were so incensed
that they held a meeting on June 20 and asked the Scots to leave.

[47] Harrell, *Loyalism in Virginia*, p. 78; *Virginia Magazine of History and Biography*, XIV (1906), 328–329.
[48] Cresswell, *Journal*, pp. 208–209; McIlwaine, ed., *Official Letters*, I, 153–154.
[49] Wilbur H. Siebert, *The Loyalists of Pennsylvania* (Columbus, O., 1920),
p. 45.

The governor, with the advice of the Council, issued a proclamation prohibiting the expelled merchants from returning.[50]

A student of the Virginia loyalists has stated that the group was never large. Only 320 inquests were held over enemy property, and only 140 claims for damages were lodged with the British government by Virginia loyalists.[51] Even this small number represented only 90 claimants. The many other references to the Scots loyalists in Virginia, however, suggest that the true total of Scots loyalists alone was a good deal larger than the loyalist claims and official Virginia records indicate. The number of Scots who owned no property, or insufficient property, to figure in these standard sources of information about the loyalists must have been considerably larger than the property-owning class itself. The fate of the store boys as a whole is difficult to ascertain, but isolated references in the *Virginia Gazette* make it clear that some joined the rebels either from conviction or for the sake of a peaceful life while others took part in the exodus. In any case, there is abundant evidence to demonstrate that the economic, social, and political importance of the Scots merchants and loyalists in Virginia and the tobacco country generally was out of all proportion to their numbers.

IV

A few other states experienced some trouble with Scottish loyalists. The various St. Andrew's clubs were disrupted by the Revolution. At the outbreak of the war, the St. Andrew's club of Charleston had 109 members. Of these at least 32 committed themselves openly to the royal cause during the course of the war. On the other hand, 15 members are known to have contributed directly to the struggle for independence. But of these some—the three sons of Dr. John Moultrie, for example—were born in America. The sympathies of the remaining 62 members are unfortunately not known. During the British occupation of Charleston, the loyalists revived the society. At the first meeting in 1780, 20 of the old members attended, and 64 other persons applied for membership. Extinguished

---

[50] *Virginia Gazette,* Dixon, Oct. 9, 1779, p. 2; Harrell, *Loyalism in Virginia,* pp. 136–137.

[51] Isaac S. Harrell, "Some Neglected Phases of the Revolution in Virginia," *William and Mary Quarterly,* 2nd ser., V (1925), 165.

once more by the British evacuation of 1782, the club went through a second rebirth in 1787, when the surviving members in the city elected new officers, who included two former loyalists.[52]

Like North Carolina and Virginia, the state of South Carolina passed measures to ensure the loyalty of the inhabitants. The requirement of an oath abjuring allegiance to the Crown in 1777 forced a number of Scots, some of whom were merchants, to leave the colony. A much larger departure of loyalists took place in 1778, when the state required all male inhabitants over sixteen years of age to swear to defend it against George III. More Scots left at this time, including a former student of medicine at Edinburgh, a veteran of the French and Indian War who had settled down as a storekeeper, and a rice planter and merchant who had come over in 1756. But the biggest migration of all occurred in 1782, when the British evacuated Charleston. Nearly four thousand persons dispersed to Florida, Jamaica, Halifax, New York, and England, in that order of importance. In 1777 Colonel Hamilton, a Scot, had gone from Halifax to Florida to organize a regiment of North Carolina loyalists. Now, in 1782, John Stuart, the former Indian Superintendent in the South, formed at Pensacola the West Florida Rangers. His former deputy to the Cherokees, Alexander Cameron, like Stuart a Scot, commanded one of the two companies of the new unit.[53]

Maryland's problem was similar to that of Virginia. In both colonies some of the clergymen of the Church of England were Scots. Since these men had been bred in the Jacobite tradition of the Aberdeen doctors, they were justifiably suspected of Toryism. Maryland, like Virginia, experienced some difficulties with Scots store boys. In July, 1775, the patriots' committee of St. Marys County censured Archibald Campbell, factor for John Glassford and Company at Leonardtown on the Potomac, and William Lilburn, factor for James Buchanan and Company at St. Inegoes, for refusing to sell goods for cash and insisting on payment in tobacco, which they

[52] Easterby, *St. Andrew's Society of Charleston*, pp. 50, 52–53, 56–57.
[53] Robert Barnwell, Jr., "The Migration of Loyalists from South Carolina," *Proceedings of the South Carolina Historical Association*, 1937, pp. 34–36; Ella Pettit Levett, "Loyalism in Charleston, 1761–1784," *ibid.*, 1936, p. 12; Walter Clark, "Prefatory Notes," *N.C. Recs.*, XI, xviii; Barnwell, "Migration of Loyalists," pp. 37–38.

were accustomed to accept for shipment to Glasgow. The committee resolved that no attorney should prosecute any suit for debts due to John Glassford at the firm's Leonardtown store. The two Scottish factors petitioned the provincial convention, stating that they had "undesignedly fallen under the censure of the Committee of St. Marys County for a supposed breach of the Resolves of the late Provincial Convention." [54] The life of a storekeeper in Maryland in 1775 was as troubled as in her neighbor to the south.

New York had no such close connections with Scotland as Virginia. The New York merchants shipped to Glasgow potash, iron, flour, staves, whale fins, and hard woods; they imported from Glasgow woolens, carpets, tartans, and haberdashery. This trade amounted to very little in value. In 1764–1765, imports and exports between New York and Glasgow each came to a little over £8,000. The corresponding figures for Virginia were £126,500 and £244,700 respectively. [55] Clearly the Scottish mercantile community, confined as it was to a few wealthy merchants and a small number of shopkeepers, did not play a significant part in New York's loyalist opposition. But the battles of the Mohawk Valley entitle the state to third place among the theaters of Scots loyalist activity. The opponents of independence in New York were Highlanders for the most part. As in North Carolina, they were recent immigrants. Lowland Scottish loyalism was confined to a handful of people at a few places between New York and Albany.

In April, 1775, Colonel Allan McLean handed to Lieutenant Governor Colden a letter from the Earl of Dartmouth which contained instructions from the king under the sign manual. George III authorized the colonel to exercise his well-known influence with the emigrants from the Western Highlands with a view to extracting promises of active support against "all illegal Combinations and Insurrections whatsoever." [56]

[54] Rev. Nelson Waite Rightmyer, "The Character of the Anglican Clergy of Colonial Maryland," *Maryland Historical Magazine*, XLIV (1949), 247–248; Journal of the Proceedings of the Maryland Convention, 1775, in *Md. Archives*, XI, 41–44.

[55] Virginia Draper Harrington, *The New York Merchant on the Eve of the Revolution* (New York, 1935), p. 174.

[56] Earl of Dartmouth to Lt.-Gov. Cadwallader Colden, April 5, 1775, in *Colden Papers*, VII, 281.

Many of the Highlanders gave such active support by serving in Butler's Rangers under Sir John Johnson. The story of the Cherry Valley massacre, of Joseph Brant and Johnson's Indian allies, and of the Highlanders' ultimate defeat and withdrawal into Ontario is too well known to need recapitulation here. But it has been too often assumed that the Scots left the Mohawk Valley *en masse*. It seems far more likely that the Macdonells or Macdonalds of Glengarry provided the backbone of loyalist resistance and that the rest of the Highlanders, not having compromised themselves, remained behind when the Macdonalds went to Canada. The Highlanders of Johnson's force founded Glengarry County, the most easterly county in Ontario. Their acknowledged leader built himself a large, two-story mansion which he named Glengarry House. There were still plenty of Scots around Johnstown, New York, in 1791, when Patrick Campbell described the Genesee country in his *Travels*. At Albany Bush, near Johnstown, many Scots still resided. They formed a well-organized community, maintaining solidarity when necessary for their political advantage and electing one of their number to assess the rest for state taxes. Fifty or sixty of them would gather at Johnstown on these occasions, some dressed in Highland plaids and bonnets. Their views on emigration were exactly those of their fellow countrymen before the war: "They blessed their stars that they had left Scotland, while they had something left to pay their way [and] regretted only [the lack of] the beautiful sight of the Highland hills." Most of them owned land in severalty and lived comfortably. Campbell recommended to them the superior soil of Upper Canada and told them that they would be much happier under the British government. Many of them said they had heard the same from everybody to whom they spoke and that they intended selling their farms and getting free land in Canada. A little earlier there were many Scots at Niagara in Canada. Of six hundred loyalists examined at that place in 1787 by Commissioner Dundas about half had been born in America and half of the remainder in Scotland. Five-sixths of them were former New Yorkers.[57]

[57] Patrick Campbell, *Travels in the Interior Inhabited Parts of North America in the Years 1791 and 1792*, ed. by H. H. Langton and W. F. Ganong (Toronto, 1937), pp. 221, 224, 231–232; Pryde says that in 1777 the whole people of both sexes and all ages transferred themselves in a body to Canada ("Scottish Colonization," pp. 152–153), but this statement is inconsistent with the evidence of

As a result of the American Revolution the focus of Scots emigration shifted from the Carolinas and New York to Canada. The initial impetus toward the settlement of Ontario came from the loyalist migration which consisted largely of Scots from the revolted colonies. The Scottish immigration to Nova Scotia and Prince Edward Island, which had begun soon after 1770, continued on a growing scale after 1783. Prince Edward Island received the discharged Royal Highland Emigrants. New Brunswick, like Ontario, received its first large immigration from the Scots loyalists. Robert Pagan, brother of John who helped Witherspoon settle Pictou in Nova Scotia, had been a merchant in Maine. He was the principal founder of St. Andrews, New Brunswick. The prewar Highland immigrants to Nova Scotia were intensely loyal to the Crown. The only exceptions among the Scots there are said to have been a few rigid Presbyterians of the strict covenanting tradition, who still dwelt in the emotional climate of Bothwell Brig and Drumclog Moss and regarded resistance to the Crown as next to godliness.[58]

V

As compared with the frequent references to Scottish loyalism in the period, one may find few examples of active sympathy for the American cause among the immigrants from Scotland. A number of individual careers are fairly well known. The reputations of John Paul Jones, John Witherspoon, James Wilson, Arthur St. Clair, Hugh Mercer, and a few other American patriots among the Scots have given a misleading tone to much of what has been written of the so-called "Scottish contribution" to American independence. These few swallows did not make a summer, and most of the Scots found the egalitarian climate of 1776 too chilly for comfort.

Even among the Virginia merchants, however, there was at least one notable supporter of the patriotic cause. James Hunter the elder of Fredericksburg put his large ironworks at the service of the Revo-

---

Campbell's *Travels; N.Y. Cal.*, I, 448–449; Charles Clifford King, "The Fate of the New York and New England Loyalists during the Post-War Period 1783–1793" (unpublished master's thesis; Urbana, Ill., 1940), p. 7.

[58] Hugh Murray, *Historical Account of Discoveries and Travels in North America* (London, 1829), II, 484–485; Campbell, *Travels*, p. 300, n. 1; Rattray, *The Scot in British North America*, I, 275.

lutionary armies. Although Hunter held aloof from Virginian society, another Scot, a young merchant named Jack Cunningham,
"noisy, droll, waggish, yet civil in his way and wholly inoffensive,"
appeared in Virginia drawing rooms. At one party he was observed
to join a crowd who were toasting the Sons of America and singing
"Liberty Songs." Cunningham was very much the exception to the
rule. It has been said, indeed, that the failure of the Scots merchants
to adapt themselves to the social life of Virginia and to become
absorbed and accepted in Virginia society partly explains their
inability to furnish a permanent mercantile class strong enough to
survive the Revolution.[59]

Even in New England, apparently, where Scottish immigration
presented no problem, the Scots had been maligned for lack of enthusiasm in the name of liberty. But a few rabid Scots patriots
there were. "It is a great injustice to the Patriots on your side of
the water," wrote a gentleman from Boston late in 1774, "to charge
the Scots here with being enemies to the Americans. A Scotch shoe-
maker was the leader of all our mobs, during the time of the Stamp-
act." Another Scot, William Hyslop, of Brookline, Massachusetts,
had been a member of the local committee of correspondence and
an organizer of the Boston Tea Party. The writer of this letter hoped
that his London correspondent would make all this public, "that the
stains that have been thrown upon the Scotch in New England, for
their want of patriotism, and for their taking part with Government,
may be wiped off."[60] In spite of a few exceptions, it appears that the
comparatively few Scots in New England conformed on the whole
to the loyalist pattern found elsewhere in the colonies.

In June, 1775, occurred what seems to have been a unique incident. A certain Donald McLeod, who had just arrived from Scotland and had "nothing to Recommend himself but the vanity of
Calling himself a Highlander from North Britain," petitioned the
New York congress for permission to raise a company of one hundred Highlanders from among the distressed immigrants then subsisting on charity in the city. He was moved, he said, "by a voluntary
Spirit of Liberty." He could find the men without difficulty, and his
only stipulation was that they be put in the Highland dress and

---

[59] Coakley, "Two James Hunters," pp. 3–21; Fithian, "Journal," p. 301.
[60] Willard, ed., *Letters on the Revolution*, pp. 16–17.

under pay during their service "in defence of our Liberties." There is something a little strained about an American of a few days' residence talking about "our Liberties." In a second petition, McLeod pointed out that a ship had just arrived from Scotland with a number of Highlanders aboard. He had spoken to them that morning and they "all seemed to be very desirous to form themselves into Company's [*sic*] with the Proviso of having Liberty to wear their own Country Dress Commonly called the Highland Habit." Moreover, they wished to serve under Highland officers as some of them could not speak the English language. As for arms, the Highlanders were "already furnished with Guns, Swords, Pistols and Highland Dirks which . . . are at this Time very difficult to be had." [61] This is perhaps the only instance recorded of a large number of Highland immigrants serving, or being ready to serve, the patriotic side. No doubt the deciding factor was the prestige of the petitioner, who was probably a member of the tacksman class and guessed correctly that his long-term interests would be served best by joining the rebels. If he added conviction to convenience, it is difficult to imagine in what part of the Highlands he could have absorbed libertarian principles. But perhaps he had traveled abroad before emigrating to America.

A Philadelphia gentleman, writing to a friend in London in May, 1776, asserted that

many of the Scotch have particularly signalized themselves in the cause of freedom. . . . Messrs. Sproat, Semple, and Milligen, merchants in Front-Street . . . with many others of their countrymen, . . . have raised companies of their own countrymen of a hundred men each, who are equipped in the Scottish dress, and make a very warlike appearance. . . . I mention this, as I see many reflections on the Scotch in the English papers. Thank God, they are here the very warmest advocates for liberty.[62]

Here again is an illustration, albeit a striking one, of the exceptional character of Scottish-American patriotism. Like the Boston writer, this Philadelphia correspondent feels the necessity of exonerating the Scots from the charges almost universally leveled at them by citing some notable exceptions to the rule. As in Donald McLeod's

[61] *N.Y. Cal.*, I, 99–100.
[62] Willard, ed., *Letters on the Revolution*, pp. 314–315.

case, hundreds are said to be involved; this and the mention of the "Scottish dress" suggest that the Philadelphia men were Highlanders. Perhaps the organizers had been in America since childhood and had become assimilated to American habits of thought and feeling. Perhaps some of them were in fact Scotch-Irish. Whatever the truth about this unusual episode, it is difficult to believe, in the face of so much evidence to the contrary, that they were direct emigrants from Scotland of recent vintage.

VI

The question of the Presbyterian, as distinct from the native Scottish, contribution to the achievement of American independence (a question touched upon here only in the introductory chapter) is not properly a part of the present study. Investigation of this large subject is being carried on at present by a quondam student of the impact of the American Revolution upon public opinion in Scotland.[63] It is enough to emphasize here that the universality of Presbyterian patriotism is a fallacy, for the great majority of the Scottish immigrants, especially the recent ones, were loyalists. With the exception of a few Highlanders and Aberdonians, all the Scots in America were Presbyterians. By the 1770's Jacobitism was no longer closely associated with Roman Catholicism. Presbyterian Jacobites from the Highlands and Episcopalian Jacobites from Aberdeenshire formed the backbone of loyalist resistance in North Carolina. It is the confusion of the Scots with the Scotch-Irish that has resulted in the assumption that Presbyterian loyalists were practically unknown during the American Revolution.

In spite of similarities of religion and speech, the Scots and the Scotch-Irish were distinct peoples by the beginning of the eighteenth century. The Scotch-Irish had their own reasons for emigrating to America. The causes behind the direct emigration from Scotland were in the main peculiar to Scotland. These were incidental to long-term economic changes going on in the country during the eighteenth century. The chief causes were poverty, overpopulation, rising rents, social readjustment in the Highlands, and the increasing facilities for transportation to America that arose after the Union of the Parlia-

[63] Dalphy A. Fagerstrom, of the University of Minnesota.

ments in 1707. In spite of a widespread impression to the contrary, evictions in general, and eviction for sheep pasture in particular, were not an important cause of Scottish emigration in the period.

The Scots can be distinguished from the Scotch-Irish, too, in the peculiarities of their pattern of settlement. While the latter, as is well known, filtered down the Appalachian valleys, the Scots proper scattered themselves up and down the seaboard, the Lowlanders dispersing as individuals in both town and country, and the Highlanders founding their own communities on the farming frontier. Certain districts in Scotland were closely associated with certain areas of settlement in America, and there was a tendency for sizable groups to migrate in a body to such regions as the Cape Fear Valley of North Carolina and the large frontier county of Albany in New York. This tendency was encouraged by the actions of the Highland tacksmen, or middleman leaseholders, whose declining status after the failure of the 1745 rebellion induced them to lead their under-tenants to America *en masse*, in the hope that they might build a new quasi-feudal society in the colonies, and themselves enjoy the rights and prerogatives of clan chiefs.

The tacksmen's attempt to set up the clan system in the American environment was as much a failure as John Locke's aristocratic constitution for Carolina. Coming as late as it did, it missed having even as much success as the English model of squirearchy in the tidewater area. The short-lived experiment was caught in its early stages by the advent of the American Revolution. The loyalism of the Highlanders in that struggle was the final blow to the aristocratic element among them. For many decades after the Revolution, Highland immigrants continued to pour into North Carolina, but the phase in which the tacksmen played such an important role had passed for good. The immigrants who fled before the Highland clearances of 1790–1890, the century of evictions for sheep pasture, were poor crofters whose resistance to assimilation in their new country was much less than that of their eighteenth-century forebears.

After the Revolution, Highland immigration to the United States grew in volume with each succeeding decade. Checked by the first French war (1793–1801) and by the War of 1812, the Highlanders recommenced the flow as soon as peace came.

Many of those who left during the nineteenth century, of course, went to more recently opened colonies of the British Empire. Canada was a favorite target of the Highlanders. The earliest settlements in Nova Scotia antedated the American Revolution, while those in Ontario and New Brunswick had been established in 1783, largely by Scottish loyalists from the south.

By 1890 so much of the Highlands had been depopulated that the sources of supply for immigrants were almost cut off. Many of the Western Isles of Scotland had lost three-quarters of their population. The monuments to this century of uprooting are the thousands of ruined cottages whose stunted walls now give shelter only to sheep.

Yet the greatest decade of Scottish emigration to the United States, so far as sheer numbers go, was the 1920's. In these ten years of postwar blight, the exodus consisted largely of unemployed Lowlanders. More than 300,000 of them went to America in that period, putting the whole movement of the eighteenth century in the shade.

In spite of the relatively small scale of the eighteenth-century migration, the influence of Scots as a national group, and even as individuals, was far greater than at any subsequent time. Filling political and administrative offices, the professions, and the ranks of commerce with energetic leaders, the Scots of the Age of Reason aroused the envy and malice of many Englishmen and Americans. In the nineteenth century, the Scots immigrants, in spite of their greater numbers, were lost in the general ferment of mass movement to the New World and the rapid growth of the United States. The names of a few important individuals alone have stood the test of time in the history books—Frances Wright, Andrew Carnegie, Alexander Graham Bell, Philip Murray.

Since the Irish were Celts like the Highlanders of Scotland, it is interesting to speculate upon the difference in their attitudes toward the British government during the American Revolution. The Irish were traditional foes of English rule, against which they had frequently rebelled. Although many of the Highlanders had fought the House of Hanover in 1715 and 1745–1746, their rebellion was not against the English as such. Many clansmen of the western Highlands in the eighteenth century looked upon the Dukes of Argyll as their principal enemies. The predatory Campbells had appropriated by force a great part of the lands bordering the older

Campbell country. The Breadalbane estates, for example, were carved out of conquered territory. It was the aggrieved or threatened victims of Campbell ambitions who hurried to raise the Stuart standard. From this point of view the '15 and the '45 were essentially Scottish civil wars. The Highlander's first loyalty was to his chief. The Campbell landowners were enemies of the House of Stuart from Cromwell's days forward, and they drew many to their side once the Hanoverians were established. When the chiefs had finally accepted the rule of the Germans, the tacksmen and crofters followed suit from their ingrained habit of obedience, as well as from self-interest. The Highland Celt's loyalty went to his social superiors, and so did the Irish Celt's. But the outcome was different. In Ireland, the Irish nation was irrevocably opposed to the English, while in Scotland, the Highlander and the Lowlander were coming to see themselves as members of a single nation, in equal partnership with England under the flag of the United Kingdom. In Scotland the first two Georges were no more and no less foreign than in England. In Ireland they represented the alien and superimposed rule of the English. The fact that Scotland had never been permanently subdued by England in war was of cardinal importance in distinguishing her attitude to England from that of the Irish.

After 1707 Scotland showed an amazing energy in exploiting the right of free trade with the English colonies. In this as in many other ways the role of the Scots in the history of the American provinces is clearly distinguishable from that of other immigrant groups. Scotland went on, after 1783, to play an equally conspicuous part in the development of a new British Empire. But the age of Scotland's bid for a lion's share of influence in the old English empire in North America drew to a conclusion amidst the ruins of that empire.

Appendix:

The Numbers of the Emigrants

AS FAR as the numbers of the emigrants from Scotland to North America in the eighteenth century are concerned, interest centers upon the period from 1763 to 1775. Only in these twelve years was there anything that might be called "mass migration." Even at this peak of Scots emigration, the numbers involved are not to be compared for a moment to those of the Scotch-Irish emigrants in the same years. The sporadic emigration from Scotland in the period 1707–1763 cannot be estimated even vaguely. But it is fairly certain that no span of twelve years witnessed such an "epidemical fury" as took place in the interval between the Seven Years' War and the outbreak of the Revolution.

Mention has been made in the body of the present work of the numbers of persons who left Scotland at various times before 1763. The whole number was probably not very great. At no time before the Peace of Paris did "depopulation" alarm the Scottish gentry as it did after that event. It is impossible to make an intelligent guess as to the actual numbers who left Scotland in the half century or more from the Union of the Parliaments to the conclusion of the French and Indian War. But the following twelve years are much more open to exploration.

Miss Margaret Adam, the only systematic student of the Scots emigration of the period, made no attempt to arrive at an independent estimate of their numbers. She cited the nearly contemporary figures given by Knox and Garnett.[1] The former gave 20,000 for the numbers emigrating

[1] Adam, "Highland Emigration of 1770," pp. 281–282.

in the period 1763–1773; the latter gave 30,000 for the period 1773–1775. Garnett's statement is, in the opinion of the present writer, a wild exaggeration. But Knox's, on the other hand, is seemingly very close to the truth. In fact, with the addition of about 5,000 for the years 1774 and 1775, Knox's figure matches exactly that arrived at independently by the present writer. There is, unfortunately, no way of knowing what method Knox used to calculate the numbers, if indeed his estimate is not simply a lucky guess.

In his study of emigration from the United Kingdom in the nineteenth century, Stanley C. Johnson mentioned an article in the *Gentleman's Magazine* for 1774 which gave figures to show that in five years (1769–1774) no less than 43,720 people sailed from five ports in the north of Ireland. This is not the place to call in question the figures given in the 1774 account, which were the result of the assumption that every departing ship carried a number of emigrants equal to her tonnage (or one emigrant per ton burthen). But Johnson went on to make the statement that "Scotland was contributing even more, at this time, to the exodus than was Ireland." He cited as his authorities the *Annual Register, The Scots Magazine,* and the *Gentleman's Magazine* of contemporary date.[2] In fact, the two London publications contain very little on the subject, and most of what they do have is relayed from Scots papers. *The Scots Magazine* is the best single periodical source, and the only one of the important sources used by Margaret Adam. As she admits, the whole number of emigrants in the period 1763–1775 mentioned or hinted at by *The Scots Magazine* is not over 10,000. The present writer's computation for this source comes to about 8,000. The figure is necessarily a little vague, as many of the magazine's general estimates have to be scrapped in case they overlap somewhere with the specific mentions of ship departures. But the actual number, as will presently appear, was perhaps three times that figure.

The very page of the *Gentleman's Magazine,* which Johnson cites for the emigration of 43,000 Scotch-Irish (a figure he suggests was exceeded by the Scots' emigration of the same years), gives a list of immigrants arriving at American ports from August to November, 1773. In this record year of Scottish migration the magazine reports that 6,222 arrived from Ireland, and 1,400 from England, Scotland, and Germany *combined.*[3] Johnson's guess cannot be taken seriously.

It has been emphasized that *The Scots Magazine,* upon which Miss Adam leaned so heavily, gave figures totaling only about 8,000. But

[2] S. C. Johnson, *History of Emigration,* pp. 1–2.
[3] *Gentleman's Magazine,* XLIV (1774), 332.

this author did not mention other important sources for the movement of people out of the country. She made no attempt to calculate numbers from the abundant records of ships' departures and arrivals to be found in the Public Record Office, colonial records and newspapers, and contemporary writings of various kinds.

In the absence of sustained and accurate official statistics, the only sound basis for an estimate of the numbers involved lies in the accounts of individual ships' sailings and arrivals. But before tackling the task of summing up the numbers mentioned in these accounts, it may be worth while to describe the limitations of the official figures.

The official returns in the Public Record Office are in two groups. These groups were compiled by different methods and they cover different short periods. The earlier group is among the State Papers for Scotland. It covers emigration from eight Highland counties only, and for a mere two years before November, 1773. The numbers of emigrants from various parishes were reported by the parish ministers to the five sheriffs who had charge of these eight counties, and by them to Thomas Miller, the Lord Justice Clerk.[4] It is said that some of the ministers feared a government plan to halt emigration, which was recognized even then by many as a useful solution to the poverty problem. The ministers' returns are therefore suspect from the outset. Further examination shows them to be very inadequate. The whole number of emigrants mentioned by the ministers in 1772–1773 was only 3,169, far short of the true total that can be arrived at by more comprehensive methods of calculation.

The second group of official statistics is to be found among the Treasury Papers. It was compiled from returns submitted by the customs officials all over Scotland. A letter from John Robinson, Secretary to the Treasury, dated December 8, 1773, required the customs officers of both England and Scotland to register all emigrants leaving Great Britain. They were to record names, ages, occupations, places of former residence, and reasons for emigrating. All names of emigrant ships and their masters were to be taken down. These records were kept from the end of 1773 until about September, 1775, when emigration practically ceased.[5] They do not represent complete information on emigration from Scotland in the period. Many ships sailed from remote Highland sea lochs without being registered, as is sufficiently clear from occasional reports in the newspapers of unregistered emigrant ships that were forced by bad weather into some port large enough to have a customhouse, where they

[4] Fagerstrom, "American Revolutionary Movement," ch. iii, *passim.*
[5] Newsome, "Records of Emigrants," pp. 39–40.

were added to the lists from which they would otherwise have been missing.

The total number of emigrants mentioned in both groups of official statistics is a little over 6,000. This was about one-third of the true figure.

The present writer arrived at his own estimate in the following manner. The figures given by the parish ministers for 1772–1773 were ignored, because they were incomplete and are not reconcilable with figures derived from other sources. Accounts of the departures of emigrant ships became common in the Scottish press in and after 1768. A truly systematic approach to the question of numbers had to be confined to the years 1768–1775.

The author compiled a table of emigrant ship departures from Scotland in these years from the following sources: *The Scots Magazine;* *Boswell's Tour; The Celtic Magazine;* the various editions of the *Virginia Gazette;* C. M. Andrews, *Guide to the Materials in the P.R.O.;* and V. R. Cameron, ed., *Emigrants from Scotland, 1774–5* (a transcript of the customhouse returns for those years). The resulting table is too long and involved for inclusion here. Every item had to be weighed and evaluated and all duplications eliminated. A similar table of arrivals in the colonies was made, relying upon the *Boston Records; North Carolina Records; The Scots Magazine; The Dalhousie Review;* Ezra Stiles's *Diary;* the various editions of the *Virginia Gazette; The Pennsylvania Magazine of History;* and a number of other less important sources. It should be noted that the *Virginia Gazette* reported arrivals in all the colonies, not just those in Virginia itself. Names of ships and masters, as well as other information, served as checks to prevent inclusion of the same figure twice in the total compiled from both arrivals and departures.

To this total was added the number of emigrants indicated in contemporary press reports, about which sufficient evidence was available to show that they were not covered by the accounts of ships' departures and arrivals. It was found that there were 9,511 departures from the Highlands in the years 1768–1775, and 6,478 from the Lowlands. The grand total of departures, therefore was found to be 15,989. It may be assumed that any overestimates by writers in the newspapers which have been included in this figure are more or less compensated by sailings which have nowhere been recorded, or of which the records have been lost. The total arrivals in the colonies, which did not overlap the departures, was 4,256. The final figure for Scots emigration to North America in the years 1768–1775 was, therefore, found to be 20,245. To this must be added an estimate of the numbers for the years 1763–1767 inclusive. Since the rate of emigration was clearly much less in those years than in the later period, one is fairly safe in saying that the total emigration in the twelve years before the Revolution broke out was less than 25,000. By nineteenth-century standards this seems a ridiculously small figure, even for emigration from a small country like Scotland. But it represented a far greater loss of people than the country had ever known before, and it was not a negligible loss in relation to the then-total population of Scotland.

It may be of interest to note, as an illustration of the inadequacy of the official figures, that the total arrived at by the above method for the area of Scotland and for the period covered by the parish ministers' returns was 6,513. For the same area and period, the State Papers give a total of only 3,169. For the period March–July (inclusive), 1774, the newspaper reports estimated the departures from Greenock at 5,000. For the same period, the customhouse returns in Treasury Papers give a total of only 274 departures from Greenock. It is impossible to say how this extraordinary discrepancy arose, especially when one considers that there was a customhouse at that port.

By far the most important receiving colony was North Carolina. From 1768 to 1775, North Carolina took in over 5,000 Scots immigrants, about a quarter of the total for the period.

Bibliography

PRIMARY SOURCES

Printed document collections:

Boston, Mass., Registry Department. *Records Relating to the Early History of Boston.* 39 vols. Boston: Rockwell and Churchill, 1876–1909.

Elgin, Scotland. *The Records of Elgin.* Comp. by William Cramond. 2 vols. University of Aberdeen, 1903–08.

Georgia. *Collections of the Georgia Historical Society.* 10 vols. Savannah: Georgia Historical Society, 1840–1952.

Georgia. *The Colonial Records of the State of Georgia.* Ed. by Allen D. Candler. 20 vols. Atlanta, 1904–16.

Glasgow, Scotland. *Extracts from the Records of the Burgh of Glasgow A.D. 1691–1717.* Glasgow: Scottish Burgh Records Society, 1908.

Glasgow, Scotland. *Extracts from the Records of the Burgh of Glasgow A.D. 1718–38.* Corporation of Glasgow, 1909.

Maryland. *Archives of Maryland.* 65 vols. Baltimore: Maryland Historical Society, 1883–1952.

New Jersey. *Documents Relating to the Colonial History of the State of New Jersey.* 1st ser. 33 vols. Newark, 1880–1928.

New York State. *Calendar of Historical Manuscripts, Relating to the War of the Revolution.* 2 vols. Albany, 1868.

North Carolina. *The Colonial Records of North Carolina.* Ed. by William L. Saunders. 10 vols. Goldsboro and Raleigh, 1886–90.

Scotland. *Publications of the Scottish History Society.* 1st ser., 61 vols.,
    Edinburgh, 1887–1911; 2nd ser., 20 vols., Edinburgh, 1911–20; 3rd ser.,
    45 vols., Edinburgh, 1921–53. (See separate titles under "Primary
    Sources, Miscellaneous.")
Stirling, Scotland. *Extracts from the Records of the Royal Burgh of Stirling,
    A.D. 1667–1752.* Ed. by R[obert] Renwick. Glasgow: Glasgow Stirling-
    shire and Sons of the Rock Society, 1889.
Virginia. *Official Letters of the Governors of the State of Virginia.* Ed. by
    Henry Read McIlwaine. 3 vols. Richmond, 1926.

Newspapers and periodicals:

Boston Evening-Post, The, 1735–75.
Gentleman's Magazine, The, London, 1731–1907.
Pennsylvania Gazette, Philadelphia, 1728–89.
Political State of Great Britain, The, London, 1710–40.
Scots Magazine, The, Edinburgh, 1739–1803.
Virginia Gazette, The, Williamsburg, 1736–80.
    Series used:
        William Parks, 1736–46.
        William Hunter, 1751–61.
        Alexander Purdie, March–June, 1766.
        Alexander Purdie and John Dixon, 1766–74.
        John Dixon and William Hunter, 1775–78.
        William Rind, 1766–73.
        Clementina Rind, 1773–74.
        John Pinkney, Sept.–Dec., 1774.
        Alexander Purdie, 1775–78.
Weekly Journal, The, New York, 1733–51.

Miscellaneous:

Anderson, James. *Observations on the Means of Exciting a Spirit of Na-
    tional Industry; Chiefly Intended to Promote the Agriculture, Com-
    merce, Manufactures, and Fisheries, of Scotland, in a Series of Letters
    to a Friend, Written in the Year One Thousand Seven Hundred and
    Seventy-five.* London: T. Cadell, and Edinburgh: C. Elliot, 1777.
Andrews, Charles M., ed. *Guide to the Materials for American History to
    1783, in the Public Record Office of Great Britain.* 2 vols. Washington,
    D.C.: Carnegie Institution of Washington, 1912–14.
*Annual Register, The, or a View of History, Politics, and Literature, for
    the Year 1773.* 5th ed. London: W. Otridge & Son, 1803.

Boswell, James. *Journal of a Tour to the Hebrides.* Ed. by Frederick A. Pottle and Charles H. Bennett. New York: Viking Press, 1936. [This version contains material not in the 1785 ed.]

Boswell, James. *The Journal of a Tour to the Hebrides with Samuel Johnson, LL.D.* In R. W. Chapman, ed., *Johnson's Journey to the Western Islands of Scotland and Boswell's Journal of a Tour to the Hebrides with Samuel Johnson.* London: Oxford University Press, 1924. [1st ed., 1785.]

Cameron, Viola Root, comp. *Emigrants from Scotland to America 1774–1775: Copied from a Loose Bundle of Treasury Papers in the Public Record Office, London, England.* London: 1930 (mimeographed).

Campbell, Patrick. *Travels in the Interior Inhabited Parts of North America in the Years 1791 and 1792.* Ed. by H. H. Langton and W. F. Ganong. (Champlain Society, *Publications,* vol. XXIII.) Toronto: Champlain Society, 1937. [1st ed., 1793.]

Carter, Robert, of Corotoman. *Letters of Robert Carter 1720–1727: The Commercial Interests of a Virginia Gentleman.* Ed. by Louis B. Wright. San Marino, Calif.: Huntington Library, 1940.

Chastellux, Marquis de. *Travels in North-America in the Years 1780, 1781, and 1782.* 2 vols. London: G. G. J. and J. Robinson, 1787.

Colden, Cadwallader. *The Letters and Papers of Cadwallader Colden.* 9 vols. (New York Historical Society, *Collections,* vols. L–LVI, LXVII–LXVIII.) New York: Printed for the Society, 1918–37.

Cresswell, Nicholas. *The Journal of Nicholas Cresswell 1774–1777.* 2nd ed. New York: Lincoln Macveagh, 1928.

Crèvecoeur, J. Hector St. John. *Letters from an American Farmer.* New York: Fox, Duffield & Company, 1904.

[Douglass, Dr. William.] *Postscript, To a Discourse Concerning the Currencies of the British Plantations in America.* Reprinted in Andrew McFarland Davis, ed., *Colonial Currency Reprints,* vol. IV. Boston: Prince Society, 1911.

Fithian, Philip. "Journal of Philip Fithian, Kept at Nomini Hall, Virginia, 1773–1774," ed. by John Rogers Williams, *American Historical Review,* V (1900), 290–319.

[Martyn, Benjamin.] *An Account Showing the Progress of the Colony of Georgia.* Reprinted in Georgia Historical Society, *Collections,* vol. II (1842). [1st ed., London, 1741; Annapolis, Md., 1742.]

Forbes, Rev. Robert. *The Lyon in Mourning: Or a Collection of Speeches Letters Journals etc. Relative to the Affairs of Prince Charles Edward Stuart.* Ed. by Henry Paton. 3 vols. (Scottish History Society, *Publications,* vols. XX–XXII.) Edinburgh: Printed at the University Press by T. and A. Constable for the Scottish History Society, 1895–96.

Forbes, Sir William, of Pitsligo. *Memoirs of a Banking-House.* Ed. by Robert Chambers. London and Edinburgh: William and Robert Chambers, 1860.

Fries, Adelaide L., ed. *Records of the Moravians in North Carolina.* 6 vols. Raleigh, N.C.: Edwards and Broughton Company, State Printers, 1922–43.

Gilpin, William. *Observations, Relative Chiefly to Picturesque Beauty, Made in the Year 1776, on Several Parts of Great Britain; Particularly the High-Lands of Scotland.* 2nd ed. 2 vols. London: R. Blamire, 1792.

[Gordon, Lord Adam.] "Journal of an Officer's Travels in America and the West Indies 1764–1765." In Newton D. Mereness, ed., *Travels in the American Colonies.* New York: Macmillan, 1916.

Gottesman, Mrs. Rita Susswein, comp. *The Arts and Crafts in New York, 1726–1776: Advertisements and News Items from New York City Newspapers.* (New York Historical Society, *Collections,* vol. LXIX.) New York: Printed for the Society, 1938.

Grant, Mrs. [Anne McVicar], of Laggan. *Memoir and Correspondence of Mrs. Grant of Laggan.* Ed. by J. P. Grant. 3 vols. London: Longman, Brown, Green, and Longmans, 1844.

Gregory, William. "William Gregory's Journal," *William and Mary College Quarterly Historical Magazine,* 1st ser., XIII (1904–05), 224–229.

Hamilton, Henry, ed. *Selections from the Monymusk Papers* (1713–1755). (Scottish History Society, *Publications,* 3rd ser., vol. XXXIX.) Edinburgh: Printed at the University Press by T. and A. Constable Ltd. for the Scottish History Society, 1945.

Harrower, John. "Diary of John Harrower, 1773–1776," *American Historical Review,* VI (1901), 65–107.

Hartwell, Henry, James Blair, and Edward Chilton. *The Present State of Virginia, and the College.* Ed. by Hunter Dickinson Farish. Williamsburg, Va.: Colonial Williamsburg, Incorporated, 1940. [Written in 1697; 1st ed., London, 1727.]

[Hepburn, Rev. Thomas.] *A Letter to a Gentleman from His Friend in Orkney, (Written in 1757) Containing the True Causes of the Poverty of That Country.* Edinburgh: William Brown, 1885. [1st ed., London, 1760.]

Honyman, Robert. *Colonial Panorama 1775: Dr. Robert Honyman's Journal for March and April.* Ed. by Philip Padelford. San Marino, Calif.: Huntington Library, 1939.

Jefferson, Thomas. *The Life and Selected Writings of Thomas Jefferson.* Ed. by Adrienne Koch and William Peden. New York: Random House, 1944.

Johnson, Samuel. *Journey to the Western Islands of Scotland.* In R. W. Chapman, ed. *Johnson's Journey to the Western Islands of Scotland and Boswell's Journal of a Tour to the Hebrides with Samuel Johnson.* London: Oxford University Press, 1924. [1st ed., London, 1775.]

Johnson, Sir William. *Calendar of the Sir William Johnson Manuscripts in the New York State Library.* Comp. by Richard E. Day. Albany: University of the State of New York, 1909.

Johnson, Sir William. *The Papers of Sir William Johnson.* 10 vols. Albany: University of the State of New York, 1933.

"Journal of a French Traveller in the Colonies, 1765," *American Historical Review,* XXVI (1921), 726–747.

"A Journal of the Managers of the Scotch American Company of Farmers." In Vermont Historical Society, *Proceedings,* 1926–28, pp. 181–203.

Law, John. *Money and Trade Considered: With a Proposal for Supplying the Nation with Money.* Glasgow: R. and A. Foulis, 1760. [First ed., 1705.]

McArthur, Margaret M., ed. *Survey of Lochtayside 1769.* (Scottish History Society, *Publications,* 3rd ser., vol. XXVII.) Edinburgh: Printed at the University Press by T. and A. Constable for the Scottish History Society, 1936.

[Martyn, Benjamin.] *An Account Showing the Progress of the Colony of Georgia.* Reprinted in Georgia Historical Society, *Collections,* vol. II (1842). [1st ed., 1741.]

Mason, Frances Norton, ed. *John Norton & Sons Merchants of London and Virginia: Being the Papers from Their Counting House for the Years 1750 to 1795.* Richmond, Va.: Dietz Press, 1937.

Millar, A. H., ed. *A Selection of Scottish Forfeited Estates Papers 1715; 1745.* (Scottish History Society, *Publications,* vol. LVII.) Edinburgh: Printed at the University Press by T. and A. Constable for the Scottish History Society, 1909.

Murray, Hon. Charles Augustus. *Travels in North America during the Years 1834, 1835, & 1836.* 2 vols. London: Richard Bentley, 1839.

Murray, Hugh. *Historical Account of Discoveries and Travels in North America; Including the United States, Canada, the Shores of the Polar Sea, and the Voyages in Search of a North-west Passage; with Observations on Emigration.* 2 vols. London: Longman, Rees, Orme, Brown, & Green, 1829.

Naismith, John. *Thoughts on Various Objects of Industry Pursued in Scotland, with a View to Enquire by What Means the Labour of the People May Be Directed to Promote the Public Prosperity.* Edinburgh: Printed for the author, 1790.

Newsome, A. R. "Records of Emigrants from England and Scotland to North Carolina, 1774–1775," *North Carolina Historical Review*, XI (1934), 39–54, 129–143.

Pennant, Thomas. *A Tour in Scotland, and Voyage to the Hebrides; MDCCLXXII.* 2 vols. Chester: John Monk, 1774–76.

Pococke, Richard, Bishop of Meath. *Tours in Scotland, 1747, 1750, 1760.* Ed. by Daniel William Kemp. (Scottish History Society, *Publications*, vol. I.) Edinburgh: Printed for the Scottish History Society, 1887.

[Schaw, Janet.] *Journal of a Lady of Quality; Being the Narrative of a Journey from Scotland to the West Indies, North Carolina, and Portugal, in the Years 1774 and 1776.* Ed. by Evangeline Walker Andrews and Charles McLean Andrews. New Haven: Yale University Press, 1921.

"Scotus Americanus." *Informations Concerning the Province of North Carolina, Addressed to Emigrants from the Highlands and Western Isles of Scotland.* Printed for James Knox, Glasgow, and Charles Elliott, Edinburgh, 1773. Reprinted in William K. Boyd, ed., *Some Eighteenth Century Tracts Concerning North Carolina.* Raleigh, N.C.: Edwards & Broughton Company, 1927. Pp. 427–451.

Sinclair, Sir John. *The Statistical Account of Scotland Drawn Up from the Communications of the Ministers of the Different Parishes.* 21 vols. Edinburgh: William Creech, 1791–99.

Smith, William. *The History of the Late Province of New York, from Its Discovery, to the Appointment of Governor Colden, in 1762.* 2 vols. New York: New York Historical Society, 1830.

Stiles, Ezra. *Extracts from the Itineraries and Other Miscellanies of Ezra Stiles, D.D., LL.D. 1755–1794 with a Selection from His Correspondence.* Ed. by Franklin Bowditch Dexter. New Haven: Yale University Press, 1916.

Stiles, Ezra. *The Literary Diary of Ezra Stiles, D.D., LL.D. President of Yale College.* Ed. by Franklin Bowditch Dexter. 3 vols. New York: Charles Scribner's Sons, 1901.

Tailfer, Patrick, Hugh Anderson, and David Douglas. *A True and Historical Narrative of the Colony of Georgia.* Charleston, S.C.: Printed for the authors by P. Timothy, 1741. Reprinted in Georgia Historical Society, *Collections*, vol. II (1842).

Tucker, Josiah. *The True Interest of Great-Britain Set Forth in Regard to the Colonies; and the Only Means of Living in Peace and Harmony with Them.* In Robert Livingston Schuyler, ed., *Josiah Tucker: A Selection from His Economic and Political Writings.* New York: Columbia University Press, 1931. [1st ed., London, 1774.]

"United Empire Loyalists: Enquiry into the Losses and Services in Consequence of Their Loyalty: Evidence in the Canadian Claims." In Ontario Bureau of Archives, *Second Report, 1904.* Toronto: L. K. Cameron, 1905.

Watts, John. *Letter Book of John Watts Merchant and Councillor of New York, January 1, 1762–December 22, 1765.* (New York Historical Society, *Collections,* vol. LXI.) New York: Printed for the Society, 1928.

Webster, Alexander. *An Account of the Number of People in Scotland in the Year One Thousand Seven Hundred and Fifty Five.* In James Gray Kyd, ed., *Scottish Population Statistics Including Webster's Analysis of Population 1755.* (Scottish History Society, *Publications,* 3rd ser., vol. XLIV, wrongly printed "XLIII.") Edinburgh: Printed by T. and A. Constable Ltd. for the Scottish History Society, 1952.

Wesley, John. *The Journal of the Rev. John Wesley A.M. Sometime Fellow of Lincoln College, Oxford.* Ed. by Nehemiah Curnock. 8 vols. London: Charles H. Kelly, 1909–16.

Whitelaw, James. "Journal of General James Whitelaw, Surveyor-General of Vermont." In Vermont Historical Society, *Proceedings,* 1905–06, pp. 119–157.

Willard, Margaret Wheeler, ed. *Letters on the American Revolution 1774– 1776.* Boston: Houghton Mifflin Company, 1925.

SECONDARY MATERIALS

Adam, Margaret I. "The Causes of the Highland Emigrations of 1783– 1803," *Scottish Historical Review,* XVII (1919–20), 73–89.

Adam, Margaret I. "Eighteenth Century Highland Landlords and the Poverty Problem," *Scottish Historical Review,* XIX (1921–22), 1–20, 161–179.

Adam, Margaret I. "The Highland Emigration of 1770," *Scottish Historical Review,* XVI (1918–19), 280–293.

Alden, John Richard. *John Stuart and the Southern Colonial Frontier: A Study of Indian Relations, War, Trade, and Land Problems in the Southern Wilderness, 1754–1775.* Ann Arbor: University of Michigan Press, 1944.

Alexander, Samuel Davies. *Princeton College during the Eighteenth Century.* New York: Anson D. F. Randolph & Company, 1872.

[Alexander, William.] *Notes and Sketches Illustrative of Northern Rural Life in the Eighteenth Century.* Edinburgh: David Douglas, 1877.

Alvord, Clarence Walworth. *The Mississippi Valley in British Politics: A Study of the Trade, Land Speculation, and Experiments in Imperialism Culminating in the American Revolution.* 2 vols. Cleveland: Arthur H. Clark Company, 1917.

American Council of Learned Societies. "Report of Committee on Linguistic and National Stocks in the Population of the United States." In American Historical Association, *Annual Report for the Year 1931,* I, 107–125.

Bailey, Kenneth P. *The Ohio Company of Virginia and the Westward Movement 1748–1792: A Chapter in the History of the Colonial Frontier.* Glendale, Calif.: Arthur H. Clark Company, 1939.

Ballagh, James Curtis. *White Servitude in the Colony of Virginia: A Study of the System of Indentured Labor in the American Colonies.* (Johns Hopkins University, *Studies in Historical and Political Science,* 13th ser., vols. VI–VII, June–July, 1895.) Baltimore: Johns Hopkins Press, 1895.

Banks, Charles Edward. "Scotch Prisoners Deported to New England by Cromwell, 1651–2." In Massachusetts Historical Society, *Proceedings,* LXI (1928), 4–29.

Barker, Charles Albro. *The Background of the Revolution in Maryland.* (*Yale Historical Publications,* vol. XXXVIII.) New Haven: Yale University Press, 1940.

Barker, Howard F. "National Stocks in the Population of the United States as Indicated by Surnames in the Census of 1790." In American Historical Association, *Annual Report for the Year 1931,* I, 126–359.

Barnwell, Robert W., Jr. "The Migration of Loyalists from South Carolina." In South Carolina Historical Association, *Proceedings,* 1937, pp. 34–42.

Bassett, John Spencer. "The Regulators of North Carolina (1765–1771)." In American Historical Association, *Annual Report for the Year 1894,* pp. 141–212.

Bassett, John Spencer. "The Relation between the Virginia Planter and the London Merchant." In American Historical Association, *Annual Report for the Year 1901,* I, 553–575.

Beard, Charles Austin. *Economic Origins of Jeffersonian Democracy.* New York: The Macmillan Company, 1915.

Berkley, Henry J. "Extinct River Towns of the Chesapeake Bay Region," *Maryland Historical Magazine,* XIX (1924), 125–134.

Berkley, Henry J. "The Port of Dumfries, Prince William Co., Va.," *William and Mary College Quarterly Historical Magazine,* 2nd ser., IV (1924), 99–116.

Bidwell, Robert Leland. "The Morris Reading-Houses: A Study in Dissent." Master's thesis (unpublished), William and Mary College, 1948.

Black, George Fraser. *Scotland's Mark on America.* New York: Published by the Scottish Section of "America's Making," 1921.

Bolton, Ethel Stanwood. "Immigrants to New England, 1700–1775." In Essex Institute, *Historical Collections,* LXIII (1927), 177–192, 269–

284, 365–380; LXIV (1928), 25–32, 257–272; LXV (1929), 57–72, 113–128, 531–546; LXVI (1930), 411–426, 521–536; LXVII (1931), 89–112, 201–224, 305–328.

Brebner, John Bartlet. *The Neutral Yankees of Nova Scotia: A Marginal Colony during the Revolutionary Years.* New York: Columbia University Press, 1937.

Buck, Solon J., and Elizabeth Hawthorn Buck. *The Planting of Civilization in Western Pennsylvania.* Pittsburgh: University of Pittsburgh Press, 1939.

Buell, Augustus C. *Sir William Johnson.* New York: D. Appleton and Company, 1903.

Burton, John Hill. *The History of Scotland from Agricola's Invasion to the Extinction of the Last Jacobite Insurrection.* 2nd ed. 8 vols. Edinburgh: William Blackwood and Sons, 1905.

Butterfield, L. H., ed. *John Witherspoon Comes to America: A Documentary Account Based Largely on New Materials.* Princeton: Princeton University Library, 1953.

Canby, Courtlandt. "Robert Munford's *The Patriots*," *William and Mary Quarterly*, 3rd ser., VI (1949), 437–447.

Chalmers, George. *An Estimate of the Comparative Strength of Great-Britain, during the Present and Four Preceding Reigns,* "A New Edition." London: Printed for John Stockdale, 1794.

Chamberlain, George W. "The New York Scotch Colony," *Magazine of History*, IV (1906), 43–46.

Coakley, Robert Walter. "The Two James Hunters of Fredericksburg: Patriots among the Virginia Scotch Merchants," *Virginia Magazine of History and Biography*, LVI (1948), 3–21.

Coakley, Robert Walter. "Virginia Commerce during the American Revolution." Doctoral dissertation (unpublished), University of Virginia, 1949.

Collins, Varnum Lansing. *President Witherspoon: A Biography.* 2 vols. Princeton: Princeton University Press, 1925.

Comrie, John D. *History of Scottish Medicine to 1860.* London: Published for Wellcome Historical Medical Museum, by Bailliere, Tindall & Cox, 1927.

Connor, R. D. W. *Race Elements in the White Population of North Carolina.* (North Carolina State Normal & Industrial College, *Historical Publications*, no. 1.) Raleigh, N.C.: Published by the College, 1920.

Coulter, Calvin B., Jr. "The Import Trade of Colonial Virginia," *William and Mary Quarterly*, 3rd ser., II (1945), 296–314.

Crittenden, Charles Christopher. *The Commerce of North Carolina 1763–*

1789. (*Yale Historical Publications,* vol. XXIX.) New Haven: Yale University Press, 1936.

Cruikshank, E. A. "A Memoir of Lieutenant-Colonel John Macdonell, of Glengarry House, the First Speaker of the Legislative Assembly of Upper Canada." In Ontario Historical Society, *Papers and Records,* XXII (1925), 20–59.

Cunningham, A. "The Revolution Government in the Highlands," *Scottish Historical Review,* XVI (1918–19), 29–51.

Cunningham, William. "Differences of Economic Development in England and Scotland," *Scottish Historical Review,* XIII (1915–16). 168–188.

Curtis, Edward E. *The Organization of the British Army in the American Revolution.* New Haven: Yale University Press, 1926.

Darroch, John. "The Scottish Highlanders Going to Carolina," *Celtic Magazine,* I (1875–76), 142–147.

Dicey, Albert V., and Robert S. Rait. *Thoughts on the Union between England and Scotland.* London: Macmillan and Co., Limited, 1920.

Dickie, John M. "The Economic Position of Scotland in 1760," *Scottish Historical Review,* XVIII (1920–21), 14–31.

Easterby, J. H. *History of the St. Andrew's Society of Charleston, South Carolina 1729–1929.* Charleston, S.C.: Published by the Society, 1929.

Eaton, Cyrus. *Annals of the Town of Warren: With the Early History of St. George's, Broad Bay, and the Neighboring Settlements on the Waldo Patent.* Hallowell, Me.: Masters, Smith & Co., 1851.

Ettinger, Amos Aschbach. *James Edward Oglethorpe: Imperial Idealist.* Oxford, England: Clarendon Press, 1936.

Fagerstrom, Dalphy A. "The American Revolutionary Movement in Scottish Opinion, 1763–1783." Doctoral dissertation (unpublished), University of Edinburgh, 1951.

Finley, John H. *The Coming of the Scot.* New York: Charles Scribner's Sons, 1940.

Ford, Henry Jones. *The Scotch-Irish in America.* Princeton: Princeton University Press, 1915.

Fothergill, Gerald. "Emigrants from England," *New England Historical and Genealogical Register,* LXII (1908), 242–253, 320–332; LXIII (1909), 16–31, 134–146, 234–244, 342–355; LXIV (1910), 18–25, 106–115, 214–227, 314–326; LXV (1911), 20–35, 116–132, 232–251.

Fraser-Mackintosh, Charles. "The Depopulation of Aberarder in Badenoch, 1770," *Celtic Magazine,* II (1877), 418–426.

Ganter, Herbert L. "William Small, Jefferson's Beloved Teacher," *William and Mary Quarterly,* 3rd ser., IV (1947), 505–507.

Geiser, Karl Frederick. *Redemptioners and Indentured Servants in the Colony and Commonwealth of Pennsylvania.* (Supplement to the *Yale*

Review, vol. X, Aug. 1901.) New Haven: Tuttle, Morehouse & Taylor Co., 1901.

George, John A. "Virginia Loyalists, 1775–1783." In Richmond College, *Historical Papers,* I (1916), 173–221.

Goodville, Thomas. "Life of General James Whitelaw." In Vermont Historical Society, *Proceedings,* 1905–06, pp. 103–118.

Goodwin, Edward Lewis. *The Colonial Church in Virginia.* Milwaukee: Morehouse Publishing Co., 1927.

Grafton, C. W. "A Sketch of the Old Scotch Settlement at Union Church," Mississippi Historical Society, *Publications,* IX (1906), 263–271.

Graham, Henry Grey. *The Social Life of Scotland in the Eighteenth Century.* 4th ed. London: A. & C. Black, 1937.

Graham, William. *The One Pound Note in the History of Banking in Great Britain.* 2nd ed. Edinburgh: James Thin, 1911.

Grant, Isabel Frances. *Every-Day Life on an Old Highland Farm, 1769–1782.* London: Longmans, Green and Co., 1924.

Gray, Lewis Cecil. *History of Agriculture in the Southern United States to 1860.* 2 vols. New York: Peter Smith, 1941.

Gray, Lewis Cecil. "The Market Surplus Problems of Colonial Tobacco," *William and Mary College Quarterly Historical Magazine,* 2nd ser. VII (1927), 231–245; VIII (1928), 1–16.

Hansen, Marcus Lee. "The Population of the American Outlying Regions in 1790." In American Historical Association, *Annual Report for the Year 1931,* I, 398–408.

Harrell, Isaac Samuel. *Loyalism in Virginia: Chapters in the Economic History of the Revolution.* Durham, N.C.: Duke University Press, 1926.

Harrell, Isaac Samuel. "North Carolina Loyalists," *North Carolina Historical Review,* III (1926), 575–590.

Harrell, Isaac Samuel. "Some Neglected Phases of the Revolution in Virginia," *William and Mary College Quarterly Historical Magazine,* 2nd ser., V (1925), 159–170.

Harrington, Virginia Draper. *The New York Merchant on the Eve of the Revolution.* New York: Columbia University Press, 1935.

Harrison, Fairfax. "The Equine F F Vs: A Study of the Evidence for the English Horses Imported into Virginia before the Revolution," *Virginia Magazine of History and Biography,* XXXV (1927), 329–370.

Harrison, Fairfax. "Western Explorations in Virginia between Lederer and Spotswood," *Virginia Magazine of History and Biography,* XXX (1922), 323–340.

Harvey, D. C. "Early Settlement and Social Conditions in Prince Edward Island," *Dalhousie Review,* XI (1931–32), 448–461.

Haywood, John. *The Civil and Political History of the State of Tennessee, from Its Earliest Settlement up to the Year 1796.* Knoxville, Tenn.: Printed for the author by Heiskell & Brown, 1823.

Heaton, Herbert. "The Industrial Immigrant in the United States, 1783–1812." In American Philosophical Society, *Proceedings,* XCV (1951), 519–527.

Herrick, Cheesman A. *White Servitude in Pennsylvania: Indentured and Redemption Labor in Colony and Commonwealth.* Philadelphia: John Joseph McVey, 1926.

Hill, William H. *Old Fort Edward Before 1800: An Account of the Historic Ground Now Occupied by the Village of Fort Edward, New York.* Fort Edward, N.Y.: Privately printed, 1929.

Honeyman, A. Van Doren. "The Early Scotch Element of Somerset, Middlesex and Monmouth Counties," *Somerset County Historical Quarterly,* VI (1917), 1–23.

Hume, Edgar Erskine. "A Colonial Scottish Jacobite Family: Establishment in Virginia of a Branch of the Humes of Wedderburn," *Virginia Magazine of History and Biography,* XXXVIII (1930), 1–37, 97–124, 195–234, 293–346.

Insh, George Pratt. *The Company of Scotland Trading to Africa and the Indies.* London: Charles Scribner's Sons, 1932.

Insh, George Pratt. *The Darien Scheme.* London: Published for the Historical Association by Staples Press Limited, 1947.

Insh, George Pratt. *Scottish Colonial Schemes 1620–1686.* Glasgow: Maclehose, Jackson & Co., publishers to the University, 1922.

Insh, George Pratt. *The Scottish Jacobite Movement: A Study in Economic and Social Forces.* Edinburgh: Moray Press, 1952.

Johnson, Cecil. *British West Florida, 1763–1783.* (*Yale Historical Publications,* vol. XLII.) New Haven: Yale University Press, 1943.

Johnson, Stanley C. *A History of Emigration from the United Kingdom to North America, 1763–1912.* London: George Routledge & Sons, Limited, 1913.

Keith, Theodora. *Commercial Relations of England and Scotland, 1603–1707.* (*Girton College Studies,* no. 1.) Cambridge, England: University Press, 1910.

Kemmerer, Donald L. *Path to Freedom: The Struggle for Self-Government in Colonial New Jersey 1703–1776.* Princeton: Princeton University Press, 1940.

Kerr, Andrew William. *History of Banking in Scotland.* 2nd ed. London: Adam and Charles Black, 1902.

"Kidnapping System of the Last Century," *Chambers's Edinburgh Journal,* VIII (1839), 182.

King, Charles Clifford. "The Fate of the New York and New England Loyalists during the Post-War Period 1783–1793." Master's thesis (unpublished), University of Illinois, 1940.

Lang, Andrew. *A History of Scotland from the Roman Occupation.* 4 vols. Edinburgh: William Blackwood and Sons, 1900–07.

Levett, Ella Pettit. "Loyalism in Charleston, 1761–1784." In South Carolina Historical Association, *Proceedings,* 1936, pp. 3–17.

Livingston, Edwin Brockholst. *The Livingstons of Livingston Manor.* New York: Knickerbocker Press, 1910 (275 copies only printed by private subscription).

MacBean, William M. *Biographical Register of the St. Andrew's Society of the State of New York.* 2 vols. New York: Printed for the Society, 1922–25.

McCormac, Eugene Irving. *White Servitude in Maryland 1634–1820.* (Johns Hopkins University, *Studies in Historical and Political Science,* ser. XXII, nos. 3–4.) Baltimore: Johns Hopkins Press, 1904.

McCrady, Edward. *The History of South Carolina under the Proprietary Government, 1670–1719.* New York: Macmillan Company, 1897.

McCrady, Edward. *The History of South Carolina under the Royal Government, 1719–1776.* New York: Macmillan Company, 1899.

Macdonald, Lachlan, of Skaebost. "The Past and Present Position of the Skye Crofters," *Celtic Magazine,* XI (1886), 323–330.

MacDougall, D[onald], ed. *Scots and Scots' Descendants in America.* New York: Caledonian Publishing Company, 1917.

Mackenzie, Alexander. "First Highland Emigration to Nova Scotia: Arrival of the Ship 'Hector,' " *Celtic Magazine,* VIII (1883), 140–144.

Mackenzie, Alexander. *The History of the Highland Clearances.* 2nd ed. Glasgow: P. J. O'Callaghan, 1914.

McKerral, A. "The Tacksman and His Holding in the South-West Highlands," *Scottish Historical Review,* XXVI (1947), 10–25.

Mackinnon, James. *The Social and Industrial History of Scotland from the Union to the Present Time.* London: Longmans, Green and Co., 1921.

MacLean, J. P. *An Historical Account of the Settlements of Scotch Highlanders in America Prior to the Peace of 1783.* Cleveland: Helman-Taylor Company, 1900.

MacLeod, Roderick C. "The Western Highlands in the Eighteenth Century," *Scottish Historical Review,* XIX (1921–22), 33–48.

Mark, Irving. *Agrarian Conflicts in Colonial New York, 1711–1775.* New York: Columbia University Press, 1940.

Mason, John. "Conditions in the Highlands after the 'Forty-Five,' " *Scottish Historical Review,* XXVI (1947), 134–146.

Morriss, Margaret Shove. *Colonial Trade of Maryland 1689–1715.* Baltimore: Bryn Mawr College, 1914.

Mowat, Charles Loch. *East Florida as a British Province 1763–1784.* (University of California, *Publications in History,* vol. XXXII.) Berkeley and Los Angeles: University of California Press, 1943.

Namier, Lewis B. *England in the Age of the American Revolution.* London: Macmillan and Co., Ltd., 1930.

Nettels, Curtis P. *The Roots of American Civilization: A History of American Colonial Life.* New York: F. S. Crofts & Co., 1938.

O'Callaghan, E. B. "Early Highland Immigration to New York," *Historical Magazine,* 1st ser., V (1861), 301–304.

Pell, John. "Philip Skene of Skenesborough." In New York State Historical Association, *Quarterly Journal,* IX (1928), 27–44.

Pitman, Frank Wesley. *The Development of the British West Indies 1700–1763.* New Haven: Yale University Press, 1917.

Porter, Kenneth Wiggins. *The Jacksons and the Lees: Two Generations of Massachusetts Merchants 1765–1844.* 2 vols. (*Harvard Studies in Business History,* vol. 3.) Cambridge, Mass.: Harvard University Press, 1937.

Pryde, George S. "The Scots in East New Jersey." In New Jersey Historical Society, *Proceedings,* n.s., XV (1930), 1–39.

Pryde, George S. "Scottish Colonization in the Province of New York." In New York State Historical Association, *Proceedings,* XXXIII (1935) (*New York History,* XVI), 138–157.

Pryde, George S. *The Treaty of Union of Scotland and England: 1707.* London: Thomas Nelson and Sons Ltd., 1950.

Rait, Robert S. *The History of the Union Bank of Scotland.* Glasgow: John Smith & Son Ltd., 1930.

Rattray, W. J. *The Scot in British North America.* 4 vols. Toronto: Maclean and Company, [1880–83].

Rightmyer, Nelson Waite. "The Character of the Anglican Clergy of Colonial Maryland," *Maryland Historical Magazine,* XLIV (1949), 229–250.

Risch, Erna. "Encouragement of Immigration as Revealed in Colonial Legislation," *Virginia Magazine of History and Biography,* XLV (1937), 1–10.

Robertson, David. *The Princes Street Proprietors and Other Chapters in the History of the Royal Burgh of Edinburgh.* Edinburgh: Oliver and Boyd, 1935.

Robertson, R. S. "The Scot in America," *Magazine of American History,* XXVII (1892), 42–49.

Ross, Peter. *The Scot in America.* New York: Raeburn Book Company, 1896.

Russell, Nelson Vance. *The British Regime in Michigan and the Old Northwest 1760–1796.* Northfield, Minn.: Published by Carleton College, 1939.

Sabine, Lorenzo. *Biographical Sketches of Loyalists of the American Revolution.* 2 vols. Boston: Little, Brown and Company, 1864.

Sawtelle, William Otis. "Acadia: The Pre-Loyalist Migration and the Philadelphia Plantation," *Pennsylvania Magazine of History and Biography,* LI (1927), 244–285.

Schlesinger, Arthur Meier. *The Colonial Merchants and the American Revolution 1763–1776.* New York: Facsimile Library, Inc., 1939.

"Scotch Prisoners Sent to Massachusetts in 1652, by Order of the English Government," *New England Historical & Genealogical Register,* I (1847), 377–380.

Scott, Hew. *Fasti Ecclesiae Scoticanae: The Succession of Ministers in the Church of Scotland from the Reformation.* 7 vols. Edinburgh: Oliver and Boyd, 1928.

Scott, Sir Walter. *Manners, Customs, and History of the Highlanders of Scotland.* Glasgow: Thomas D. Morison, 1893.

Sellers, Leila. *Charleston Business on the Eve of the American Revolution.* Chapel Hill: University of North Carolina Press, 1934.

Seton, Sir Bruce Gordon, and Jean Gordon Arnot, eds. *The Prisoners of the '45 Edited from the State Papers.* 3 vols. (Scottish History Society, *Publications,* 3rd ser., vols. XIII–XV.) Edinburgh: Printed at the University Press by T. and A. Constable Ltd. for the Scottish History Society, 1928.

Shipton, Clifford K. "Immigration to New England, 1680–1740," *Journal of Political Economy,* XLIV (1936), 225–239.

Siebert, Wilbur H. *The Loyalists of Pennsylvania.* (Ohio State University, *Bulletin,* vol. XXIV, no. 23.) Columbus: Published by the University, 1920.

Smith, Abbot Emerson. *Colonists in Bondage: White Servitude and Convict Labor in America 1607–1776.* Chapel Hill: Published for the Institute of Early American History and Culture at Williamsburg, Virginia, by the University of North Carolina Press, 1947.

Stevens, Wayne Edson. *The Northwest Fur Trade, 1763–1800.* (University of Illinois, *Studies in the Social Sciences,* vol. XIV, no. 3.) Urbana: University of Illinois, 1928.

Van Tyne, Claude H. *The War of Independence: American Phase.* Cambridge, Mass.: Houghton Mifflin Company, Riverside Press, 1929.

Wallace, David Duncan. *The History of South Carolina.* 4 vols. New York: The American Historical Society, Inc., 1934.

Wertenbaker, Thomas Jefferson. *Early Scotch Contributions to the United States: Being a Lecture Delivered within the University of Glasgow on 8th March, 1945.* Glasgow: Jackson, Son & Company, Publishers to the University, 1945.

Wertenbaker, Thomas Jefferson. *Norfolk: Historic Southern Port.* Durham, N.C.: Duke University Press, 1931.

Wheeler, John H. *Historical Sketches of North Carolina, from 1584 to 1851.* Philadelphia: Lippincott, Grambo and Co., 1851.

Whitehead, William A. *East Jersey under the Proprietary Governments: A Narrative of Events Connected with the Settlement and Progress of the Province, until the Surrender of the Government to the Crown in 1702.* (New Jersey Historical Society, *Collections*, vol. I.) New York: New Jersey Historical Society, 1846.

Wittke, Carl. *We Who Built America: The Saga of the Immigrant.* New York: Prentice-Hall, Inc., 1948.

Wright, Robert. *A Memoir of General James Oglethorpe, One of the Earliest Reformers of Prison Discipline in England, and the Founder of Georgia, in America.* London: Chapman and Hall, 1867.

Index

Martin, Josiah, governor of N.C., 95, 154-159

Martinique, French West Indies, 45

Martyn, Benjamin, secretary to the Ga. trustees, 136

Maryburgh, Scotland, 87, 93

Maryland, 44, 45, 92, 102, 109, 116, 121, 123
  Scottish loyalism in, 174-175

Massachusetts, 10

Mecklenburg County, N.C., 95

Mercer, Hugh, 177

Middleton, Peter, 133

Miller, Thomas, Lord Justice Clerk, 65, 97, 99, 187

Mississippi, state of, 106, 109

Mississippi Company, 167

Mohawk Valley, N.Y. Colony, 81, 83, 106

Montgomery, Sir James, 77

Montgomery Act (1770), 54-55

Montgomery's Highlanders, 48, 49

Monymusk, Aberdeenshire, Scotland, 57

Moore, Colonel James, 159

Moore's Creek Bridge, battle of, 76, 150, 154, 157-159, 160

Morris, Lewis, 143

Moultrie, John, 142

Mull (Inner Hebrides), 36

Nansemond County, Va., 122, 172

Navigation Laws, English, 9, 12, 14-15, 142, 143
  cease to apply to Scotland after 1707, 16

Neilson, George, 131

New Brunswick, 177

New Edinburgh (Darien Colony), 13

New England, 20
  Scottish settlers in, 87
  Scottish-American patriots in, 178
  see also names of individual colonies

New Hampshire, 18

New Jersey, 142-146

New Jersey, East, 11, 94

New Jersey, West, 14

New York City, 28, 102, 132
  Scottish merchants in, 125

New York Colony, 13, 37, 47-49, 77-85, 89, 92, 93, 152
  Scottish loyalists in, 175-176
  Scottish-American patriots in, 178-179

Newbern, N.C., 146, 170

Nicholas, Robert Carter, treasurer of Va., quoted, 167-168

Norfolk, Va., 32, 121, 141, 169

North Carolina, 19-20, 23, 41, 60, 89, 92, 94, 96, 106, 108, 121, 122, 150-151, 152, 172
  Scottish loyalists in, 154-161
  number of Scots emigrating to, 1768-75, 189
  see also Cape Fear Valley, N.C., and Cumberland County, N.C.

Northern Isles, 2, 66-68

Northumberland County, Va., 165

Nottingham, Md., 123

Nova Scotia, 11, 35, 86-88, 92, 97, 157, 177

Oglethorpe, Edward, governor of Ga., 115, 134-139

Ohio Company, 167

Olyphant, David, 133-134

Ontario, 177

Orkney Islands, 66-67

Pagan, John, 87-88

Pagan, Robert, 177

Pagan, William, 125

Paisley, Scotland, 28, 31

Parker, Richard, 165, 167

Parliament, Scots, 5, 15

Patillo, Henry, 20

Pennsylvania, 14, 20, 25, 30, 33
  Scottish-American patriots in, 179

Perth Amboy, N.J., 11, 143

Perthshire, Scotland, 64, 77

Petersburg, Va., 119, 120, 172

Philadelphia, Penna., 30, 70, 108, 179

"Philadelphia Plantation," N.S., 86-88

Pictou, N.S., 86-88, 100-101, 106, 108

Piscattaway, Md., 123

Pollock, Thomas, 147

Port Tobacco, Md., 123

Portree, Scotland, 41, 50, 87, 102

Portsmouth, Va., 169

Presbyterianism:
  in America, 21, 180
  in the Scottish Highlands, 34

Presbyterians, Scottish, in the American colonies, 120-121

Prince Edward (St. John's) Island, 49, 50, 77, 106, 177

Privy Council, British, discourages emigration, 97

Privy Council, Scots, 5, 9, 12, 90
Proclamation of 1763, 47, 48, 74
Pryde, George S., on the term "Scotch-Irish," 18

Quebec Province, 126
Highland veterans settle in, 49

Raasey (Inner Hebrides), 69-70
Rand, William, 160
Regulation, War of the, 20, 150, 155
Rents, rising, as a cause of emigration, 23, 63
Revolution, American, *see* American Revolution
Revolutions of 1688–89, 15
Richmond, Va., 119, 121
Richmond County, Va., 165
Ritchie, Archibald, 167
Ritchie, James, & Co., merchants, 124
Robinson, John, Secretary to the Treasury, 98, 187
Robinson, Patrick, 14
Roman Catholic Church, in the Highlands, 34
Ross, John, 88, 101
Ross-shire, Scotland, 50, 62, 83, 88
Royal Highland Emigrants, 49
"Runrig" (Scottish open field system), 52-53
Ryegate, N.Y. (later in Vt.), 29-31

St. Andrews, N.B., 177
St. Andrew's Societies in America, 125
as centers of Scottish influence, 130-134
St. Clair, Arthur, 177
St. Inegoes, Md., 174
St. John, N.B., 125
St. Marys County, Md., 174
Savannah, Ga., 134
Schoharie, N.Y. Colony, 82
Scot, George of Pitlochy, 11
Scotch-Irish, 112
history of the term, 18-19
emigration contrasted with Scottish, 19-21, 180-181
in western Pennsylvania, 110
numbers emigrating to North America, 185, 186
Scotland:
poverty of, 1

compared with countries of northern Europe (1700), 4-5
economy of, compared with that of England, 5
exports of, in 18th century, 5, 27-28
economic growth of, in 18th century, 8
trade with America before 1707, 13-15
effects of Union of 1707 on, 16
Church of, 34
absence of customary rights in, 53
agricultural improvements in, 54-57
trade with tobacco colonies, 116-125
exploits American trade after 1707, 126-127
influence on America curtailed by Revolution, 148-149
Scots-American Company of Farmers, 29-31
Scott, Sir Walter, quoted, 34
Seven Years' War, discharged Scottish veterans of, settle in colonies, 46-49
Shedden, Robert, 169
Shetland Isles, 67-68
Skene, Alexander, 132
Skene, Philip Wharton, 85-86
Skenesborough, N.Y. Colony, 83, 85-86
Skye (Inner Hebrides), 36, 41, 50, 69-70, 75-76, 96
Smith, Guy, quoted, 164-165
Smith, William, champions Lachlan Campbell, 78
Sonmans, Peter, 143-145
South Carolina, 44, 115, 141
Scottish loyalists in, 173-174
South Uist (Outer Hebrides), 50
Spiers, Alexander, & Co., merchants, 124
Sprowle, Andrew, 169
Stafford County, Va., 120
Stephens, Thomas, 134
Stephens, William, 134-135, 138
Stiles, Ezra, quoted, 130
Stirling, William, 136
Stirling, Me., 25
Stirling, Scotland, 10, 25
Stockton, Richard, 87
Stuart, Prince Charles Edward, 34